Teacher Education

and the

Agency for International Development

A Study Prepared

by

Louis W. Normington

THE AMERICAN ASSOCIATION OF COLLEGES FOR TEACHER EDUCATION

The study reported herein was developed pursuant to a contract with the Agency for International Development, Contract AID/csd 1811. Contractors are encouraged to express freely their professional judgment in the conduct of the project. Points of view or opinions stated do not, therefore, necessarily represent official AID policy.

Published 1970 by
The American Association of Colleges for Teacher Education
One Dupont Circle, Washington, D. C. 20036

Library of Congress Catalog Card Number: 77-111405
Standard Book Number: 910052-42-5

TABLE OF CONTENTS

118 **SECTION II—RANGE OF ASSISTANCE PROGRAMS**

APPENDIXES

iv

FOREWORD

From whatever perspective one views the concept of human resources and their relationship to national development, the need to develop an appropriate educational system is crucial. Those who would put a nation's human resources to the best possible use for the common weal are charged with the responsibility for the development of an educational system capable of transforming human potential into human productivity—a productivity that supplies new momentum to a society's economic, political, esthetic, and humanitarian life.

The teacher in such an educational system performs a significant function since his role is to perpetuate society's heritage and simultaneously to energize human resources toward social progress. If it is accepted that the teacher is a central element in the formal education of a nation's human capital and that the level of education cannot rise far above the quality of the teacher in the classroom, then the selection and preparation of these teachers are of significant social concern. Concerted effort must be made, therefore, to produce the best teacher that a nation can afford.

Furthermore, teacher education provides a vital link between a nation's institutions of higher learning and the public they are designed to serve. Not all youth, even in the most affluent societies, can personally and directly be enrolled in a college or university, even though these institutions are usually supported by the public at large. The benefits of higher or tertiary education to the majority of the population are thus generally transmitted by the teacher who is a product of this higher education. The institutions that educate teachers, the teacher educators themselves, and the governmental departments concerned with teacher training are thus clearly a part of the nation's overall strategy in the development process.

Any international, technical assistance operation that supports the preparation and the improvement of a country's teachers is, therefore, involved in several vital and sensitive areas of a nation's life. It does so in the following ways:

- By affecting the quality of the teachers' performance, the donor reaches into the lives of a people at a much deeper level than that achieved merely by an exchange or donation of material goods. The teaching process affects attitudes, emotional commitments, and societal involvements, as well as the development of skills and vocational viability.

- In undertaking assistance to an institution of tertiary or higher education for the preparation of teachers, the donor, theoretically at least, provides a link between the institution of higher education and the public at large. It thereby provokes in institutions of higher learning a concern for urgent societal needs to which its knowledge can be applied and directed. In such a situation the potential for collaboration between the traditional academic disciplines and the professions, such as teacher education, is expanded and the application of knowledge to socially relevant needs is accelerated.

- By providing technical assistance to a foreign country's educational system, American institutions and educators tend to broaden the context within which teacher education takes place. The representatives of the American institutions serving in foreign nations open, by their very presence and their activities, windows on a world heretofore unknown by the future teachers whom they tutor. Thus, teacher education, in addition to providing a vital link between higher education and its public, can also serve as a vital bridge between the peoples of many nations in this era of multilateral cooperation.

- In their positions as colleagues, consultants, or advisors to foreign colleges, universities, and government officials, American educators serve as an additional resource for the infusion of alternative solutions to educational problems. But, in involving American personnel in the teacher education process overseas, the very quality and pace of social change is being affected. By providing alternatives to existing educational processes, technical assistance disturbs, however subtly, the status quo. The positive contributions, as well as those that jeopardize the existing social order, are rapidly multiplied by the unique character of a teacher education institution.

The success of American teacher education in coping with the problems of development overseas is not the prime focus of this book. But the contemporary American effort to establish an effective relationship between human resource development and the achievement of broad societal aspirations, through the medium of teacher education, is amply documented.

This volume differs from many documents that have focused on AID's activities insofar as it provides detailed descriptions of programs conducted by university contractors. Professional students of international development education are thus provided with case studies that lend themselves to a variety of analytical exercises and open additional avenues for research into specialized areas of teacher education and technical assistance.

Finally, the AACTE Committee on International Relations was aware of the ever-present danger that besets action-oriented endeavors of the type described in this volume. Too often the need to initiate a course of action and to sustain its momentum provides little time for the contractor or his agents to reflect on the process itself or to feed back into the institution's supporting network the lessons he has learned. In recent years a number of studies have concentrated their efforts on this problem. TEACHER EDUCATION AND AID presents an additional analysis to this growing body of literature as seen from the perspective of individuals, institutions, and processes involved specifically in the preparation of teachers. Hopefully, this perspective supports and complements the other efforts that have been made in this direction.

FRANK H. KLASSEN
*Associate Secretary**

December 1969

---

* With staff responsibility for AACTE Committee on International Relations.

PREFACE

The research for this volume was undertaken by the American Association of Colleges for Teacher Education. The Association's interest in this area stems from its own fifty-year concern for the improvement of teacher education in America and its increasing involvement in the technical assistance process abroad. AACTE's interest was also motivated by a series of assumptions regarding the significant role of teacher education in the life of any nation, and by a belief that America's higher education community has a responsibility to those nations whose aspirations for improved educational opportunities are restricted by manpower and economic limitations and the many problems that accompany the process of achieving political independence.

As a voluntary association of over 800 colleges and universities which prepare more than ninety percent of America's teachers, AACTE is particularly interested in the problems and achievements of its member institutions in the field of teacher education overseas. Since World War II, the Agency for International Development and its predecessor agencies have carried the major burden in directing the application of American technical skill and economic resources to the problems of educational advancements abroad. In doing so, AID has relied heavily on the leaders of American teacher education to initiate, conduct, and sustain programs of teacher improvement overseas, whether on a direct-hire basis, through university contracts, or through other means. The extent of AID's contribution in manpower and money, and in the range and breadth of professional programs that have been fostered in recent decades, is unknown to the broad professional public involved in international relations and teacher education.

Individual participants fortunate enough to have become involved in teacher education projects in Afghanistan or Zambia often returned to their American campus with little opportunity to relate their international experience to the domestic curriculum. Nor did they have access to a literature that provided a comprehensive description and analysis of the global dimension of America's teacher education efforts overseas or of AID's long-term international commitment in this field.

This volume represents an attempt to rectify this knowledge gap. But it does so only partially, because it reflects the work of only one governmental agency, AID, and concentrates on the contemporary state of affairs. The total history, which will incorporate the efforts of other branches of government, the foundations, and institutional projects of a non-government nature, has yet to be written. With these limitations, TEACHER EDUCATION AND AID pays tribute to the dedication of a host of government workers, legislators, administrators, and dedicated teacher educators, from the earliest days of President Truman's Point Four Program to the present, for their firm belief that the wealth of the nation, as Frederick Harbison has remarked, "consists not of its natural resources or its capital, but its human resources."

The AACTE is particularly grateful to Dr. Louis W. Normington of Pacific Union College who served as project director for this study. Dr. Frank H. Klassen, associate secretary, AACTE, coordinated the project in his capacity as director of international programs for the Association. During the course of Dr. Normington's investigation, he was assisted by the comments, suggestions, and reports of AID officials in the United States and overseas, as well as a host of institutional representatives who have participated in one way or another in the AID/teacher education process overseas. To the director and the many persons who assisted Dr. Normington in this investigation, AACTE extends its thanks and acknowledges their contributions to this study.

EDWARD C. POMEROY
Executive Secretary

December 1969

INTRODUCTION

Purpose of the Study

This research project has two major functions:

1. *To describe the extent of AID involvement in teacher education.*

It seeks to answer such questions as types of assistance given, institutions involved, operational methods used, difficulties encountered, elements contributing to success or failure, and values accruing to the American institutions participating.

2. *To see if generalizations can be extracted, with particular reference to the factors underlying success or failure, which may be useful as guidelines to AID or to other institutions participating in similar future projects.*

It is recognized that the present research is merely a modest beginning to a task of enormous size and complexity. Any recommendations or guidelines will be tentative in nature and may be said to represent hypotheses rather than established findings.

Scope and Limitations

This study is limited to technical assistance in the preparation of elementary and secondary teachers and teacher educators, as sponsored by the Agency for International Development and its predecessor agencies, such as the International Cooperation Administration. It is further limited to programs that were reported operational in 1967. These limitations were imposed in part by two considerations: one, the objectives of the study; the other, availability of information in AID files and time available to the investigators.

Analysis of Available Information

Originally, it was hoped to review all programs sponsored by AID, including those already phased out. AID, however, has been described as "the agency without a memory." In some cases, files were incomplete or past practical reassembly, having already been shipped to the archives. Some university contracts had been phased out. In these cases, it was impossible in the available time to find material that had been sent to the archives. The situation was even more difficult with regard to direct-hire activities. It would have been impossible without the generous assistance of Miss Edna Falbo, director of the Historical and Technical Reference Section, who made a determined effort to collect and catalog material such as the *Country Assistance Plans* going back to 1962. The study was, therefore, limited to projects being carried on in 1967.

Since World War II, there has been a tremendous outpouring of assistance to the so-called underdeveloped countries. Many member countries and organizations of the United Nations have participated. In the United States, private foundations such as Carnegie, Ford, Rockefeller, and Kettering, as well as many different government agencies, have been involved. However, this study was limited to projects sponsored by AID.

It is equally true that assistance has been given in many areas such as agriculture, health, roads, engineering, and business and public administration. Even in the field of education, aid has been given to a diversity of activities. It has involved buildings, textbooks, equipment; primary, secondary, higher, and adult or community education; and even such areas as medicine or dentistry could be considered, since they involve the upgrading of professors. In order to keep the task to manageable proportions, and to focus on an area where the expertise of the AACTE could best be utilized, *the inquiry was limited to technical assistance to teacher education.* This was defined as the preparation of elementary and secondary teachers and teacher educators.

A further limiting factor should be noted. The study was primarily a documentary analysis and interpretation with minimal opportunity for visiting the projects overseas. During the investigation it became evident that a complete, and accurate, picture could *not* be obtained solely from the documents in the files. While the field visits were extremely valuable, unfortunately not enough time was available to assess contributions or outcomes through an in-depth study of the impact of the projects on local educational systems.

Value of Study of Results

This study must, therefore, be regarded as the first phase of a much broader survey that would develop priorities and strategies for future assistance to teacher education in developing countries.

This *second phase* might be conducted on two fronts. In one, attention would be focused on a field study of the project. It would compare original objectives with actual results. The reactions of the foreign "consumers"— ministries of education and local communities—would be investigated. In the second approach, leading American educators who have participated in technical assistance programs—from both government and the academic community—would be involved in a searching review of the whole process of selecting, planning, staffing, administering, and evaluating technical assistance projects in teacher education in a series of regional or national conferences.

Sources of Data

Four major sources of information were analyzed:

1. Reports in AID files and the Historical and Technical Reference Section.
2. Field investigation in a limited number of overseas projects.
3. Interviews with AID/Washington officials and university personnel, including returned contract team members.
4. Studies conducted by other investigators, such as Education and World Affairs and the American Council on Education.

1. AID FILES AND HISTORICAL AND TECHNICAL REFERENCE SECTION

These AID reports included such materials as contracts, progress reports, end-of-tour reports, and contractor performance evaluations. The *Country Assistance Plans* for each country, for the years 1962 through 1967, also provided condensed reports on both institutional projects and direct-hire programs. The usefulness of the latter was somewhat limited because they were devoted mainly to plans, and their relatively brief reports on accomplishments often failed to bear much resemblance to the plans so glowingly described the year before.

2. FIELD INVESTIGATION

The contract provided no funds for visiting actual projects. However, authorization was gained to visit a number of the projects at the same time as a follow-up study of administrative interns was carried out. Three investigators thus made brief visits to a sampling of the projects and interviewed chiefs of party, team members, United States Mission education officers, and national educators.

Dr. Frank Klassen, associate secretary of AACTE, visited projects in Brazil, Jamaica, and Peru.

Dr. Howard Jones, dean of the College of Education, Iowa University, and a member of the Committee on International Relations of AACTE, visited projects in Liberia, Nigeria, Kenya, Tanzania, and Ethiopia.

Dr. Louis Normington, project coordinator for AACTE, visited projects in Afghanistan, India, East Pakistan, Nepal, Korea, Thailand, the Philippines, and Indonesia.

A list of those interviewed is in the appendix (see page 186).

3. INTERVIEWS WITH AID/WASHINGTON PERSONNEL, CAMPUS COORDINATORS, AND RETURNED CONTRACT TEAM MEMBERS

Descriptive reports of institutional contracts and direct-hire projects, based on material in the AID files, were sent to AID/Washington personnel and to the campus coordinators involved, for comment and correction. Their suggestions were incorporated in the final reports included in Chapter 4 (page 69). In addition, selected campus coordinators, returned team members, and AID/Washington personnel were interviewed to identify the significant factors which appeared to them to underlie success or failure.

4. RESEARCH REPORTED BY OTHER INVESTIGATORS

Beginning about 1962, a number of studies have been published on the general subject of America's developmental assistance abroad. Among the organizations sponsoring such research are Education and World Affairs, the American Council on Education, the Brookings Institution, and a number of universities, including Teachers College, Columbia University, Syracuse University, and Stanford Research Institute.

In addition, there are numerous unpublished reports such as "The Development of the National Institute of Education in India," by Paul Leonard; "A Follow-up of a Technical Assistance Project in Education in West Pakistan," by John J. Hanitchak; and "AID-University Rural Development Contracts and U.S. Universities," by William Thompson et al., which have been sponsored by AID and usually carried out by contract team members. These studies are listed in the bibliography and their findings cited in the report where applicable.

Organization of the Report

This report is presented in four chapters:

Chapter 1 places teacher education within the frame of reference of the world educational crisis.

Chapter 2 contains a survey of the scope of the technical assistance program in teacher education and brief reports of the projects carried on in 1967.

Chapter 3 reports trends—an analysis of the factors underlying success or failure, with recommendations.

Chapter 4 contains detailed descriptions of a number of projects which illustrate the range and variety of teacher education activities.

The appendix has a bibliography and a list of those consulted during the study.

Acknowledgements

The AACTE is most grateful for the assistance of the many people who took time to correct reports or to make suggestions and recommendations. Particular mention should be made of AID personnel, foreign educators, campus coordinators, and past and present contract team members who went out of their way to arrange interviews, give thoughtful consideration to the questions raised, and share the benefits of their experience. It should be made clear, however, that the AACTE alone is responsible for the ideas expressed in the report.

The manuscript was ably edited and prepared for publication by W. L. Robinson.

Chapter 1

Teacher Education

and

A World in Crisis

THE CRISIS

There is little doubt that both the developing countries and the industrialized nations face an educational crisis. It is more extreme with the developing countries, however, because of both their lesser resources and their continuing struggle to build educational systems which will raise whole populations from illiteracy into the modern age.

Using the techniques of systems analysis, Dr. Philip H. Coombs of the International Institute for Educational Planning has traced five forces which have led to this crisis:[1]

1. *"The student flood,"* triggered both by rising expectations and the population explosion.

2. *"Acute resource scarcities"* to provide teachers, buildings, scholarships, and instructional materials.

3. *"The rising costs"* of attempts to improve quality in a labor-intensive industry.

4. *"Unsuitability of output,"* in relation both to "the rapidly altering needs of national development and to the similarly changing needs of individuals in changing societies."

5. *"Inertia and inefficiency"* in educational systems which, by holding on to traditional procedures in the face of changing requirements, have actually contributed to a deterioration in quality.

To meet this crisis Dr. Coombs suggests we must develop not only innovations, but a habit of innovating in education. In this process he draws attention to the central role of teacher preparation. "Educational systems," he states, "will not be modernized until the whole system of teacher-training is drastically overhauled, stimulated by pedagogical research, made intellectually richer and more challenging, and extended far beyond preservice training into a system for continuous professional renewal and career development for all teachers."[2]

This, he points out, has implications for international cooperation. The need for the industrialized nations to help the developing nations will continue for a long time to come. But "such support should not be a conveyor belt for conventional educational forms from 'donor' countries to 'recipient' ones, but rather a common act of exploration to find patterns that really fit the needs and pocketbooks of the developing nations."[3]

Importance of a Study of America's Role in Technical Assistance to Teacher Education

In the light of these factors, a careful study of the world scope of United States technical assistance to teacher education is of extreme importance at the present time.

1. EDUCATIONAL DEVELOPMENT IS VITAL TO SOCIAL, ECONOMIC, AND POLITICAL DEVELOPMENT IN THE EMERGENT COUNTRIES.

In the early years of technical assistance, education was thought to be of secondary importance to economic development. With further experience, it became clear, as Arthur G. Wirth writes in a foreword to *American Education in International Development*, that "education, far from being auxiliary, is a factor of intrinsic importance for successful change in all other spheres—political, social, psychological, as well as economic."[4]

The same idea has been expressed in various ways by many different people. In his message on international education in 1966, President Johnson, for example, declared: "Education lies at the heart of every nation's hopes and it must be at the heart of our international relations."

Writing in the *Harvard Educational Review*, Adam Curle states that countries are undeveloped mainly because most of their people are undeveloped.[5] The main reason for their lack of opportunity lies within the social structure, and can be remedied only when there are enough people with a new attitude to society. Education, he emphasizes, is the chief vehicle for changing such attitudes.

"Education is the single biggest enterprise in developing countries," points out John Hanson. "It employs more people and influences directly the lives of more people than any other organization apart from government itself."[6]

2. DEVELOPING THE CAPACITY TO PREPARE EFFECTIVE TEACHERS IS CRUCIAL TO A NATION'S EDUCATIONAL DEVELOPMENT.

Just as educational development is vital to social, economic, and political development, the improvement of teachers both as to the numbers available and their effectiveness in the classroom is vital to educational development. "Teachers are to education and economic development," writes William Platt of the Stanford Research Institute, "as machines-to-make-machines (machine tools) are to plants and production."[7]

This problem cannot be solved by attempting to provide expatriate teachers for the underdeveloped countries—the needs are far too immense —nor even by erecting buildings and passing on technical skill. As Harold Enarson, president of Cleveland State University, at one time director of educational services for AID, points out, "When we began our technical assistance under AID, we were fairly naive about it. We have now found

3

over the years that the task is not to pass on technical knowledge, but rather a knowledge of how to build institutions."[8]

And they must develop the capacity to build institutions, we might add, that will train teachers who will themselves be innovators—"seed corn" of educational and even community development. At this point we become aware of all that is involved in a cross-cultural task. It is of little value to attempt to transplant American models, for they are not likely to "fit" the expectations of a different society.

Perhaps the strongest statement comes from Freeman Butts. Writing in *Education and the Development of Nations,* he declares that "we must view the education of teachers as belonging at the very heart of any human resource development plan that hopes to contribute to the modernization and building of a free nation."[9]

3. There Has Been Inadequate Exchange of Information Between Technicians on Different Assistance Projects.

Too little cross-fertilization has taken place between projects. What has been learned so painfully in one country tends to be lost sight of when new projects are started. Philip Coombs points out that "all along, the AID agency has acted as if it had no past. This is due in part to the high rate of turnover and shifting about of personnel, with no systematic effort being made to collect their experience. This has resulted in the same lessons having to be learned over and over again. A new AID expert sent to a foreign country is as likely as not to begin over, where his predecessor did, instead of where he left off."[10]

In consequence, it is frequently reported by chiefs of party that one of their major problems is occasioned by new education officers urging radical shifts of philosophy, but having little understanding of the past developments and rationale of the project.

The same difficulty exists all too often among university teams. In some cases, where there has been strong and continuous leadership from the home institutions, a systematic and successful effort has been made to use the "feedback" from past participants to orient new team members. This is not the picture everywhere, however.

There is another tremendous area of loss. Reports like those published by Education and World Affairs are, of course, known to the academic community. But many unpublished studies, such as the report by Willis A. Porter on the building of the College of Education in Thailand, tend to get buried in the archives. As a result, a wealth of experience is lost.

4. Research Is Needed Specifically on Technical Assistance to Teacher Education.

A number of studies have already been mentioned that deal with technical assistance to education. Most of these, however, have been related to education in general, or to a detailed study of one project or institution.

It must be recognized that teacher education is but one thread in the total fabric of a country's development. Inevitably there will be overlap between the findings of a study on, for example, institution building at the university level, or one on rural development, or a study on teacher education. There are unique differences, however. Research focused directly on teacher education is needed to develop guidelines for those involved in planning and carrying out such projects. Emerging countries require help in building educational systems that will be responsive to national concerns and values—that will be agents for change. This demands the development of the capacity for long-range planning within a complex framework —one that includes the cultural context, the efficient use of all available human resources, and the distinctive characteristics of teacher education.

5. A LARGER PROPORTION OF TEACHER EDUCATION INSTITUTIONS IN THE UNITED STATES SHOULD BE INFORMED ABOUT AND INVOLVED IN THE TECHNICAL ASSISTANCE PROGRAM.

There are about 1,200 U.S. universities and colleges which have teacher education programs. Of these, 830 are members of the American Association of Colleges for Teacher Education. They prepare over 90 percent of America's teachers. In 1967, 71 of these were engaged in carrying out 134 AID-financed contracts providing technical assistance in 39 countries.[11] Twenty-two institutions were carrying on 33 projects specifically in teacher education, and a number of other projects were conducted by such organizations as the National Education Association or the National Science Foundation.

Twenty-two out of 1,200 or even 830, suggests that too few members of the educational community are being involved, and possibly some institutions with several contracts may be straining their resources. Of course, many institutions are too small to staff projects by themselves, but could be involved in consortia.

Research such as this study of AID projects, undertaken by AACTE, should perform a service in bringing to the attention of its member institutions the opportunities, problems, and rewards of involvement in this phase of technical assistance.

6. THERE IS A GREAT NEED TO INVEST LIMITED RESOURCES IN PROJECTS THAT WILL HAVE THE MAXIMUM IMPACT.

The needs of the underdeveloped nations are immense. They could use help in every aspect of their economies. In fact, rising populations have faced most of these countries with a tremendous challenge just to maintain their standard of living, let alone raise it. On the other hand, the developed countries, no matter how willing, have limited resources with which they can provide assistance.

Because of this, it has always been clear that projects should be selected which would have the maximum impact or multiplier effect. At the present time, this need has become even more urgent. The comments of Jerome Bruner have particular pertinence in this connection. Declaring that there is no single problem in the field of educational assistance more important than teacher education, he goes on to say that it is "the single form of activity that has a known multiplier effect built into it," and that this is particularly true when educating the teachers of teachers.[12]

FOOTNOTES

[1] Coombs, Philip H. *The World Educational Crisis.* New York: Oxford University Press, 1968. pp. 164-165.

[2] *Ibid.,* p. 168.

[3] *Ibid.,* p. 172.

[4] Wirth, Arthur G. *American Education in International Development.* Foreword.

[5] Curle, Adam. "Some Aspects of Educational Planning in Underdeveloped Areas." *Harvard Educational Review* 32 : 300; Summer, 1962.

[6] Hanson, John W., and Brembeck, Cole S., editors. *Education and the Development of Nations.* New York: Holt, Rinehart and Winston, 1966. p. vi.

[7] Platt, William J. *Conflict in Education Planning.* Menlo Park, California: Stanford Research Institute. 1962. p. 27.

[8] Enarson, Harold, in *Conference on World Education.* (Edited by Harold Taylor). Washington: American Association of Colleges for Teacher Education, 1967. p. 17.

[9] Butts, R. Freeman, in *Education and the Development of Nations.* (Edited by John W. Hanson and Cole S. Brembeck.) New York: Holt, Rinehart and Winston, 1966. p. 375.

[10] Coombs, Philip H., and Bigelow, Karl W. *Education and Foreign Aid.* Cambridge, Massachusetts: Harvard University Press, 1965. p. 25.

[11] Wood, Richard H. *U. S. Universities: Their Role in AID-Financed Technical Assistance Overseas.* New York: Education and World Affairs, 1968. p. 11.

[12] Bruner, Jerome S., editor. "Educational Assistance for Developing Nations: Techniques and Technology." *Education and Training in the Developing of Countries.* New York: Praeger, 1966. p. 94.

Chapter 2

Teacher Education and
The Developing Countries —
The Technical Assistance Program

THE TECHNICAL ASSISTANCE PROGRAM—A SURVEY

Chapter 1 emphasized the critical need for teacher education in the developing countries. Chapter 2 reports the efforts the United States, working through the Agency for International Development, has made to help meet these needs. The scope of this technical assistance program is described, with detailed information on the number of projects, countries involved, types of contractors, and major types of assistance. Projects operational in 1967 are described briefly by regions and countries.

The Range of Technical Assistance

A review of the projects (pages 9-12) makes it obvious that technical assistance is being given to every level and phase of teacher training in one country or another. This is, perhaps, not surprising since the countries included in this report are at vastly different stages in their development. Indeed, different areas of the same country often face dissimilar educational problems.

For some, the most urgent need is to respond to the demand of illiterate rural peoples for education of their children. Even an inadequate education is *now* politically compelling. Today's urgent needs must be confronted today, even if a more gradual and balanced approach might be educationally more defensible since it would certainly encourage a climate in which more and better education would be demanded in the future. The program for preparing teachers for the hamlet schools in Vietnam may provide such an illustration.

For others, the point of urgency is at the middle level of manpower. For a country to meet the demand for a better standard of living, a basic need is for a large number of broadly educated youth who can be trained for all the tasks of an industrial society. Here, assistance is needed to provide not only a greater number of secondary teachers, but many more who can handle a curriculum that helps youth face and meet the demands of their culture. Illustrations of this situation are in the project summaries (pages 13-31), which include numerous ones for training teachers for comprehensive high schools.

But for some countries, the most useful technical assistance may be helping them develop the capacity to carry on their own planning for teacher education as an integral part both of educational programs and of nation-wide human resource utilization. Indeed, *helping the emerging nations develop the capacity for solving their own educational problems, rather than attempting to solve those problems for them,* may well be at the heart of all technical assistance.

In all these areas the preparation of teacher educators presents a critical challenge. Simply to build up the institutional capacity to prepare the number of teachers required is a staggering problem. An even greater problem is to prepare teacher educators who will stir up in prospective teachers a willingness to change, and help them develop the skills to become innovators in their own classrooms.

It might be added that when a nation is well on the way to self-sustained growth, the task is to help its peoples understand that the phasing out of technical assistance is not desertion, but a necessary step toward the partnership of equals.

The Countries Included

In 1967, AID provided technical assistance to 69 countries. In 47 of these, help was given to education, and in almost all of the latter, 40 to be exact, *teacher education* was a major target. The countries were as follows:

Far East Region: Korea, Laos, Thailand, Vietnam

Near East and South Asia Region: Afghanistan, India, Nepal, Pakistan, Turkey; Regional (American University of Beirut)

African Region: Cameroon, Congo, Ethiopia, Kenya, Liberia, Malawi, Mali, Nigeria, Sierra Leone, Somalia, Sudan, Tanzania, Zambia, East African Regional (Kenya, Tanzania, Uganda)

Latin American Region: Bolivia, Brazil, Chile, Colombia, Costa Rica, Dominican Republic, Ecuador, El Salvador, Guatemala, Honduras, Jamaica, Nicaragua, Paraguay, Peru, Uruguay, Venezuela

The number of countries, 40, was identical with the number reported by Verna Carley as being assisted by the International Cooperation Administration in 1959. There are, however, a number of significant changes for several reasons. Some countries achieved self-sustaining growth and no longer receive U.S. assistance; or there were breakdowns in diplomatic relations or shifts in U.S. policy.

In the Far East, Taiwan and the Philippines no longer received assistance for teacher education, while Laos was added. In the Near East and South Asia, Iran, Greece, Jordan, Ceylon, Cambodia, and Indonesia were not listed. In Africa, Libya, Morocco, and Tunisia had stopped receiving assistance, while nine of the "new" nations were included: Cameroon, Congo, Kenya, Malawi, Mali, Somalia, Sudan, Tanzania, and Uganda. In Latin America, Panama and Haiti no longer received assistance, but Chile, El Salvador, Jamaica, Uruguay, and Venezuela had been added.

9

The Number of Projects

In the 40 countries receiving technical assistance for teacher education, 64 different projects were reported as operational in 1967. This compared with 1,431—the total number of agency technical service contracts. However, due to differences in reporting, these figures may not reflect an accurate or total picture of AID involvement in teacher education. Sometimes, a university would be listed as being involved in two different projects at the same institution and, at other times, in a combined one. In Latin America, all technical assistance activities relating to teacher education in one country appear to have been reported as one project. In other areas, as for example India or Nigeria, each different contract was listed separately. There were also differences from year to year. Projects were combined or divided depending on shifts of emphasis. And one or two programs, as for example that at the University of Nigeria at Nsukka in Eastern Nigeria, were inactive because of war conditions.

The Estimated Costs Involved

In the fiscal year 1967, $24 million was reported as being spent on contracts involving technical assistance to teacher education. In the same year, the agency reported that it had spent $189 million for educational and training projects, including all phases of education, agriculture, and health. In the life of the projects, which date back in one case to 1952, over $104 million was spent. The total value of all technical assistance contracts in effect in 1967 was reported at $537 million.[1] Again, it must be emphasized that the two figures are not strictly comparable. In some cases, it was not possible to separate the teacher education component of projects that included other phases of educational assistance. The figures do demonstrate, however, that a considerable proportion of America's technical assistance abroad is in the field of teacher education.

The Contracting Agencies

In 35 of the projects, AID utilized the services of a university, college, or technical institute; in 16, a professional association or other agency was used; and, in the remainder, the overseas mission used direct hire or personal contract technicians. A combination of methods was used on the same project in a number of cases.

Twenty-two universities, colleges, and technical institutes participated in these 35 projects. As can be seen from Table 2 (see appendix, page 169), the majority of institutions handled only one project, but Teachers College, Columbia University, had four; Ohio University, Southern Illinois University, and the University of Wisconsin each had three; and Colorado State University, Dunwoody Technical Institute, Ohio State University, and San Diego State College Foundation each had two.

AID also called on the resources of professional associations and other independent agencies for specific kinds of projects. The *National Science*

Foundation, for example, was asked to give assistance to the Science Education Improvement program in India. The *American Vocational Association* was involved in technical teacher training in Turkey. The *National Education Association* sponsored the Teach Corps—teacher volunteers who conducted workshops in many countries; the *Texas Education Agency* pioneered a new approach to in-service training for science teachers in Guatemala; and the *American Association of Colleges for Teacher Education* utilized the resources of its members in providing internship experience in American universities for administrators of teacher education institutions from developing countries.

Types of Technical Assistance Programs

The 64 technical assistance programs in teacher education are of an almost bewildering variety, and do not easily lend themselves to organization or analysis. Some are long-term institution-building projects concerned with developing an elementary teacher-training institute, for example. Others, such as the NEA Teach Corps, are usually short-term. They have, as one of their principal effects, the development of a climate for change by exposing teachers to American methods and materials, and getting them excited about what can be done. Still others, such as the Teachers College, Columbia University, projects in Peru and Afghanistan, are comprehensive in nature with a wide variety of objectives.

Among the principal kinds of programs, even though there is obviously some overlapping, are the following nine typical ones:

1. *Institution Building*—The technicians help develop the institution from "the ground up" and, working with national counterparts, attempt not only to produce curricula and materials of instruction that will meet local needs, but also to train a faculty, administration, and staff to run it. Among the institution-building projects are those for elementary teachers; trade and technical, including agricultural and commercial teachers; those for teachers for secondary, including multipurpose, schools; and those for graduate schools for the preparation of supervisors, administrators, and researchers.

2. *Teacher Supply Programs*—Here the emphasis is on providing a supply of faculty members for the teacher education program until there are enough national educators ready to carry on. By their presence and example it is hoped that the American educators will be sources of innovation and new ideas. The International Voluntary Services program in Laos is of this nature.

3. *In-service Programs*—Not only are workshops, seminars, vacation evening classes, evening classes, and radio/correspondence schools introduced, but national educators are helped to develop the skills needed to run them. An example is the program carried out by a University of Ohio team in Nigeria.

4. *National Education Planning Study*—A somewhat more recent development has been the provision of consultant help to the ministries of edu-

11

cation to assist them in national educational planning as a prelude to programs of reform in teacher education. Programs in Brazil and Korea are examples. Along with these should be mentioned Human Resource Studies like the one carried on in Bolivia by Ohio State as a prerequisite for more efficient planning for teacher education.

5. *Science Education Improvement*—One of the most successful in-service programs has been the series of summer science institutes started in India in 1963 and since carried out in other countries.

6. *Program Building*—Here the emphasis is on working with existing faculties to develop curricula, and to find ways of improving teaching techniques and materials of instruction. University of Wisconsin teams are working with a number of elementary teacher education institutions in this way in Northern Nigeria.

7. *Administrative Internships*—This is one approach to meeting the need for qualified administrators for teacher education institutions in developing countries. Through the sponsorship of the American Association of Colleges for Teacher Education, young administrators are given the opportunity of working for a year with the president of an American college or university, or the dean of a school of education, to become acquainted with modern techniques and skills in educational administration.

8. *Programs Which Develop a "Climate for Change"*—The National Education Association Teach Corps is an example of a program which helps produce a desire on the part of national teachers to improve. Corps teachers work with them to show how modern methods can be used in their surroundings.

9. *Comprehensive Programs*—In such activities, the contract team work with the national ministry of education to carry out a wide variety of projects. Examples are the Teachers College, Columbia University, projects in Afghanistan and Peru.

Worldwide Impact

Much of the most important work of technical assistance to teacher education does not lend itself to statistical treatment—helping local educators improve curricula, for example. What statistics are available, however, do suggest that the impact is impressive. In 1962,[2] there were 73,000 student teachers in college-level AID-assisted teacher education programs, and 107,000 prospective teachers in AID-assisted schools below the college level. In addition, in-service training was provided with AID help to 108,000 teachers.

During the past five years, it was estimated that almost 300,000[3] teachers participated in in-service training programs sponsored by AID with the assistance of American universities and professional associations. Of these, 24,000 were in the Far East; almost 82,000 in the Near East and South Asia; 33,000 in Africa; and more than 160,000 in Latin America.

12

Brief Summaries of Individual Projects

Brief summaries have been made of the major features of each of the 64 projects reported operational in 1967. Some were initiated in 1967, while others began as long ago as 1952. They are organized by regions and countries, the four regions reported below being Far East (including Vietnam); Near East and South Asia; Africa; and Latin America. Programs such as the National Educational Association Teach Corps, which are carried out on a world-wide basis, are listed under "International."

In noting any cost-of-project figures in the summaries below, two points should be emphasized. Some of the projects received support from other sources, the figures quoted being only those from AID appropriations. Secondly, in many of the countries, there were earlier projects which were phased out before 1967, and not included in this study.

FAR EAST (INCLUDING VIETNAM)

In the Far East there were 11 projects in four countries. They involved five universities and the International Voluntary Services, as well as direct hire personnel. The cost in 1967 was $2,030,000; and the total cost of the projects, some of which date back to 1955, has been $12,926,000.

KOREA

Vocational Training

Technical assistance for the training of trade and industrial teachers and agricultural teachers was provided by AID through the project "Vocational, Technical and In-Service Training." Beginning in 1956, a number of agencies, including AID, UNESCO, the Federal Republic of Germany, and Australia, assisted the government of Korea in a program designed to replace the shops and equipment destroyed by the war, and to both improve and expand vocational training.

A teacher-training center in trade and industrial education and one in agricultural education, with a combined enrollment of over 300 students, were established at Seoul National University. New curricula in vocational education were developed, and by 1967 nearly 500 trade and industrial and agricultural teachers had received three months of in-service training emphasizing both teaching methods and skill training.

During the project, over 60 Koreans received training in the United States. They returned to become principals and supervisors of technical or agricultural high schools or instructors at the teacher-training centers.

Educational Planning

In 1967, a new program was introduced in response to a request from the ministry of education for assistance in the development of policies for a long-range science education program, and in the coordination of United

States-sponsored science education activities. Efforts to improve science education were currently being sponsored by the Asia Foundation, the Fulbright Commission, the National Science Foundation, the Peace Corps, and other United States organizations. These were, however, uncoordinated and did not fit into a comprehensive national plan.

The project, "Educational Policy and Planning," was designed to lead to the development of a modern, effective, indigenous educational system for the country. Experimentation in teacher education, particularly in science and technical vocational education, were included. Five U.S. technical advisors were made available to the ministry. For the first year they were mainly involved in vocational education, basic science education, and aptitude testing.

LAOS

Normal Schools

Through a contract with International Voluntary Services, teaching assistance, primarily in English, science, and industrial arts, has been given to the Ecole Supérieure de Pédagogie (National Education Center), and to Ecoles Normales des Instituteurs (Regional Training Centers) at Pakse and Luang Prabang.

The International Voluntary Services team grew from eight in 1959 to 40 in 1967. By 1966, over 1,600 students were enrolled in the various teacher-training programs. There was an annual graduating class of about 300, all of whom were qualified to teach in the elementary schools of Laos. By 1966, over 50 participant trainees had been sent abroad for training.

In-service Training for Elementary Teachers

Beginning in 1964, educational leaders and teachers have been trained through in-service training courses or by participant training. Over 200 Lao teachers have been trained, most of them in Thailand; and 2,000 elementary teachers have taken part in one-month in-service training courses. In 1967, over 60 participants were sent to the U.S. or to a third country for training.

Secondary Education

In 1967, a team of four technicians from the University of Hawaii assisted in the opening of a comprehensive Lao secondary school as a pilot for the improvement of the country's secondary schools. The Vientiane Comprehensive School opened with an enrollment of 100 out of 800 applicants. It included both academic and pre-vocational education, with programs in agriculture, home economics, and industrial arts. As the project develops, a program for training secondary teachers for comprehensive high schools will be developed.

14

THAILAND

Vocational Training

Technical assistance was given for the preparation of trade and industrial teachers, and agricultural teachers. This was one phase of a program to improve and extend vocational training supported in part by a loan of $6 million from the International Bank for Reconstruction and Development.

The California State Polytechnic College accepted a contract with AID to work on the agricultural phase of the project. In 1967, five team members began to develop a three-year certificate curriculum for secondary agriculture teachers at the Bangpra Agricultural Teachers College.

Oklahoma University was asked by AID to work on the trade and industry aspect of the program at the Thewes Vocational Teacher Training College. By December 1967, the project was reported to be still in the planning stages.

VIETNAM

Hamlet Schools

Beginning in 1963, a major effort was made to assist in the training and upgrading of teachers for the rural schools. Eleven thousand six hundred prospective teachers received three months of instruction, and over five thousand teachers participated in some form of in-service training. Over ninety ministry and provisional officials were given a three-month study tour in the United States and Taiwan.

Elementary Education

A contract team from Southern Illinois University assisted the faculties of five normal schools in the improvement of their curriculum; the development of laboratory schools, and practice teaching programs; the writing of textbooks; and the introduction of an organized plan for in-service education. They also worked on a twelve-month course for normal school professors which was started in the faculty of pedagogy of the University of Saigon in 1967. Over sixty participant trainees were sent to the U.S. to work for advanced degrees in elementary education.

Mobile Science Units

A program of mobile science units was developed and laboratory methods of teaching science were demonstrated to elementary teachers in many of the rural areas of Vietnam by the International Voluntary Services.

Vocational Education

A teacher-training program for technical-vocational teachers was established in Saigon at the Phu-Tho Polytechnic with the advisory assistance

15

of members of the Southern Illinois University contract team. It reported 59 teacher graduates in 1967.

Secondary Education

A contract team from Ohio University worked with the faculty of pedagogy of the University of Saigon in the development of curricula for comprehensive high schools, and in the preparation of three-year curricula in business education, home economics, industrial arts, and library science as well as the more traditional subjects for the secondary teachers who would be needed. Instructional materials were prepared for the new courses, which were introduced in the demonstration school at the University of Saigon. The team members worked with the faculties of 12 provincial high schools in pilot programs to introduce the methods and materials developed in the Thu Duc demonstration school at Saigon. In July 1967, over 110 teachers had received, or were currently enrolled in, participant training in the U.S.

NEAR EAST AND SOUTH ASIA

In the Near East and South Asia region there were ten projects in five countries, and the regional project at the American University of Beirut which provided training for nationals from both the African, and Near East and South Asia regions. This involved six universities and technical institutes, the National Science Foundation, the American Vocational Association, the Institute of International Education, and the National Education Association. The cost in 1967 was $7,422,000; the total cost of the projects, some of which date back to 1951, was $55,449,000.

AFGHANISTAN

Since 1954, a contract team from Teachers College, Columbia University, has worked on a wide variety of projects designed to improve the preparation of primary and secondary teachers.

Primary Teacher Education

Assistance was given in the development of both regular and emergency primary teacher-training programs which produced about 950 teachers by 1967. The emergency program was operated at 29 centers and consisted of preparation for teaching in Grade 10 based on a modified middle school (Grades 7-9) curriculum. The regular teacher-training program was carried on at four D.M.A.'s (teacher-training schools), and continued the training through Grade 12.

Faculty of Education, Kabul University

A faculty (school) of education was established at the Kabul University. Degree programs in education for prospective school administrators and teachers in teacher-training schools were developed with an enroll-

16

ment of over 250. A bachelor of arts program in the teaching of English, with an enrollment of about 200, was introduced.

Lycée Project in Science and Mathematics

A program of in-service training in science and mathematics was carried on in six lycées which comprised about half the secondary teachers in the country. It involved the introduction of new textbooks; instruction in math-science subject matter; and workshops designed to help the teachers understand the new materials and change their teaching techniques from a lecture activity to one of discussion and fact finding. By 1967, 130 Afghan students had been sent to the U.S. for participant training.

INDIA

Multipurpose Secondary Education

Ohio State University assisted in developing four regional colleges, with a combined enrollment of 3,000, for the preparation of teachers for multipurpose high schools. Four-year degree courses were developed combining content and pedagogy in science, commerce, and technology. A program of in-service training was developed at 74 extension centers, and the new technical curricula were introduced to over 2,100 schools. Special assistance was given 26 multipurpose schools which were selected from the different states. Fifty Indian staff members received training in the U.S.

National Institute of Education

Over a six-year period, 30 consultants from Teachers College, Columbia University, assisted in the establishment of the National Institute of Education at New Delhi. The institute was the agent of the newly-formed National Council of Educational Research and Training. It brought under one organization six earlier institutes concerned with various aspects of education. It was designed to be, in effect, a graduate professional school conducting research and training educational leaders. Graduate curricula were established for administrators and those wishing to teach in teacher-training colleges. An in-service training program, attended by over 12,000 teachers, was carried on; textbooks were written; and a national staff was trained to carry on a program of research and publication. Forty-eight Indian members of the institute were sent to the U.S. for advanced education.

Science Education Improvement

This program began in 1963 with three summer science institutes sponsored by Teachers College, Columbia University, at the National Institute of Education. Its purpose was to introduce Indian secondary science teachers to modern methods of teaching science. The program proved most successful and was expanded over the years. In 1967, the National Science Foundation assumed responsibility for coordinating United States technical assistance to the program. By the end of 1967, approximately 14,000 university, college, and high school teachers had taken part in 375 institutes over the five-year period.

Central Training Institute, Bombay

From 1960 to 1967, Dunwoody Industrial Institute assisted in the development and operation of a one-year technical teacher-training program at the Central Training Institute. Instruction was given in the teaching of 18 trades to teachers from industrial training institutes who were given a one-year leave to improve their skills. About 200 were enrolled each year.

NEPAL

Technical Education

The main thrust of the Southern Illinois team in Nepal has been directed toward the training of teachers for multipurpose secondary schools. It worked with the Nepali staff to equip and establish the National Vocational Training Center, and introduced a degree program in cooperation with the College of Education of Tribhuvan University to train secondary teachers for home economics, agriculture, and trades and industry. In-service workshops were held for about 80 teachers in 1966, and again in 1967, to give technical instruction to teachers responsible for vocational courses. Seven participants received training at Southern Illinois University.

Primary Teacher Education Workshop

In the summer of 1967, the National Education Association Teach Corps worked with the staff of the College of Education of Tribhuvan University to conduct an eight-week workshop for 200 Nepali teachers, headmasters, and inspectors.

PAKISTAN

Summer Science Institutes

In 1966, the Institute of International Education organized a program of institutes similar to the ones which had proved successful in India. Four institutes in math and physics were conducted for high school and college teachers. In 1967, five institutes were held in mathematics, chemistry, and physics for about 120 college teachers, and plans were made to add biology to the program in the following year.

Institute of Education and Research

Since 1960, a Colorado State College team has assisted in the development of an Institute of Education and Research at the University of Dacca.

By 1967, the institute had been established with a Pakistani faculty of 49, and enrollment of over 300 students.

One-year and two-year M.Ed. programs were developed, and an Ed.D. program was introduced in 1967. A B.S. program for industrial arts teachers was also initiated in cooperation with the faculty of science. Centers for educational research, testing and guidance, and curriculum development were established. An in-service training program offering short courses, workshops, and seminars was reported to reach over 1,000 teachers and educational officers each year. Participant training in the U.S. was provided for over 50 Pakistani educators.

Commercial Institutes

In November 1967, Colorado State College signed a contract to assist the government of East Pakistan in developing 14 commercial institutes for the training of clerical and business personnel. One aspect of the project was to devise a program whereby the graduates of the commercial institutes could continue their education and obtain a teaching certificate in commercial subjects.

TURKEY

Technical and Vocational Education

A team of technicians sponsored by the American Vocational Association worked for two years with the staff of the Men's Technical Teacher Training College in Ankara. Four seminars, each two weeks in length, were held for vocational and technical teachers throughout Turkey.

REGIONAL PROJECT

American University of Beirut

Since 1951, AID has provided training for students from Africa and the Near East and South Asia regions at the American University of Beirut. One of the largest groups has been prospective teachers. In 1967, for example, 185 prospective teachers from 13 countries were reported to be attending the university.

AFRICA

There were 22 projects in 14 countries in Africa. They involved 13 universities and institutes, the National Education Association, Educational Development Center (formerly E.S.I.), and direct hire personnel. The cost in 1967 was $8,469,000 and the total cost of the projects, some of which date back to 1958, was $40,854,000.

CAMEROON

Teach Corps Workshop

In 1965, a workshop in library procedures was conducted by an NEA

Teach Corps volunteer. Sixteen teachers from primary, secondary, and teacher-training colleges met at the Cameroon College of Arts, Science, and Technology for two weeks.

CONGO

National Pedagogic Institute

Assistance was given in the training of secondary school English teachers. In 1967, two English specialists were provided for the faculty of the National Pedagogic Institute. This represented a shift of objective from a program initiated in 1964 for the direct teaching of English to government employees selected for training in the U.S. or others needing to learn English.

ETHIOPIA

Faculty of Education, Haile Selassie I University

The University of Utah assisted in the creation of a faculty (college) of education at the Haile Selassie I University. By 1967, it had a faculty of over 70 and an enrollment of 900. Degree curricula were developed for secondary teachers, for instructors in elementary teacher-training institutions, and for elementary school directors and supervisors. In addition, a one-year diploma program was introduced to prepare elementary directors and supervisors. In-service programs for elementary and secondary teachers were attended by over 1,000 teachers in 1966 and 1967. Sixteen participants received advanced training in the U.S.

Beginning in 1966, the Utah team was asked to develop a vocational and technical teacher-training program. Two one-year diploma programs were introduced for teachers in business, home economics, and industrial education, and plans were made to introduce degree programs in 1967.

KENYA

English-Language Teacher Training

A National Education Association team of primary school specialists was one of a number of groups which worked to introduce English as the medium of instruction in Kenya's primary schools. "PEAK" (Primary Education for Africans in Kenya) methods and materials, first tried on an experimental basis with the aid of a Ford Foundation grant, were introduced through in-service activities to the majority of the primary schools of the country.

Agriculture Education

A vocational agricultural curriculum was established at the Agriculture Diploma College at Edgerton by a team from West Virginia University.

In 1967, a specialist in secondary school agriculture developed a training program for teachers of agriculture on the secondary level.

Radio/Correspondence Courses

In 1967, three technicians from the University of Wisconsin wrote correspondence courses in English, geography, history, Kiswahili, and math, and produced lessons to be broadcast by radio to go along with them. By December 1967, it was reported that course enrollment exceeded 1,400.

LIBERIA

Elementary Teacher-Training Institutes

Tuskegee Institute supplied a team of specialists to assist in the development of two teacher-training institutes with a combined capacity of 375 students. By 1967, seven years after the project was started, the two institutes, at Zorzor and at Kakata, were fully operational with Liberian faculty and administration, and had graduated over 250 elementary teachers. Thirty-three Liberians received training in the U.S.

In-service Training

In addition, a program of in-service training for teachers and principals had been introduced and, by 1967, it was reported that over 1,000 had participated. AID also provided the services of technicians under direct hire to assist in a number of projects involving the in-service training of teachers in English, in science, in reading, and in the improved use of local teaching materials.

MALI

Pedagogic Institute

Technicians from Southern Illinois University worked with the Pedagogic Institute of the Higher Teacher Training Center in Bamoko. They developed an in-service training program for secondary English teachers, established an audiovisual center, and introduced a vocational guidance testing program. Four participants received training in the U.S.

NIGERIA

Eastern Region: University of Nigeria, Nsukka

In the Eastern region, assistance to the College of Education of the University of Nigeria was one phase of a contract by which Michigan State University assisted in the development of a university based on the land-grant philosophy and designed to meet the economic, social, and intellectual needs of Nigeria. Four-year degree programs for secondary teachers and three-year certificate programs for junior high school vocational teachers were developed. An Institute of Education was established with the

52 higher elementary teacher-training colleges in the region. In-service courses and workshops were given on campus or in 37 continuing education centers, and by 1967 were reported to have reached over 10,000 adults, including teachers. A research program directly related to Nigerian education was being carried on when the university was forced to close because of the outbreak of hostilities between Eastern Nigeria and the central government. Fifty Nigerians received participant training.

Western Region: Advanced Teachers Colleges

In the Western region, Ohio University at Ibadan and the University of California at Los Angeles in Lagos assisted in the development of Advanced Teachers Colleges. Three-year programs leading to the Nigerian certificate in education were established which prepared teachers to teach their major subjects in secondary schools and in Grade 2 teacher-training colleges. Six participants from Lagos and 18 from Ibadan received training in the U.S.

The Ohio team was particularly successful in establishing an in-service training program which, by 1967, had over 7,000 teachers registered. In-service centers to make available teaching aids were also established in 26 locations and reported that in 1967 their services were utilized by 12,000 teachers.

Northern Region: Teacher-Training College, Kano

In the Northern Region, Ohio University assisted in the development of the Kano Teacher-Training College. Three programs were developed: a five-year curriculum for Grade 2 primary teachers was planned for students who had completed elementary school; a three-year program for secondary school graduates was developed leading to the Nigerian certificate in education and preparing secondary teachers and tutors for primary teachers colleges; and a two-year program for secondary school graduates who wished to be primary teachers. In addition, in-service activities, including correspondence courses, vacation classes, and in-service centers, helped several thousand teachers each year. Eighteen participants received training in the U.S.

Primary Teacher-Training Colleges

Four-member teams from the University of Wisconsin worked in a unique program-building project in seven of the larger primary teacher-training colleges. The major purpose was to design and demonstrate ways to stretch the contributions of qualified teachers to serve greater numbers of students. Recognizing that program building is a long-term project, the Wisconsin team developed a two-phase approach. In the first phase, teams with expertise in English, mathematics, geography, history, and principles of education worked with Nigerian faculties in each of the primary teacher-training colleges to try out new materials and new approaches. In the second phase, those materials which seemed promising were selected for modification in terms of the needs of Nigeria so that they could be introduced in the country as a whole.

SIERRA LEONE

University College, Njala

Technical assistance in the creation of an agriculturally- and educationally-oriented university college at Njala, a rural location 125 miles from Freetown, was given through a contract with the University of Illinois. By 1967, the college had a faculty of 60 and an enrollment of 300. Four-year degree curricula combining subject matter and professional training were developed with emphases in biological science, agriculture, English, and home economics. Three-year curricula leading to the higher teacher certificate were also prepared. Fourteen Sierra Leoneans received training in the U.S.

An in-service summer workshop program carried out by the NEA Teach Corps provided assistance to over 800 primary teachers over a five-year period.

SOMALIA

National Teacher Education Center

The major AID project was the building and equipping of the National Teacher Education Center for the preparation of elementary teachers. Technical assistance to establish the program was provided by a team from Eastern Michigan University. A basic three-year program for elementary teachers was developed and put into operation and, by 1967, over 150 teachers had been graduated. An in-service training program was also introduced for primary teachers and secondary teachers in English, mathematics, and science. By 1967, over 50 had received participant training.

SUDAN

Khartoum Senior Trade School

Teacher education was one phase of a project in which Dunwoody Industrial Institute provided technical assistance to the Khartoum Senior Trade School. A one-year program of teacher training was introduced. Teacher trainees in six trade areas spent half a day in skill improvement, in addition to half a day in teacher preparation. The project came to an end with the breaking of diplomatic relations in 1967 as a consequence of the Israeli-Egyptian conflict. Seventeen participants received training at the Dunwoody Institute.

TANZANIA

Teach Corps Workshop

In 1966, a five-week workshop for primary school teachers was conducted by the National Education Association for about 240 primary teachers. Emphasis was placed on English-language instruction.

ZAMBIA

In-service Workshop

Direct hire technical assistance was provided to the Zambian Ministry of Education in a program designed to improve the quality of teaching in mathematics, geography, and English at both the primary and secondary levels. Education Services, Incorporated, provided the services of American professors to conduct workshops in the use of modern mathematics textbooks.

EAST AFRICA REGIONAL

Teacher Education in East Africa

Teacher education in Kenya, Tanzania, and Uganda has been assisted through a contract with Teachers College, Columbia University. The project has two main aspects. Beginning in 1964, about 80 tutors (teachers) were supplied to the secondary teacher-training colleges to assist in developing and upgrading their programs. They are maintained under an arrangement whereby salaries at the local level are paid by the respective African governments and AID supplies additional salary and teaching materials.

Institutes

Educational specialists were also provided to assist in developing institutes of education which would devise degree programs for secondary teachers, give direction to in-service training programs, and supply leadership in educational planning. Among the additional contributions they reported were the sponsoring of East African Conferences on Teacher Education and assistance to the ministries of education of the three countries in the development of plans for the reorganization of their elementary teacher-training programs.

LATIN AMERICA

There were 18 projects in 16 countries. They involved six universities or colleges, the National Education Association, the Texas Education Agency, and direct hire personnel. The cost in 1967 was $6,167,000; total cost of the projects, the earliest of which dates back to 1955, was $19,403,000.

BOLIVIA

Seminar Program

In 1966 and 1967, contract technicians assisted in a program of seminars for elementary and secondary teachers, normal training instructors, supervisors, and principals. They were designed to introduce modern instructional methods, and were attended by about 2,300 Bolivian educators. It was hoped that through these seminars an understanding of the need for educational change, and a climate for change, might be developed.

Human Resource Study

Statistical data necessary for the efficient planning of teacher education and other manpower training programs was expected to be available in 1968 as the result of a Human Resource Study conducted by Ohio State technicians.

BRAZIL

Since 1957, the United States has provided technical assistance to many phases of teacher education in Brazil. Among the projects reported were:

A National Center for Teacher Training, established at Belo Horizonte to train supervisors and normal school professors and to sponsor in-service programs.

The training of staff for 60 regional supervisory and teacher-training centers in the Northeast.

In-service training for 6,000 elementary and junior secondary teachers and 1,000 supervisors and school directors in the Northeast.

Training for 500 secondary agriculture teachers.

The development of four vocational teacher-training centers in which, by 1957, over 2,000 vocational teachers had been trained.

Coordinated Plan

In 1966, AID agreed to assist the government of Brazil and state governments to develop coordinated plans for education in the nation. A team from the State University of New York worked at the elementary level and one from San Diego State College Foundation, at the secondary level. A year later, the two projects were combined under the leadership of the San Diego State College Foundation.

Educators' Study Program

In 1966 and 1967, the University of Wisconsin-Milwaukee provided a nine-month program of study, observations, and internship in elementary education for 47 educators from Northeast Brazil.

CHILE

Primary and Secondary Reform

An education sector loan agreement was signed in September 1967 to provide the resources for major reports in primary and secondary, including vocational, education. The project includes technical assistance for both in-service and preservice teacher preparation programs.

COLOMBIA

Regional Education Center

Consultant help was provided for a National Education Planning Study Group which made plans for reforms at the elementary, secondary, and teacher-training levels. By 1967, 23 regional education centers had been established to provide in-service training for teachers.

COSTA RICA

Normal Schools

Direct hire specialists assisted in developing programs at three newly-built normal schools. The curriculum was revised to include a year of general education designed to prepare elementary teachers in the mathematics, science, and social science areas, followed by a year of professional training. Special attention was given to working with the laboratory school staff. Teachers, principals, and supervisors were encouraged to visit the laboratory schools and observe the new techniques. In addition, all 80 Costa Rican district supervisors received six weeks of training in supervisory techniques.

Teach Corps Workshop

In 1967, 175 elementary teachers, supervisors, and principals participated in a five-week workshop conducted by the NEA Teach Corps. Particular attention was given to techniques for handling multiple-grade situations and group teaching methods. The workshop participants were then used in a series of workshops conducted by the ministry of education in which 2,000 teachers of small schools received training.

DOMINICAN REPUBLIC

Comprehensive High School Pilot Project

Assistance in converting the curriculum at two secondary schools from their traditional programs to those of comprehensive high schools was given by a team from San Jose State College. They offered programs in commercial, industrial, agricultural, and primary teacher education in addition to the university preparatory curriculum. The objective was to use these two schools as a pilot project preparatory to establishing such schools in 17 areas throughout the country.

In-service Workshops

The San Jose Team also worked in cooperation with UNESCO, the Peace Corps, and the Teach Corps, in providing summer workshops for elementary and secondary "guide" or master teachers, who were then used in connection with additional in-service programs. For example, the 125 elementary master teachers who participated in the Teach Corps workshop were later used in connection with in-service programs for the 8,000 Dominican Republic teachers with only eight years of education.

ECUADOR

In-service Seminars

AID initiated a program in 1967 to assist in the reform and expansion of secondary and technical education. Following a comprehensive survey of the country's public high schools, in-service seminars were held for about 1,000 secondary teachers. Involved in the project were the Pittsburgh and New Mexico Universities, UNESCO, the Fulbright Commission, and local universities.

EL SALVADOR

Teach Corps Workshops

Beginning in 1967, the emphasis of AID assistance was redirected from elementary, where a surplus of teachers had developed, to secondary, including technical, teacher training. The NEA Teach Corps conducted workshops for 80 secondary teachers of science and mathematics who were then used for in-service programs with other teachers in their local schools.

GUATEMALA

Assistance to Ministry

Technical assistance has been provided to the ministry of education to develop a comprehensive countrywide educational plan for in-service training of primary teachers and industrial arts teachers, and for a pilot in-service program for secondary science teachers.

In-service Program for Primary Teachers

Direct hire technicians assisted in a two-year in-service training program for about 1,200 unqualified primary teachers. It included two summer school periods of eight weeks each, correspondence work in the various subject areas, attendance at workshops, supervisory visits, and observation of teaching in a demonstration school.

In-service Program for Science Teachers

In 1966, the Texas Education Agency undertook a pilot program to provide in-service training for science teachers. The plan provided for a group of 10 Guatemalan science teachers to go to Texas for observation and training, and then to work with 10 science teachers from Texas in conducting a series of in-service training seminars for Guatemalan science teachers.

HONDURAS

In-service Programs

A training program was carried on for 140 elementary teachers in the use of the new textbooks prepared under the ROCAP (Central America and Panama) textbook program. These teachers were then used in 126 short training courses in different parts of the country. As a result, about 5,000 teachers received instruction. Workshops for over 400 primary teachers and student teachers were held in 1966 and 1967 by the Teach Corps.

JAMAICA

Elementary and Junior Secondary Programs

Technical assistance to teacher education was given in support of a World Bank loan of $3,400,000 for the construction of secondary schools and the expansion of teacher-training institutions. A team from the California state college system organized in-service seminars to introduce teachers and administrators to curricular changes in the proposed new junior secondary schools. In cooperation with the NEA Teach Corps, a workshop was held for 275 teachers and principals of junior secondary schools. New methods were presented in social studies, science, and school administration. They also worked with the elementary teacher-training colleges, and helped develop an intern program for 600 prospective teachers in Jamaican schools.

NICARAGUA

Training Centers

Direct hire technicians assisted the ministry of education in the improvement of both elementary and secondary teaching. Training centers were established for both preservice and in-service training programs; 50 librarians were introduced to modern library techniques; 50 science teachers received training in laboratory science; and workshops were held for both elementary and secondary teachers.

PARAGUAY

In-service Program for Rural Teachers

Technical assistance to teacher education was a small part of the Rural Education Development Project which was concerned with the building and staffing of schools in the rural areas. Direct hire technicians assisted in an in-service program for rural teachers and the establishment of a curriculum center for the purpose of developing curricula and teaching materials.

PERU

Broad-based Educational Assistance

Since 1963, a team of technicians from Teachers College, Columbia University, has assisted in a program to expand and improve the educational system in Peru. Members worked on the preparation of a *Five-Year Plan for Improving Education in Peru* and the improvement of the administrative structure of the ministry of education and the decentralization of a number of its functions. Specifically in the field of teacher education, they worked on the consolidation of many small normal schools into regional normal schools; the development of a four-year curriculum to replace the old three-year one; the establishment of training centers for teachers in "nucleo" (central or consolidated) schools in the rural areas; and the improvement of the training of vocational and technical teachers. They also sponsored a nationwide action research program, called CRECER, in which teachers studied their school communities and tried to link educational development to social, cultural, and economic improvements. By 1967, 105 participant trainees had been sent for study to the United States, Puerto Rico, Mexico, Brazil, and Colombia.

URUGUAY

In-service Training for Science Teachers

In 1967, AID, in cooperation with the National Science Foundation, assisted in an in-service training program for secondary science teachers. In cooperation with the Peace Corps, AID also initiated a project that will utilize educational television to raise the level of classroom instruction at both the primary and secondary levels.

VENEZUELA

Vocational Education

Teacher education was one aspect of the technical assistance program in Venezuela which included the whole area of manpower training and development. The major efforts of the University of Wisconsin-Milwaukee in teacher education were focused on participant training, consultant help, and intensive study tours for senior education personnel. Eighty-four professional personnel from the ministry of education were sent to the United States for a 10-month non-credit course in which they studied vocational education and the comprehensive high school curriculum. This program was later modified to a two-year M.A. program in which 31 Venezuelans studied vocational education either at Stout State Vocational College or in Puerto

29

Rico. Short-term and long-term consultant services were given to a number of projects. For example, four technicians were sent to the Barquisimeto Vocational Training Institution to help initiate a program of training secondary vocational teachers in agriculture, commerce, and vocational technical subjects.

INTERNATIONAL

National Education Association Teach Corps

Since 1961, the National Education Association (NEA) has sponsored a program called the Teach Corps. Classroom teachers at both the elementary and secondary levels have volunteered to hold workshops lasting about four to eight weeks for teachers overseas. In the fiscal year 1967, for example, 65 volunteers held workshops in eight countries with an attendance of over 1,600 teachers and school administrators. The countries were: Colombia, Costa Rica, Dominican Republic, El Salvador, Honduras, Kenya, Sierra Leone, and Tanzania. Modern methods of teaching were demonstrated, and, wherever possible, national educators were involved as counterparts so that they could gain skill in holding similar workshops. Among the subjects selected for the various workshops were English, language arts, social studies, mathematics, science, reading, multiple-grade teaching, audiovisual methods, and the production of teaching aids using indigenous materials.

In a number of cases, the Teach Corps workshops were used as an integral part of a coordinated program for in-service teacher training. In Tanzania, for example, the Teach Corps taught English as part of an upgrading program to permit Class C teachers to qualify for Class A rank and salary. The total program, consisting of three major summer sessions, included work in English, Swahili, mathematics, science, history, and geography. In Costa Rica, a workshop was held for 125 elementary teachers, supervisors, and principals who then participated in a series of workshops attended by about 2,000 teachers from one-, two-, and three-classroom schools.

Administrative Internships

The American Association of Colleges for Teacher Education sponsors a program in which outstanding young administrators from colleges, universities, and ministries of education in developing countries are brought to this country for a period of six to nine months. While here they work closely with a college president, or the dean of a school of education, in what might best be described as an on-the-job training experience.

One of the unique features which has contributed considerably to the success of this program is the provision for the American host administrator to travel to the participating country in order to take part in the final selection of the candidate. While there, he also spends from two to three weeks in a program designed to familiarize him with the educational system of the country and to provide opportunity for him to meet and confer with key educational administrators in the country. These experiences enable him to design a more individualized and concentrated program for the intern, and also help to develop a deeper sense of commitment to the program.

During the intern's stay in the U.S., he attends an orientation conference, conducted by the AACTE staff in Washington, D.C., and is also visited on his assigned campus by the director of the program.

By July 1967, about 20 interns had participated in this experience and had returned to key educational positions in their home countries.

Participant Training Program

The training of host country nationals in the United States or in a third country has been an important part of most technical assistance programs in teacher education. In some cases, the contract provided for a certain number of counterparts who had worked with American technicians to receive additional training. In others, the participant training program was entirely separate, but the contract team was usually involved, together with the host country ministry of education and the local mission education officer, in the selection of candidates.

In the majority of cases, the participant training was programmed for the United States. In some cases, because of language problems or the special needs of the program, the training was given in a third country.

In the fiscal year 1967, participant training was provided for over 2,100 in the field of education.[4] Of these, approximately 1,600 came to the United States and the remainder went to a third country.

The domestic programs of a large number of American colleges and universities thus played a significant role in the development of foreign educational leaders and specialists and made an important contribution to the overall manpower training objectives of AID and the recipient countries.

FOOTNOTES

[1] *The Foreign Assistance Program Annual Report to the Congress, Fiscal Year 1967.* Washington, D.C.: U.S. Government Printing Office, 1968. p. 16.

[2] *Ibid.,* pp. 12, 13.

[3] *New Initiatives in Economic Assistance—Agriculture, Health, and Education.* Washington, D.C.: Agency for International Development. 1966.

[4] *Horizons Unlimited—A Statistical Report on Participant Training.* Washington, D.C.: Office of International Training, Agency for International Development. 1968.

Chapter 3

The Technical Assistance Program
Past, Present, Future

THE TECHNICAL ASSISTANCE PROGRAM—AN ANALYSIS

The preceding chapter has provided a comprehensive description of AID activities as they relate to teacher education. In Chapter 3, an attempt is made to analyze observable trends; to isolate the factors which appear to underly success or failure; and to present some recommendations as to both overall strategy and the planning and carrying out of individual projects. They are not offered as final answers, but as the basis for discussion and further investigation. It should be pointed out that no evaluation of individual projects was carried out. This was not within the scope of the study, nor were data available for such purpose in records examined or in brief visits to the field.

Trends Reported Ten Years Ago

In 1959, Verna Carley reported what she described as significant trends in the International Cooperation Administration program of technical assistance to teacher education.[1] She mentioned the following 10 trends:

1. Toward extended and continuing programs of both preservice and in-service teacher education.

2. Toward an acceptance of the need for training of leaders—the administrators, teacher-trainers and supervisors—as well as of teachers.

3. Toward a legal basis of in-service education through finances provided by national legislation, for the upgrading of teachers, and certificates for satisfactory completion of requirements.

4. Toward reducing the disparity between rural and urban opportunities for education through expanded teacher education.

5. Toward a more functional type of teacher preparation which will equip teachers with the understandings and skills to help their communities improve their standards of living and adjust to the changing social and economic circumstances.

6. Toward developing multipurpose teacher education centers with several interrelated projects proceeding simultaneously to the advantage of all participants and observers (for example, in the development of curriculum and educational materials, in adult literacy and in secondary, as well as in primary, education).

7. Toward long-term planning for an adequate supply of trained teachers to allow expansion of opportunity all along the educational ladder, with consideration for the broad base of literacy and primary education, and with increasing opportunity for those most able to continue in middle school, secondary, and higher education.

8. Toward decentralization of programs by developing pilot projects in several parts of the nation, with larger reliance on local initiative and self-help activities appropriate to each region.

9. Toward assumption of responsibility by universities and technical schools for the professional preparation of teachers.

10. Toward greater utilization of available resources through improved coordination among agencies, and within a region.

Trends Observable Today

It is of interest that all 10 of the aims Verna Carley mentioned still can be observed in numbers of projects around the world. Eight additional ones have emerged with additional experience, or are being given greater emphasis than they were 10 years ago. They are:

1. DEVELOPING AN INTEGRAL LONG-RANGE EDUCATIONAL PROGRAM FOR A COUNTRY AND IMPROVEMENT, AND THE INSTITUTIONAL PLAN TO CARRY IT OUT

In the early phase of technical assistance to teacher education, there tended to be a number of projects in which help was given to limited areas of urgent need. This has tended to shift, wherever possible, to encouraging the country to develop a national program for its human resource needs, with assistance being provided for specific projects on a longer-range basis *within that context.*

In the Latin American aid program, Alliance for Progress, for example, it has been made a condition of U.S. aid that countries make adequate national plans which include allocations of manpower and resources to particular developmental goals. Such planning has also been made a precondition for I.B.R.D. loans. In this context, *a country's needs for a large number of broadly-trained secondary school students,* who can fulfill the middle manpower demands of an industrial society, *can be balanced against the demand for universal primary education,* in making plans for the allocation of scarce funds and even scarcer skilled personnel.

2. EMPHASIZING THE DEVELOPMENT OF THE CAPACITY OF THE COUNTRY TO SOLVE ITS EDUCATIONAL PROBLEMS, RATHER THAN TO PROVIDE "AMERICAN" SOLUTIONS

With increased experience in technical assistance, it has become clear that the most important task is *to help the country develop the capacity* to plan, to build institutions, to develop curricula, to write textbooks, to conduct revelant research, to train faculty, and to do all the other tasks of a live and growing educational system. Without this, the best of buildings, equipment, and even trained personnel, will not be used effectively. In Latin America, for example, textbooks which were written, produced, and provided for some countries were resented by many teachers, in a number of those countries, even though attempts had been made to involve the nationals in the program from the beginning.

Helping a country develop the capacity to solve educational problems is a long-range task and does not lend itself to quick results that can be used to justify increased appropriations. Nevertheless, in more and more programs, it is being recognized that this is the only way to produce solid and lasting results.

3. PERCEIVING TECHNICAL ASSISTANCE IN TEACHER EDUCATION AS PRIMARILY A PROBLEM OF INDUCING CHANGE IN A CROSS-CULTURAL SETTING

In the early attempts at technical assistance, consultants often fell into the trap of thinking that, if they could teach the nationals of an underdeveloped country how education was structured in the United States, they could duplicate it in their own country and the problem would be solved. This proved an oversimplification and resulted in frustration on both sides when resistance was encountered or the project proved too expensive for the resources of the country. It ignored the fact that it has taken the United States over 100 years to develop its present educational system. Even more, it overlooked the fact that many of the aims of American education are dependent upon implicit political, social, and economic assumptions that are not shared by other cultures.

It eventually became clear that the long-term goal of technical assistance, particularly in the field of teacher education, was to:
1. Help identify and clarify national goals.
2. Assist the nationals to develop their own ways of reaching those goals.
3. Help them build up their own capacity to do so.

This plunged the technicians into all the problems of any project involving change. Their efforts were complicated by the fact that the educated people within a country were frequently the products of an educational system foreign both to the United States and to the country itself.

4. SETTING UP PROGRAMS WHOSE PRIMARY FUNCTION IS TO DEVELOP A CLIMATE FOR CHANGE

A clearer understanding of the nature and importance of the change process has led to a rethinking of the timing or phasing of assistance in technical assistance projects. It is recognized that *there must be a climate for change*, if massive assistance of either a technical or material nature is to be effective. This has led to a number of projects whose primary function appears to be to encourage a climate for change. This may involve a desire for change, a willingness to accept change, or simply a better idea of what changes are possible or desirable.

The program of summer science institutes of India, now being directed by the National Science Foundation, is one of many such projects. It has resulted in thousands of science teachers becoming more receptive to trying new approaches and, in fact, to requesting better equipment and materials of instruction. One of the most important outcomes of the work of the NEA Teach Corps, in which volunteers from American classrooms have held workshops in many of the developing countries, has been to open teachers' minds to the possibility of different methods of teaching. In Bolivia, with the avowed aim of developing an awareness of need for change, seminars were held for 2,000 elementary, secondary, and normal school teachers, together with supervisors and principals. A different, but apparently successful, approach to the same problem was study tours for Brazilian educators sponsored by the University of Wisconsin.

5. PLANNING TECHNICAL ASSISTANCE AS AN INTEGRAL PART OF DEVELOP-
   MENT LOANS OR GRANTS OF FACILITIES AND SUPPLIES

There is a definite trend for technical assistance to be tied in with loans or grants for the development of facilities in teacher education. Experience has shown that the leaders of developing countries are sometimes eager to build showplaces that will bring prestige to their countries, but are at times over optimistic as to their ability to maintain and make effective use of them, once they are built. They may even be under pressure to rush into programs before it is clear that these are what the country most urgently needs, or upon which it can expend its limited financial resources.

The International Bank for Reconstruction and Development, for example, has made *the securing of technical assistance a requirement for some of its loans, which include aid to teacher education.* The growing importance attached to human resource planning has drawn attention to the need for technical assistance at the point where a projected institution is being fitted into the overall plans for the country, and not merely for assistance in getting an institution built and operational.

6. EMPHASIZING PROGRAM BUILDING IN AN EFFORT TO CHANGE THE
   QUALITY AND DIRECTION OF CLASSROOM INSTRUCTION

Some of the most obvious successes of AID projects have been where a contract team has worked to build up a new teacher education college, to structure a curriculum, and to train counterparts to take over. Changing what is actually happening in classrooms—the quality, tone, and direction of instruction—has been less successful. Of course, implicit in all programs of technical assistance to teacher education has been the assumption that what is being done will improve the quality of teaching. A number of programs, however, have made this their *primary objective.* One illustration is the project of the University of Wisconsin in Northern Nigeria. Teams of specialists worked there with the faculties of seven of the larger primary teacher-training colleges in program building, the main goal being development of improved teaching techniques, curricula, and materials of instruction.

7. GREATER EMPHASIS ON THE PREPARATION OF TEACHERS FOR SECONDARY SCHOOLS AND TEACHER-TRAINING INSTITUTIONS

Making generalizations on a program reaching 40 countries is hazardous, but there are certainly areas where the need to train primary teachers is still the most urgent. In general, however, *there seems to have been a change of emphasis to the secondary level,* including technical and vocational teaching and to preparation of teachers for teacher education institutions. Of 32 programs that were "institution building" in nature, only 6 were for the preparation of elementary teachers. Twenty-one were for secondary teachers and, of these, 10 mentioned some form of industrial arts or trade and technical teaching. Five were specifically for teacher preparation institutions, and a number of the secondary schools also included curricula for prospective elementary teachers.

In some cases, this has come about because of shifts in demand and increasing awareness of the need for more people of the middle manpower level to support the demands of a technological society. A perhaps more important factor has been the realization that available foreign resources are extremely limited in terms of the needs of the developing nations, and so must be used where they can make the greatest impact. This has led to the increasing use of the concept of the "multiplier effect." Projects are selected where the input of the American technician will be multiplied to the greatest extent. It can readily be seen that, if teachers are trained and they, in turn, train others, there is a greater multiplier effect than if the American or other expatriate is used merely to teach children themselves. When the teachers of teachers are trained, the potential is even greater.

8. USE OF MODERN TECHNOLOGY IN TEACHER EDUCATION

A number of projects have been directed to the utilization of radio/correspondence and television primarily for in-service training programs. With rising populations and increasing demands for education, the governments of underdeveloped countries have been faced with a tremendous task to maintain, let alone improve, the level of preparation of teachers in their schools. This problem has been accentuated by a continuous shifting of educated people from positions of relatively low prestige and pay, such as teaching, to jobs in government and industry. In consequence, there has been great interest in using modern mass media technology for in-service training programs to reach large numbers of teachers. Correspondence courses, which are made more vital and effective by lessons over the radio, have been tried in a number of countries. In Northern Nigeria, a recent University of Wisconsin project appears to be receiving an encouraging reception. More ambitious programs involving television are also being tried on an experimental basis. It is obvious that limiting factors exist in the capacity of a country to maintain a steady output of electrical current throughout the area and to provide the necessary facilities for maintenance.

Factors Underlying Success or Failure

Any attempt at evaluation of particular programs faces insuperable problems. For one thing, there are too many unknown variables: the social/political climate of the country; the efforts of other countries and agencies; the educational level which already exists; and the presence or absence of an intangible but very real climate for change. Nor did the planning of the projects include a research design that lends itself to rigorous evaluation. In consequence, it is virtually impossible to pinpoint the effect of the American input.

Just as baffling is the question: What are the criteria for success? A building may be put up, an institution may be in operation, and yet the project may have failed to come to grips with the critical needs of the country. Initial objectives spelled out in contracts have to be modified repeatedly as a project develops. They could hardly be used as the basis for evaluation. Moreover, the long-range nature of institution building makes it hazardous to indulge in premature judgments. And certainly a reading of written reports, followed by a quick visit, would scarcely provide adequate data for evaluation.

But even if an appraisal of whole projects cannot be made, each one has had recognizable elements of both strength and weakness. And the professional people involved—the contract team members, the mission educational personnel, as well as the national staff members—are frequently in surprisingly close agreement as to what these were.

So an attempt has been made to scrutinize the data for clues as to the factors underlying success and failure. In doing this, the following sources have been used:

1. The progress reports of chiefs of party and terminal reports of team members. Particular attention has been paid to the difficulties they reported and the achievements they felt had been accomplished.

2. The judgments of the many professional people interviewed—chiefs of party, team members, campus coordinators, education officers, and national educators—as to the critical factors.

3. The published reports of other investigators.

The number and variety of factors which have been reported as playing a critical role in technical assistance is at first dismaying. It reflects the complexity of the problems; the vastly differing conditions of different projects; and *the difficulty of defining what is meant by success*, which has been referred to earlier. A closer inspection, however, suggests that they can be grouped in clusters of factors. Of course, there is a good deal of overlap, and some specific items don't fit too easily in any category. The four clusters selected for the purpose of this report are:

- Factors Relating to the Project—Its Selection, Planning, and Timing
- Factors Relating to Support of the Project—Host Country, AID, and Home Institution

- Factors Relating to the Contract Team
- Factors Relating to the Carrying Out of the Project.

Factors Relating to the Project—Its Selection, Planning, and Timing

1. CLEAR UNDERSTANDING AND AGREEMENT AMONG THE VARIOUS PARTIES AS TO THE PURPOSES OF THE PROJECT.

There are at least six parties to any major technical assistance project involving an institutional contract. They are: (1) the national government, including its ministry of education; (2) the educators at the project level with whom the team members will be working; (3) AID staff of the overseas mission; (4) AID/Washington; (5) the contracting institution; and (6) the contract team members under their chief of party. Clear understanding and agreement as to the nature, purpose, and implications of the project on the part of all six are essential if the project is to have the kind of support which will lead to effective working relationships and permanent success.

As stated, this seems self-evident but it has wide-ranging implications. National governments sometimes request or agree to proposals for technical assistance for a variety of motives, including prestige and the expectation of financial help. Sometimes, they have no clear picture of what they want and frequently there are changes of ministry officials while a project is being developed, bringing new men with widely differing perspectives into the decision-making and implementation processes. It is also not uncommon for a project to have approval at the ministry level, but for the contract team members to discover on their arrival that the local educators do not understand, or are not in sympathy with, what has been planned.

On the American said, a fairly frequent report by contract team members is that they are not clear as to what they are trying to do, or how they are trying to do it. Turnover in both AID and contract staff also introduces new people into the project. They may have little understanding of past developments and are impatient to get immediate results, even at the expense of abrupt changes in procedure.

Where a clear understanding of and commitment to the project have been most successfully achieved, care has been taken to ensure that the planning process *did involve all the parties concerned.* Planning was also regarded as a continuous program and not something done once, prior to the contract being written. The steps taken in the development of the School of Education at the Haile Selassie I University in Ethiopia provide a good illustration.

2. COMMITMENT TO THE GOAL OF ESTABLISHING AN INDIGENOUS EDUCATIONAL SYSTEM AND NOT IMPOSING AN AMERICAN MODEL.

Some projects have been initially welcomed only to meet with increasing resistance. Others have been virtually abandoned when U.S. financial assistance came to an end. It is obvious that a program that fails to be institutionalized will have little lasting effect in a country. Where the opposite has been the case, it has been because U.S. technicians have helped the nationals decide, clarify, and carry out projects in teacher education the latter saw as meaningful. In this respect it is sometimes difficult for national educators, whose own training may be based on a European model, to see the importance of developing a truly indigenous program.

Since national educators are frequently unaware of the ways in which technical assistance can help them, the technicians face a difficult task. They must demonstrate the values of their expertise without seeking to impose solutions. One way in which this has been done is for the U.S. technicians to work on solutions for smaller problems regarded by the national educators as urgent, even as they work with the ministry or national educators to clarify more long-range goals. It has been reported that one great aid in helping national educators see the value of an indigenous system of education has been the return of participant trainees who, during their stay in the U.S., have developed a more pragmatic view of education.

Reinforcing this point of view, Paul Hanna in his "Model of National Investment in Education" draws attention to the importance of linking input for change to "dynamic national purposes," if it is to be effective.[2]

3. THE PROJECT IS DEVELOPED AS AN INTEGRAL PART OF AN OVERALL PROGRAM FOR ECONOMIC AND SOCIAL DEVELOPMENT.

One of the most noticeable of recent shifts in technical assistance has been that of developing educational priorities as a part of national programs for economic and social development. There are a number of reasons for this. In the first place, the limited funds available, both for the underdeveloped countries themselves to support educational programs and for the U.S. to assist them, have forced attention to practical educational priorities. It is not enough that a proposed program be "good"; it must be urgent.

Then, too, it has been realized that indiscriminate aid to education may produce disastrous results. As David Abernathy points out, giving rural youth a little education makes them dissatisfied with subsistence farming but provides little alternative and results in a drift to the towns of semi-literate youth without marketable skills.[3] "The shotgun approach may create more difficulties than it solves," points out Frederick Harbison, for "in any country, developed or undeveloped, education becomes socially malignant if its people do not have a chance or incentive to use it."[4] In a number of countries, India and the Philippines, for example, there are large numbers of graduates unable to find employment. The reason is that they were taught in inferior institutions by unqualified instructors under curricula that had little relevance to the kinds of work available. Abernathy goes on to suggest that, to be effective, technical assistance in teacher education must go beyond building institutions, developing techniques, and teaching problem solving. It must, he urges, "come to grips with the political ends the government intends the education system to serve, and to point out to governments the effects for good or ill which may be expected to follow from alternative courses of action."[5]

John W. Hanson offers seven criteria for a comprehensive plan for education which would well repay study by anyone involved in technical assistance projects.[6]

4. MAJOR PROJECTS ARE CONCEIVED, FROM THE BEGINNING, AS LONG-TERM AND PLANS MADE ACCORDINGLY.

Projects such as building up a teacher education institution or assisting in the reorganization of a national system of education take time—10 years or more, it has been suggested. The increasing awareness of the need to work within the cultural framework, if lasting results are to be obtained, has made this very clear. Projects in which this has been recognized from the beginning and big expectations for short-term results have not been built up, have proved more successful.

On the other hand, the contract team, AID itself, and the host country are conditioned to want visible, readily measurable results and thus to put a premium on essentially short-term activities. As Richard Humphrey points out in *Universities and Developmental Assistance Abroad*, AID is under constant pressure from "(1) the revolutionary backdrop against which the whole AID role is played out and (2) domestic reactions to its programs, which require the practicing bureaucrat at all times to be ready with 'evidences of effectiveness' for a suspicious Congress and general public."[7] The members of the technical assistance team are generally on short-term (two-year) contracts and idealistically anxious to see results from "their" contribution. And the ministry of the underdeveloped country, faced with rising demands from an impatient populace, is also inclined to grow doubtful if results are not quickly seen.

It is pointed out that other agencies in the U.S. have found ways of supporting long-term projects in spite of the need for periodic financing at relatively short intervals. Congress may have to make the decision that the U.S. does not initiate major technical assistance projects in teacher education unless it is willing to do so on a long-term basis. While recognizing that all foreign aid projects must be within the scope of the nation's foreign policy, it must also be realized that technical assistance, once initiated, should be free from the influence of day-to-day shifts in America's relationship to a particular government.

While it is true that the change process in teacher education is essentially long-term, any project has short-term components. Sometimes the relationship between the two is left unclear and the individual team member is expected to find his own task within the overall work plan. Short-term goals need to be related to the ultimate objectives and spelled out with sufficient clarity, so that they can be operational guides for both individual team members and groups. Such guides would also provide a more objective basis for the assessment of the progress achieved by the project.

5. Major Focus Is Toward Investment In People Rather than Investment in Commodities—Buildings, Equipment, and So Forth.

It is very clear that, for technical assistance to be effective, the technicians must be provided with the necessary tools—the buildings, equipment, libraries, and supplies. Where projects have been most successful, however, the main concern has been training people. In some cases, buildings intended as prototypes have been so lavish that they have defeated their purpose. The nationals have not copied them because of inadequate funds. Worse, the lack of funds to construct similar buildings has become an alibi for refusal to make any change.

In many instances, expensive equipment has not been used effectively. And there are big libraries with fine collections of books in English, where not one student in twenty knows English well enough to read them. The University of Kabul is an example. The library is beautiful and has a good book collection in English. Comparatively little is available in Pharsi, however, and few students know English sufficiently well to profit from the wealth of material available. The chief of party pointed to the difficulty he had experienced in persuading the university administration to provide enough time, in degree curricula, so that students could develop a mastery of what was in effect an essential tool skill.

"The most basic consideration of all," as J. D. Harrar, president of the Rockefeller Foundation, pointed out, "is the extent to which each project can serve as a training facility for the nationals of the countries concerned. Only by emphasizing the training aspects of foreign assistance is it possible to develop permanent roots and to achieve continuity and multiple benefits from an enlarging force of competent personnel able to serve national needs."[8]

Not only skills but even more—*attitudes, perspectives, motivations*—need to be considered if investment in human resources is to be meaningful. In this respect, there was widespread agreement among those interviewed in the study as to the importance of a strong counterpart and participant training program in each major project.

6. Effective Timing.

A major factor that seems to have contributed to the success of some projects is that *the country was ready*. There was a desire for change—and confidence in American ideas. The top leadership of the country was not only in sympathy, but had enough strength and stability to give active support. Of course, this raises the question of what can be done if these important factors are not present. The answer may lie in staying away from major, long-term programs until they are present. Instead, small-scale projects may be initiated which help prepare a climate more receptive to change by offering alternative approaches and demonstrating what can be achieved by technical assistance. There have been many such projects carried on by direct hire technicians. The summer science institutes and the NEA Teach Corps workshops are other examples. And the study tours provided for senior educational personnel in Venezuela by the University of Wisconsin-Milwaukee illustrate yet another approach.

Factors Relating to the Support of the Project by the Host Country, AID, and the Home Institution

1. FIRM COMMITMENT TO THE PROJECT AND CAPACITY TO CARRY IT OUT BY THE INSTITUTION ACCEPTING THE CONTRACT.

Few, if any, of the institutional contracts examined in the course of this study involved the "whole university." Today, institutional involvement is probably an empty phrase in this connection. There was an easily discernible difference, however, between those institutions where a campus coordinator was virtually trying to backstop the operation on his own; and others, where the top administrators in the university or a nucleus of the senior members of a department were vitally involved in it, had perhaps served on the team, or visited it, and were concerned with its success.

The difference was, of course, even more crucial on the project site. In some cases, team members spoke of the frustration of working in isolation. Others seemed to feel themselves still very much a part of their home institution, with strong lines of contact and apparent ability to draw on its resources.

Perhaps of even greater importance was the quality of person serving overseas. Due to the financial cutbacks and consequent uncertainty about the future of programs, many institutions reported difficulty in getting the best qualified staff from their own faculty to accept overseas appointments. The nature of the task, in some cases, was such that high school teachers were better qualified and, in others, the institution might have no one available for a particular specialized need. Where there was a high degree of institutional commitment, however, great pains were taken to find men who knew the institution intimately (perhaps had been graduate students) and possessed the best qualifications for the task to be done.

There was no clear agreement on the values of combining or associating all international education activities in one campus center entitled, for example, "Office for International Education and Programs." Where this practice was followed, however, there appeared to be greater campus involvement. Certainly, there was more utilization of overseas experience, both in the use of feedback for the orientation of prospective overseas staff and in the development of area studies in Latin America, Africa, or Asia.

There was agreement that the campus coordinator should have frequent opportunity to visit the project in the field. In some cases, a returned chief of party had become campus coordinator and was able to give intelligent support. It was also felt that there should be a campus committee, which would include returned technicians, to work with the coordinator.

44

To staff projects adequately proves a real strain on the faculties of most institutions. Indeed, there is some evidence to suggest that, as the project is continued over the years, it becomes difficult to continue to staff it with first-class men from the faculty of the sponsoring college or university. There have, in fact, been questions as to whether it is fair to the students for their most effective teachers to be away from campus for long periods, especially when the contract does not provide for the kind of research in which graduate students could be involved along with their professors.

Institutional commitment implies many things. The project should become an integral part of the instructional program. Time should be allowed to returned team members for feedback purposes and to participate in the recruitment and training of new staff members for overseas work. Salary and rank policy should protect the team members from loss, in comparison to those who remain on campus, and research and publication should be built into the program.

2. THE NATIONAL GOVERNMENT IS STABLE, AND THE MINISTRY OF EDUCATION IS NOT ONLY COMMITTED TO THE PROJECT, BUT CAN GAIN SUPPORT FOR ITS PROPOSALS.

Much of the success of some projects, such as the faculty of education of the Haile Selassie I University, is because they enjoyed the support of a strong and stable government. In others, due to changes of government, turnovers in ministries of education, and fluctuations in the economic position of the country, projects, which initially were soundly based, proved frustrating and discouraging.

In this connection, it has been pointed out that, for a project to succeed, the ministry of education must not only be professionally competent and sympathetic, but it must also have political ability. Education and manpower plans may be made by educators and economists, but the decisions are made by politicians. Unless the ministry of education has developed political know-how, the planning it does will not result in administrative action.

Unfortunately, the governments of underdeveloped countries frequently show instability and the rapid turnover among ministries of education presents a real problem for long-range projects. Unless there can be reasonable expectations of stability, however, the U.S. might be wiser to limit itself to shorter-range projects, as it has done in a number of places.

3. SUPPORT TO THE PROJECT IS BOTH ADEQUATE AND CAREFULLY TIMED.

In spite of the importance ascribed to technical assistance in the educational area, financial support given is still small compared with the total investment in the foreign assistance program. That is perhaps outside the scope of this study. What is pertinent, however, is that once a project has been agreed on, *it must be supported adequately and for a long enough period to achieve results.* This has been true of many projects. In some, unfortunately, the scope of work has been too ambitious for the resources provided. In others, the recipient country has been overly optimistic in the promises it has made of financial support. And in still others, misunderstandings and disagreements between the mission and the recipient country as to their mutual responsibilities for supporting the project have proved most frustrating to the technical assistance team.

Timing or phasing of assistance is of prime importance. Some projects need a relatively long period to identify and clarify the major problems and how they should be attacked, and to develop a climate for change. During this period, massive assistance is wasted, and the lack of commensurate results proves frustrating both to AID and the specialists involved. Equally important, a gradual phasing down of U.S. assistance to the project is better than an abrupt stop. It enables the recipient government to increase its financial commitment gradually, and does not leave the national educators without support when they are just taking hold. There is also need to do first things first. Curriculum change plans, for example, should precede the erection of buildings. Otherwise, costly mistakes are made and buildings are either in the wrong place or do not fit into the program eventually decided.

Factors Relating to the Contract Team

1. THE CONTRACT TEAM HAS OPERATING AUTHORITY FOR DAY-TO-DAY DECISIONS.

The best climate for success is reported when the contract team is as free as possible to make use of its experience and judgment in carrying out the project without day-to-day supervision by the AID mission. This, of course, assumes points made earlier, including a clear understanding of the project by all concerned and a firm commitment on the part of the institution accepting the contract. This need for operating authority has little if anything to do with academic freedom. Most faculty members in teacher education have had experience in working with school districts in a consultant capacity and are aware of the limitations of the consultant role. It is also clear to them that the contract team is a part of the U.S. "presence" and, as such, operates within a political framework.

Richard Wood points out: "The problem of delegation has three major dimensions: delegation from the host country to its representatives at the project site; from the U.S. university to its field staff; and from AID to the contracting U.S. university (including, and especially important, delegation from the AID country mission to the U.S. university field team)."[9] His last point was the one mentioned most frequently by those interviewed in this study. It was frequently stated that the AID education officer seemed under pressure to supervise an institutional contract in the same way he would supervise direct-hire services. As Richard Humphrey stated it, AID officials attached great importance to avoiding possible embarrassment or criticism as the result of "irresponsible" action on the part of contract teams. "In consequence, 'riding herd' on contracts often seemed to have been the agency concept of its normal functional relationship to the contracting universities."[10]

In some instances, AID officials even seemed to feel that any contact with the ministry of education should be through them. In consequence, there was a good deal of frustration and misunderstanding. Some suggested the desirability of moving back to the procedure in the earliest technical assistance contracts, where the major objectives were stated and the contract team was given considerable freedom in trying to achieve them.

2. Chief of Party Is Able To Exert Leadership.

There was widespread agreement that an effective chief of party was essential to a successful project. The five qualities identified in *The Overseas American* as the components of effective foreign service apply to all team members, but especially to the chief of party. They were: technical skill, belief in mission, cultural empathy, a sense for politics, and organizational ability.[11]

The above five points were mentioned in different ways by those interviewed. In addition, it was felt that the chief of party ought to be a senior member of the university or college faculty or at least have such a close working relationship with it as to be able to draw on the resources of the institution. It was also suggested that administrative experience, with the capacity to compromise, and willingness to capitalize on the staffs' capacities, so as to involve them in the project, were of greater value than a reputation for research ability.

Basic to any program of institution building is the need to develop a democratic process of decision making. This demands that the chief of party be able to involve all those with various perspectives on the context in which aid is being given. He must get individuals with widely differing cultural backgrounds and professional frames of reference to agree to and support a common course of action.

3. Sensitivity to the Cultural Factors Influencing Change.

Many of those interviewed stressed the point that the qualifications of the staff are of the greatest significance to the success of the project. One superior consultant, they agreed, is worth more than five mediocre ones. This is also mentioned repeatedly in reports and interviews dealing with AID education officers.

Even more important than professional competence, however, is the ability to look beyond the immediate task and see the whole project in its cultural context. "Technical assistance," writes Harold L. Enarson, "has been viewed too often as a cold, neutral, aseptic process. Assistance is 'given' from a 'better developed people' to a 'less developed people.' Not surprisingly, an unconscious arrogance infects us all. The larger truth is that we and our fellow educators in the developing countries are joint explorers, sharing our culture, our insights, and the fruits of our learning, one with another."[12]

One's effectiveness in any project in international cultural relations, points out Charles H. Malik, depends "on how much one stands firm on the good in himlself; how much one appreciates the good in others; and how much one has the humility, the grace, and the self-confidence to enter into creative intercourse with others on the basis of the good in them and the good in himself."[13]

The mixture of personal, professional, and cultural qualifications needed by the effective American advisor overseas is pointed out in the following list developed by Paul Leonard.[14] His amplification is well worth reading:

First, the consultant must be a realist.

Second, there is the need to understand the culture of the people with whom the consultant works.

Third, the consultant must be thoroughly competent in his field.

Fourth, emotional stability is imperative.

Fifth, one of the most important qualifications for the consultant abroad is patience.

Sixth, the consultant should be able to press for action without alienating his counterpart.

Seventh, the consultant should understand the pride of the Asian/African/Latin American, as well as his insecurity.

Eighth, the consultant should never forget that he is an outsider.

Ninth, the consultant should be creative with ideas and skillful in discussing them.

4. Team Members Have a Clear Idea of Their Responsibilities.

While it is obvious that one of the main qualifications of the overseas educator is flexibility, it is equally important that he must have a clear idea of what is expected of him if he is to be effective. Many end-of-tour reports and interviews attested to the fact that this was not always true.

There were two problems or areas of misunderstanding which were mentioned repeatedly. The first was whether the role of the technicians was *"operational"* or *"advisory."* Sometimes a man went out expecting to "take charge" and found the national educators thought of him as advisory only. In other cases, technicians expected to function as consultants and innovators, and have time for research. They found they were expected to carry a full teaching load and work with counterparts "on the side."

The goal of technical assistance must always be to help the national educators develop the capacity to solve their educational problems. In that sense, it is advisory. However, different projects at different stages will require varying approaches.

The American professor must avoid the very human tendency to bring "the whole plan in a suitcase" and seek to impose it on the national educators. On the other hand, the latter frequently do not see clearly what their goals are; how they will achieve them; or what the foreign technician can do to help. Under these circumstances it would be foolish for the consultant to hang back and wait until his advice is requested. He must move in.

48

Frequently, at the beginning of the development of a new teacher-training institution, there is no core of national educators to "advise" and the technician must obviously get on with the task. Then, too, before nationals are willing to place reliance on any foreigner's advice, they can be forgiven for wanting to see a demonstration.

Karl Bigelow illustrates this point in relation to teacher education in Nigeria as follows: "AID has been committed to the idea that its job of providing 'technical assistance' required the provision of 'advisors' and 'experts' who would exercise a considerable influence in the way of inducing change, and that it was not its business to produce people who would just fill job vacancies. In practice, Americans arriving in Nigeria to work with AID-supported projects have found that the exercise of much influence required a prior demonstration of ability to perform effectively in jobs that Nigerians considered essential to become members of a team in which professional competence determined status and the likelihood of being listened to."[15]

A second problem which was frequently mentioned seems to apply most often to the "first team" or the early stages of a project. The technician goes out with unrealistic dreams of how quickly he is going to make innovations. Then he faces the realities of getting an institution operational with inadequate materials, unqualified assistants, and poorly prepared students. And he becomes intensely frustrated as the two years of his contract slip away and so little of what he planned can be accomplished. *This underlines the need for candor and realism in the recruitment and orientation of team members.*

It has been suggested that training should be provided for technicians in the advisory role. The following "strategy for change," reported by Edward Medina of the Teachers College, Columbia University, team in Peru, is based on his experience.[16] There are seven steps or phases:

1. Develop an environment for discussion of the *status quo* in order to look at the rationale for current operations.
2. Initiate discussion showing that their operations are an expression of their assumptions (implicit) of the nature of society. (Illustration: supervision is tantamount to policing.)
3. Lead them to see there are alternatives. (Illustration: supervision may be a technique for providing a climate for change.)
4. Try to achieve a consensus that an alternative may have better results.
5. Seek agreement to try the alternative on a small scale.
6. Communicate the results to the educational community.
7. Try to get the community to adopt changes (assuming it is successful).

5. AN EFFECTIVE PROGRAM OF ORIENTATION IS CARRIED ON FOR NEW TEAM MEMBERS.

There was widespread agreement as to the values of the orientation of new team members and equally widespread disagreement as to how much was being done or how to improve. It was generally agreed that, while orientation could and should take place in the United States, some would only be effective in the country and within the project. There was agreement that overlap between the tours of technicians assigned to the same task would be helpful in maintaining continuity. At the same time, it was pointed out that the doubling up in housing this would mean, plus the need of the departing technician to have time to readjust before resuming stateside duties, did not make a lengthy overlap practical. In view of the importance of maintaining continuity and minimizing the confusion and uncertainty of each new technician having, in effect, to start from the beginning, ways to provide this overlap should be devised.

There was agreement that orientation should include the history of the project, with its successes and failures, in addition to a briefing about the culture, educational system, and history of the country, and practical instruction in what to bring and what not to bring. A number of those interviewed mentioned the importance of including wives in the orientation program. It was suggested also that there should be some preparation for situations that might arise in such an enterprise .

Some institutions which have a central office as a focal point for international programs (Ohio University is a noteworthy example) make a strong attempt to combine the feedback process from returning staff with the orientation of new team members. In general, however, returned team members agreed that little use had been made of their experience.

In this connection, it should be stated that there are many reports such as Paul Leonard's 1967 report on *The Development of the National Institute of Education* which, if they were published in somewhat abbreviated form, could provide valuable material for orientation purposes. Funds should be included in AID contracts to provide for this, or they should be a part of the institutional commitment to the program.

Factors Relating to the Carrying Out of the Project

1. Plans Are Clear—They Involve in Their Preparation All Those Concerned and the Planning Process Is Continuous Throughout the Project.

"A carefully developed plan, including a clear statement of purpose, a description of methods of operation that might be used, and provision for ongoing evaluation of the project" is given by Arthur Lewis as one of the three elements common to effective projects in technical assistance.[17] There is plenty of evidence that, without such a plan, there is much frustration and wasted effort. A reading of end-of-tour reports yields many examples of technicians who reported that they were never really clear as to the purposes of the project or where their contribution fitted in.

50

Dr. Lewis, in his report for Education and World Affairs, gives the three following overall guidelines which he considers need to be kept in mind for effective planning:

Guideline One: *External aid projects should be related to economic development, educational manpower development, social development, and institutional development;*

Guideline Two: *External aid projects should be related to a nation's ability to make and to implement long-range plans for educational development;*

Guideline Three: *The methods employed in developing and implementing a project should be consistent with what is known regarding processes of change.*[18]

For an understanding of what is involved in these three guidelines, the reader is referred to his report. There are two implications which are of particular pertinence in studying the guidelines:

The first is that the planning process is a continuous one and all concerned must be involved. A scrutiny of progress reports shows that, in many cases, the initial objectives have had to be modified. While great care should be taken to make the initial plans as clear as possible, there must be provision for their re-evaluation and refinement as the project is carried on.

The second point concerns the gap which is sometimes found between those who plan educational programs and those who carry them out. As one science consultant reported, "American aid is offered and accepted at top government levels and then met with polite evasion or indifference when it is delivered."[19] When planning flows both ways—from the top down, and from the bottom up and involves all concerned—the project is more likely to lead to solid success.

2. Adequate Provision Is Made for the Selection, Training, and Re-employment of Counterparts and Participant Trainees.

There is general agreement that projects such as institution building begin to move forward more rapidly when a supply of trained counterparts becomes available. These are nationals who have worked alongside the technicians, received on-the-job training, been sent to the U.S. for participant training, and have returned to take their places in the project. Where counterpart and participant training programs have been the most successful, a number of factors have been reported.

One of the most important is that the ministry of education has been helped to understand the importance of providing counterparts and of seeing that the selection of men for overseas training is made on a professional basis and that provision is made for their employment in suitable positions on their return. In a number of projects, the national educators at first regarded the counterpart as a substitute teacher and were reluctant to provide two men for one job. In some cases, men who had been out of their country for a time found that someone else had taken their position, and that no one seemed particularly interested in their new qualifications. On the other hand, some used their additional education as a stepping stone to positions of higher prestige and salary, and were unwilling to return to the project. It was pointed out, however, that since the majority of the latter stayed in the field of education, they should not be regarded as losses.

A second factor is that the training in the U.S. is carefully planned with the participant's future responsibilities in mind and that there is adequate supervision of his program while he is in the U.S. But two situations are troublesome, it was emphasized. It is very easy for a foreign student with problems in English to get confused and discouraged; or, on the other hand, for a student to get so involved in some advanced piece of scientific research that he is no longer interested in the training of teachers and would not, in fact, be able to use his specialized knowledge in his own country.

One or two universities have assigned responsibility for assigning participant trainees to a particular faculty member who oversees their programs and talks with their academic advisors, whether they are students at his university or not. In a number of cases, it was reported that care was taken to see that the research topic was directed to problems of concern in the participant's country and that, if possible, it was carried out under the supervision of technicians at the project site, or directed by someone on the staff of the university who was well acquainted with the project.

A third factor concerns the problems of participants who return to their own country after a lengthy period of overseas study. They tend to lose contact with influential people while abroad, and get out of the channels that lead to prestigious appointments. Even worse, they frequently find they have lost sympathetic contact with their own fellow nationals. It is important that firm plans for their utilization be made as early as possible, and that they receive orientation to the problems they will face on their return.

Qualified manpower is in short supply in most developing countries and it must be expected that highly-educated nationals frequently will be transferred to other "crisis" areas. As long as allowance is made for this in the number who receive participating training, the result may well be to increase the number of those in influential positions in the country who will support a program of educational change.

3. RELEVANT RESEARCH IS MADE AN INTEGRAL PART OF TECHNICAL ASSISTANCE IN TEACHER EDUCATION.

"Nothing could be more fundamentally important for an entire cooperative assistance enterprise," wrote Freeman Butts five years ago, "than well-conceived, well-executed, independent programs of basic research on the direction, character, and prediction of social change as related to education. Basic research in the theory and practice of international education could be as important for designing technical assistance programs that will genuinely aid national development as basic research in the physical sciences is important for technological and developmental improvement in industry, government, space exploration, and national defense."[20] His comments are still pertinent today.

There is abundant evidence that technical assistance programs take hold and are effective only when they help underdeveloped countries develop educational programs that meet their indigenous needs. When contract teams endeavor to do this, they are made very much aware of the almost total lack of all the kinds of information. The availability of such information is taken for granted in the U.S. They are forced by immediate operating pressure to plunge in, hopefully looking forward to the time when research can be undertaken to supply such data. Where explicit contract provision has been made for such research, and particularly where steps have been taken to build up the capacity of the national educators to conduct their own research projects, this has proved successful. The Institute for Education and Research in India, as one example, has built up a strong national team of researchers whose work is having increasing application to educational procedures in that country.

The need for research in the ways in which qualitative changes in teaching take place is underscored by a theory developed by Beeby. Pointing out that there are four stages in the growth of a school system, he suggests that innovative changes will be successful only if they take into account the "angle of reform." His four stages are: (1) *Dame School* where the teachers are ill-educated and untrained; (2) *Formalism* where they are ill-educated, but trained; (3) *Transition* where they are better-educated and trained; and (4) *Meaning* where they are well-educated and well-trained.[21]

Some projects have promoted modern "inquiry" methods which demand the educational background and inner security possessed by teachers at the *fourth stage*, when the teaching force is still at the *first or even second stage*. These attempts introduce too steep an angle of reform, he believes, and have slight possibility of success. Whether or not his theory is accepted completely, it points to the need for research in the change process in particular cultures.

Freeman Butts offers three propositions relating to the need for educational research.[22] They are placed in an African setting but are aqually pertinent in other areas:

1. The diverse, and often disparate, political, economic, cultural, and national aspirations expressed by the new African governments for their universities must be rationalized into a congruent set of educational priorities if they are to be translated into an effective program of higher education and of teacher education.

2. The fundamental academic assumptions that underlie the university traditions already established in Africa must be reckoned with and,

53

if need be, re-examined in order that their validity may be tested in the light of requirements imposed by these aspirations and by a human resource development theory that takes teacher education seriously.

3. The political, social, psychological, and cultural values that form the context of African life as it faces the prospects of change from traditional to modern forms should be the continuing subject of careful, objective, and empirical research. Such study should provide the basis upon which to formulate a congruent program of teacher education that will bring together African aspirations, inherited university patterns, and the findings of social science research.

Recommendations

The following 21 recommendations reflect the broad agreement, if not consensus, of those involved—chiefs of party, technicians, AID education officers, and others consulted in the study. In other cases, they are no more than a statement of the best practices observed. And in a few cases, they represent the judgment of the Committee on International Relations of the AACTE, which undertook the study at the request of AID. In summary, they are presented as a basis for thoughtful discussion and further investigation.

The 21 recommendations are grouped under two headings. The first relate to the *overall strategy—the grand design of technical assistance.* The second group is directed to the *planning and carrying out of individual projects.*

Recommendations Relating to the Overall Strategy

1. THAT TECHNICAL ASSISTANCE TO TEACHER EDUCATION IN UNDERDEVEL-OPED COUNTRIES BE ACCEPTED AS ESSENTIALLY A LONG-TERM PROCESS.

The conviction of the great majority of those interviewed was that short-term funding, the pressure for quick results, and abrupt changes in programs were major threats to the effectiveness of our technical assistance program. The need to work within the social cultural context; to help counterparts develop the capacity to handle problems themselves; to build confidence in national governments so that they could depend on our advice; and the slowness of the institution building processes were all cited as demanding a long-term approach.

It was recognized that there could, and must, be some short-term projects to demonstrate what technical assistance can accomplish; to help develop a climate for change; and to help solve urgent and pressing problems. Even in these cases, however, there was agreement that they should be part of a long-range plan if they were to have any real impact.

2. THAT GUIDELINES BE DEVELOPED FOR THE SELECTION OF TECHNICAL
ASSISTANCE IN TEACHER EDUCATION AS OPPOSED TO OTHER FORMS OF
ASSISTANCE.

There is urgent need to develop and enforce a strategy for the selection
of the most appropriate projects for countries in different stages of development. Neither the desires of the recipient country, often politically motivated, nor the judgment of a team of professors on a short visit is adequate.

Guidelines which take into account the many factors involved and
capitalize on the experience of the past 15 years need to be developed,
made clear to all the parties involved, and enforced. Of course, individual
AID missions have used various criteria through the years in selecting
projects, but there would appear to be a lack of an overall strategy which
is held to. In addition, the guidelines for assistance in teacher education
may be very different from those in other areas. Recognizing this, a number of writers—Philip Coombs, Jerome Bruner, and Arthur Lewis, to cite
three examples—have made significant proposals.

Such guidelines need to recognize, by way of illustration, that technical
assistance in teacher education is of a long-term nature and requires,
among other things, political stability in the recipient country. Massive
assistance may be premature unless there is a climate for change and, in
view of the limitless nature of the needs of underdeveloped nations, U.S.
assistance may have to be limited to prototypes. Moreover, to be effective,
assistance to teacher education needs to be placed within the framework
of national goals which take into account human resource planning.

3. THAT THE DESIRABILITY OF ESTABLISHING A SEPARATE INSTITUTE TO
GIVE LEADERSHIP TO TECHNICAL ASSISTANCE IN EDUCATION BE RE-
EXAMINED.

Whether it be a "National Institute for Educational and Technical Cooperation," as the Gardner report suggested,[23] or a "semi-autonomous foundation for educational and cultural exchange," as recommended by a
Brookings Institution report,[24] there have been many who have urged basic
reform in the conduct of American educational activities abroad. As
Charles Frankel pointed out, "The problem is not a matter of personalities
but of basic administrative setting." The officials, he added, are aware of
the needs of educational and cultural programs but, "in explaining and
justifying these programs to the Congress or the public, they must inevitably do so in terms of the major purposes for which their agencies or
departments exist."[25]

Among the improvements which it is claimed, could result from such an
administrative reorganization are the following:

    a. A too-close tie with American foreign policy would be minimized.
In some areas, where the countries are hostile toward U.S. policies,
such an agency might be better accepted. In addition, many of the
abrupt changes in technical assistance programs and their generally
short-term nature could be avoided more readily.

b. The present fragmentation of educational activities among different agencies could be reduced.

c. Technical assistance is a very small part of the total AID program, and, under the present structure, is given less attention than, for example, economic assistance.

d. Congress might be more willing to approve longer-term technical assistance projects if they were not tied up in a single package with the whole foreign aid program.

e. Such an agency might be better able to set up programs for training and orienting education personnel for overseas services and, by involving university centers in such programs, increase their capacity for providing consultants and technicians.

f. An agency solely concerned with education would be more able to develop the research and evaluation programs technical assistance must have if it is to have lasting impact.

There would doubtless be problems but, in view of the benefits claimed, it would seem that the feasibility of such a change should be investigated by as wide a group of those involved—both in government and in education—as is possible.

4. THAT THE RELATION OF UNIVERSITIES AND OTHER INSTITUTIONAL CONTRACTORS TOWARD AID BE RESTRUCTURED TO PERMIT THE MAXIMUM OPERATIONAL FREEDOM FOR THE CONTRACT TEAM AND THE SUPPORTING INSTITUTION.

Chiefs of party rather generally reported that one of the major constraints they faced was the tendency of the local U.S. mission educational personnel to try to "ride herd" on the day-to-day operating decisions of the contract team. Academic freedom or autonomy, as such, did not appear to be an issue. It was recognized both that technical assistance was project-oriented and that they must work under the general leadership of the U.S. mission. AID education officers, however, seemed to be trying to "run" the project. They were frequently seen, to quote one professor, "as a kind of Buddha figure sitting in an air-conditioned office and making decisions for people out in the field." It appeared to many that the values of having a university team were negated if they were to be supervised in exactly the same way as direct-hire staff and not allowed to exercise their creativity or professional judgment.

Among the points most frequently raised were the following three needs for flexibility in carrying out the provisions of the contract:

a. A high degree of operational authority.

b. Freedom from interference as a result of day-to-day changes in foreign policy or changes in AID educational personnel.

c. Simplifying and professionalizing the reporting procedures.

56

5. **That the Capacity of the U.S. Educational Institutions To Engage in Technical Assistance Be Built Up.**

To maintain a team of top-quality men in the field was reported by most universities and colleges to present a real problem. For institution building and similar long-term tasks, there was general agreement that a significant proportion of the team should be from the home institution. Building a large enough faculty to do this, without jeopardizing the primary responsibilities of the school to its students, was very difficult especially with current short-term financing procedures.

It was suggested by many that grants should be provided to build up the capacity of institutions to undertake such assignments. This practice, it was pointed out, was followed by other government agencies, such as the National Institutes of Health, the National Science Foundation, and the U.S. Office of Education.

Such assistance could also be used to extend the base of support by organizing consortia of smaller institutions which, working together, would have the strength to undertake a project.

6. **That the Goal of Technical Assistance Be To Help Educators in the Host Country Achieve an Effective, Indigenous System of Education Rather Than to Transplant American Models.**

This does not imply a passive role for the consultant. It has been earlier pointed out that national educators frequently do not see clearly what they want and may be biased in favor of a European model, rather than a truly indigenous system. But it does impose a point of view. Changes in teacher education are a type of social change, so the consultant must work within a context of social change and cross-cultural relationships. A Technical Assistance Study Group reported, for example, that "where the American personnel shed their cloak of superiority and advisory role and became colleagues and associates of the people in the university or department they were connected with—as a part of the total resources to do the job—the better that job was done."[26] This is probably most true in countries with a long tradition of education patterned on European models. It may be even more true as the educational level of the underdeveloped countries rises.

One consultant with extensive overseas experience suggested that it is all-important that we work within the pace of the host country specialists and be sensitive to any clues that they are agreeing with our recommendations out of politeness, but are not really convinced as to the wisdom or timing of our plans. It may make for a slower start, but will produce more lasting results.

7. **That Assistance to Teacher Education Be Planned Within the Framework of the Total Human Resource Problems of the Country.**

It is clear that education has other values than its contribution to the economic development of a country. It is equally clear that, unless men are given the incentive and opportunity to utilize their education, the extension of educational opportunities may only produce frustration and bitterness. Each developing nation has, for example, to strike a delicate balance between satisfying popular pressure for mass literacy programs and building up secondary education to support its middle manpower needs. Even more, it must see that the education provided, at whatever level, is relevant to the social and economic development of the country.

"An *ad hoc* piece-by-piece approach to assistance," as Frederick Harbison points out, "will no longer suffice. It is time to develop, with the collaboration of the host countries, a mentality of assistance which will stress the integrated analysis of problems of development and utilization of human resources, as well as the notion of strategy building based upon the examination of alternatives and the choice of priorities."[27]

8. THAT RELEVANT RESEARCH AND EVALUATION, INCLUDING FOLLOW-UP AFTER THE CONCLUSION OF THE PROJECT, BE INCORPORATED AS A PLANNED, FINANCED, AND INTEGRAL PART OF ALL MAJOR TEACHER EDUCATION PROJECTS.

While it is true that AID contracts ask for research, the task orientation of the agency is not supportive of a research point of view. Some overseas team members have drawn the criticism that they ignored the real purpose of a project in order to devote themselves to their personal research. Then, too, many technical assistance programs do not readily lend themselves to the establishment of research designs that yield quantifiable data. Whatever the reasons, the statement of David E. Bell, former director of AID, is still very true: "It is my impression that the organizations which carry out aid programs do not have a distinguished record of building into those programs strong elements of research and evaluation. Certainly this is true of AID, the Agency I know best."[28]

A number of reasons are cited as justifying the inclusion of research and evaluation in all major teacher education assistance projects. The most obvious is the need to make our programs more effective by sharing reliable information as to the factors underlying success and failure. This means that evaluation has to be planned from the beginning, not added as an afterthought.

A second reason is that we need to help the national educators develop the capacity to carry out the many kinds of research which are fundamental to effective long-range educational planning. That means we not only carry it out with them, but show them how to utilize the results in meaningful change. And, thirdly, if it is accepted that technical assistance in teacher education is, in fact, an experiment in social change, it is obvious that evaluation be included. We should be trying to find out if the input does, in fact, produce the predicted changes.

A strong case for research was made by Freeman Butts when he wrote: "Underlying all other means of improving our technical assistance programs is the need for continuing fundamental research in order to create a body of tested knowledge upon which to base the improvement of education so as to strengthen the economic, political, cultural, and national development of the peoples of the world. Such research should marshal the resources of scholarship in the social sciences and should probe deeply the fundamental interrelationships of education and social change. It should synthesize what has already been learned about educational cooperation; it should utilize what is being learned by the social scientists about social change; and it should bring this knowledge to bear upon the problems of education and modern nationhood in the various parts of the world."[29]

Recommendations Relating to the Planning and Carrying Out of Individual Projects

1. THAT AN INSTITUTION ONLY ACCEPT A CONTRACT IF IT IS WILLING TO COMMIT ITS RESOURCES TO THE PROJECT.

There was widespread agreement that, to be effective, a university or other institution must do much more than act as a hiring agent. A significant proportion of the project team members, including the chief of party, should be from the institution's own permanent faculty. This is to assure that they share some common points of view and can draw effectively on the resources of the institution. Where applicable, they should be drawn from other departments as well as teacher education.

The campus coordinator should be backed up by a committee, including members of the administration and senior faculty members. And there should be opportunity for regular visits to the project by the campus coordinator and administrators.

2. THAT PLANNING BE REGARDED AS A CONTINUOUS PROCESS.

There was widespread agreement as to the critical importance of involving all concerned in planning for the project and of making provisions for periodic review of the plans through what Richard Wood has described as "local adaptive research."[30]

In some cases, it was reported that the host government had been "sold" on a project by the U.S. mission without understanding its implications or really wanting it. In others, there appeared to have been a gap between the ministerial level and the operational level which caused resistance and frustration. There also developed differences of viewpoint between the university, its field team, and the AID educational officers in other instances.

Lack of enough emphasis on planning during the total life of the project was also much in evidence. Three phases were perhaps most critical: before the project was formally started, during its early stages, and as it approached time for phasing out external assistance. The need for flexibility, however, demands that planning be a continuous process.

3. That Guidelines Be Developed for an Ongoing Program of Project Evaluation As Distinct from Auditing, That Involves the Self-study Process.

There was a strong feeling that the procedure for evaluating contract performance should be improved. It was also reported that little use appeared to be made of the many reports which were required either for evaluation purposes or for modifying the program. At the time of this study, the "TAPER" (Technical Assistance Project Evaluation Report) method developed by an AID Information System Task Force had not been introduced, and this may meet some of the criticisms.

Two main points were raised. The first was that AID policy seemed to assume that evaluation must be done by an outside agency and ignored all that has been learned about the accreditation process in higher education in America. To a number of those reporting, it also seemed that such evaluation sometimes was carried out by men who were biased or who seemed to bring in pre-planned reports to justify decisions that had already been made on other grounds.

The second point was that much evaluation could more properly be described as *auditing*. It was more concerned with whether the legal requirements of the contract were met, and was often carried out by people who lacked the professional background or imagination to understand the project's nature and purpose.

It has been suggested earlier that technical assistance to teacher education is a long-term task and that planning must be regarded as a continuous process. If these points are accepted, then the need for a clear, workable system of evaluation with provision for the feedback of information into the planning is also evident. A comprehensive study of rural development projects reported by Thompson proposed that evaluation should include the following areas, all of which would also be pertinent to projects in teacher education:[31]

a. Host country and institutional setting of project:
   (1) General goals of the country-wide assistance program.
   (2) Relevance and importance of contract project in overall country development and needs.
   (3) Host government support, financial and personnel, to host institution.
   (4) Host institution personnel available and ready for training.
   (5) Previous contract or other technical assistance efforts.
   (6) Difficulties, hazards, and special problems faced by AID and the contractor.

b. Purpose of contract project:
   (1) Objectives established at the time contract was signed.
   (2) Additional goals and objectives.
   (3) Scope of operation as defined in contract and other documents.
   (4) Background for evaluation with special objectives or purposes.

c. Measures for determining progress and effective performance:

(1) A listing of appropriate bases for determining progress and effective performance as determined by the nature of the project.

(2) Evidences of accomplishments toward project goals.

(3) Staff of project: authorized positions, number filled, qualifications of contract staff.

(4) Methods of operation and acceptance of contract staff by host institution and AID mission.

d. Recommendations to AID and U.S. university:

(1) For continuing and/or phasing out project.

(2) For improving performance of contractor.

(3) For improving working relationships between AID mission, U.S. university, and host institution.

(4) For making changes that would facilitate progress toward contract goals.

4. THAT THE SERVICES OF ACTION-ORIENTED SPECIALISTS IN THE SOCIAL SCIENCES BE UTILIZED IN DEVELOPING AND EVALUATING CHANGES IN TEACHER EDUCATION.

Along with the emphasis on the cross-cultural nature of projects in teacher education, there was widespread agreement that we need to utilize the services of anthropologists, economists, political scientists, and other specialists in the social sciences. It was emphasized, however, that they must be action-oriented rather than "pure" researchers, and interested in bringing their expertise to bear on the solution of educational problems.

5. THAT CAREFUL PLANS SHOULD BE MADE FOR THE SELECTION, SUPERVISION, AND STUDY PROGRAM OF COUNTERPART AND PARTICIPANT TRAINEES, AND THEIR UTILIZATION ON RETURN TO THEIR OWN COUNTRIES.

Many of those interviewed stressed the importance of training host country educators to be capable of taking over the administrative, teaching, research, and service functions. While it was felt that every attempt should be made to see that those trained for a specific project should come back to that project when their advanced education was complete, it was stressed that if some participant trainees or counterparts went into other phases of education in the country, they should not be regarded as a loss.

Among the specific points repeatedly mentioned were the following:

The selection of candidates for advanced training should be in the hands of a continuing committee representing ministry, training officer, and contract team to ensure that the best individuals are selected, and that appropriate positions are found for them on their return.

It was suggested that, wherever possible, a group of about five who were going to work in the same institution should be selected for study at the same time so that on their return they would be able to work together to exert an influence for change.

The contracting institution must accept responsibility for supervising the program of the participant in the U.S., whether or not he is at their institution, to make it meet his needs. This would necessitate appointing someone on the staff, with personal knowledge of the project, as the liaison officer for participants and giving him the time and authority needed.

Experience in other developing countries which have moved ahead should also be included as well as that in the United States. A case in point is the use of Puerto Rico for Spanish-American programs.

Provision should also be made for reorienting the trainee for the problems he will encounter on his return to his own country.

6. THAT THE HOST COUNTRY BE REQUIRED TO GIVE INCREASING SUPPORT TO THE PROJECT.

It was felt that, in the beginning, host country support might be little more than a token contribution. As the value of technical assistance became clearer, it was suggested that increased support should be required until, by the time for phase-out, the project could be substantially financed by the recipient country.

It is clear that, unless a program is taken over by the recipient country when U.S. assistance comes to an end, little of permanent significance has been accomplished. This is made more difficult if, until that time, they have not had to support it financially. In some cases, the U.S. has maintained massive support until the very end of the contract. Then all assistance has been ended, with the host country having no provision in its budget for continuing the program. As a result, there has been a lapse of some years during which a good deal of the progress has been lost.

A different kind of problem has arisen where AID has provided the buildings and expected the host country to take care of their upkeep and the provision of necessary supplies. This has proved frustrating to the technical assistance team because the upkeep and supplies were simply not forthcoming. To avoid this, it has been suggested that, as the project goes on, there be provision for a gradual shift in responsibility, from token assistance in the beginning, to complete, or almost complete, support at the end.

7. THAT GREATER ATTENTION BE GIVEN TO THE TIMING OF TECHNICAL ASSISTANCE, INCLUDING THE PROVISION OF SOME HELP AFTER THE TERMINATION OF THE MAIN CONTRACT.

Two problems were repeatedly reported:

1. The danger of moving in too rapidly with a large team of consultants.
2. Failure to provide some follow-up after the termination of major assistance.

In regard to the first, it was pointed out there is a rhythm to assistance. In the beginning, only one or two people may be needed to work with the ministry and other educators to clarify the nature of the problem and to begin to lay plans. Too large an input at this time will raise unrealistic expectations and cause frustration both to the technicians themselves and to the host country.

There was even stronger conviction expressed that there must be some assistance after the major phase of the project is over. Such follow-up assistance, it was felt, should provide for further participant training and for short-term consultant help on request to help solve specific problems.

A four-step program was suggested by Dr. Clifford Liddle, education officer in Korea, as one approach to the problem of phasing assistance:

Step I—Small exploratory team. In this stage, a small group of "broadly developed" consultants takes time to find what the host country nationals at all levels want and how they feel the problem can be solved. There may be need during this period for some small-scale technical assistance, as it is almost impossible for a ministry of education to realize how it can draw from technicians without examples.

Step II—Managerial team. This is the period of massive assistance. The technical assistance team goes in to build an institution, working with counterparts, but doing all that is necessary to get the program operational. As counterparts become able, the technicians shift to an advisory role.

Step III—Professional advisors. In this phase, long-term advisory assistance is made available. It is recognized that the national educators, while in complete charge, can profit from the experience of American educators as they establish the new program on a firm foundation.

Step IV—Consultants available. In the final phase, short-term consultants are made available when requested by the national educators. This gradually merges into open-ended two-way cooperation within the academic community.

8. That a Roster of Top-caliber Specialists Who Would Be Willing To Give Short-term Consultant Help Be Prepared and Maintained.

There was agreement as to the need for the services of specialists on a short-term basis. This was particularly true when a project had become well-established, the exact nature of the required services was known, and all arrangements could be made beforehand. It was also reported by some host country educators that they did not get top-quality consultants for long periods and, furthermore, that they could not release their own top-ranking men to work with experts for long periods. There appeared to be a need to develop a more effective way of compiling and distributing up-to-date information as to who were available. It would seem that professional organizations such as AACTE would be well-equipped to work on the maintenance of such a roster.

9. THAT GREATER ATTENTION BE GIVEN TO THE ORIENTATION OF NEW CONTRACT TEAM MEMBERS.

Great variation was reported as to the effectiveness of orientation programs prior to overseas service. This is supported by the reports cited in Richard Humphrey.[32] It was suggested that provision be made for orientation, both in the U.S. and in the host country. In the latter, every effort should be made for a new technician to spend some time with his predecessor so that continuity of effort could be maintained. In the U.S., every effort should be made to involve returned technicians in the orientation process. The expertise of those institutions with strong orientation programs could be utilized both for new contract team workers and AID educational personnel.

Among the topics recommended for inclusion in the orientation program were the following:

The history, educational system, culture, and taboos of the country.

The cross-cultural dimensions of the task, and the dynamics of the change process as they apply to innovation in education.

The history of the project with its successes or failures.

The specific role of the new technician and how it fits into the overall project and needs of the country—as well as the attitude of flexibility necessary in any pioneering venture.

The problems of living in the specific foreign country, as well as the frustrations to be expected in dealing with the nationals of a different culture.

The structure of AID and the technician's relationship to the U.S. overseas mission.

10. THAT MODEL OR PROTOTYPE INSTITUTIONS SHOULD BE KEPT SIMPLE SO THAT HOST COUNTRIES ARE FINANCIALLY ABLE TO DUPLICATE THEM.

Buildings that are too grandiose defeat the purpose of a model or prototype because the nationals say they cannot do quality work unless they have the funds for similar buildings. Similarly, equipment that is too sophisticated for the country to maintain should not be brought in. If, however, quality work is done with modest equipment and buildings, successful graduates and counterparts, who have seen the program in action, can be used to start similar programs in other schools.

11. THAT REPORTING PROCEDURES BE STREAMLINED, THEIR PURPOSES CLARIFIED, AND SIMPLE GUIDELINES PREPARED FOR WRITING THEM.

A scrutiny of the reports in AID/Washington files show great variation in quality and clarity. This suggests a lack of understanding on the part of writers as to the function of reporting or perhaps a conviction that they are only meeting bureaucratic requirements. Many of the reports were extremely long, poorly organized, and lacking in specific information.

Assessments and value judgments were frequently made without supporting evidence and too few of them suggested that professional people were reporting to professional people.

An AID comment on one report draws attention to a problem common to many, if not most, of the reports scrutinized by this investigator. It stated: "The report contains a lot of information, much of it quite detailed. Yet it does not gather this body of information into a summary section which clearly and concisely identifies the major problems and accomplishments."

The writer went on to suggest that if the six-month report were to become a useful program tool, "*It should provide the contractor with a concise format in which to state: this is what the contract team did in the reporting period; this is what the team hoped to do but didn't; these are the team's problems; and this is what the team plans to do in the next six months to advance the program and attempt to solve the problems.*"

A major difficulty seems to be that the reporting procedure does not, in most cases, appear to have been brought into a comprehensive evaluation-planning process. As a result, reports are often treated either as necessary evils or public relations releases.

12. THAT PROVISION BE MADE FOR ADEQUATE COMMUNICATION AMONG ALL CONCERNED WITH THE PROJECT.

Many of the difficulties reported in this study revolved around problems of communication between the home institution and the chief of party; between AID/Washington and both the home institution and the field team; between the local ministry of education, the local mission, and the field team; between newly-arrived team members and the chief of party; and between the field team and host country educators involved in the project who had had no part in its planning.

While there was general agreement as to the need to improve the channels of communication, it was not so clear how to achieve this in the face of a great variety of situations and pressures. Perhaps the suggestion of Richard Wood should be seriously considered: "It is suggested that AID should sponsor a study in which the worldwide experiences of AID and university field representatives would be reviewed for the purpose of drawing up suggestions for dealing with communication problems commonly encountered on university institution-building projects."[33]

13. THAT CLEAR DISTINCTION BE MADE BETWEEN "INDUSTRIAL ARTS" AND "TRADE AND TECHNICAL EDUCATION' IN PREPARING TEACHERS FOR SUCH PROGRAMS.

The industrial arts approach in the American comprehensive high school is designed to produce a broadly educated person who is ready for training. The trade and technical institute, on the other hand, is designed to train skilled workers. Both have a unique and worthwhile function. In the United States, the former assumes that the great majority of students will attend high school before entering a trade. *This assumption is not true of the developing countries, however.* In consequence, as Frederick Harbison suggests, there appears to have been some confusion as to whether multi-purpose or comprehensive secondary schools were intended to "develop specific skills or to provide reasonable broad pre-employment education."[35]

It is clear that in setting up programs to train vocational teachers, *a clear distinction needs to be made between the two approaches,* both in discussions with host country educators, and in selecting technicians with appropriate experience and qualifications.

FOOTNOTES

[1] Carley, Verna A. *Report of Progress in Teacher Education—Technical Co-operation in Forty Developing Countries.* Washington, D.C.: Office of Educational Services, International Cooperation Administration. 1960. pp. 39-43.

[2] Hunnicutt, Clarence W., editor. *America's Emerging Role in Overseas Education.* Syracuse, N.Y.: Syracuse University School of Education. 1962. pp. 21-38.

[3] Abernathy, David and Coombe, Trevor. "Education and Politics in Developing Countries." *Harvard Educational Review* 35 (3) : 287-302, Summer 1965. p. 291.

[4] Harbison, Frederick. "Education for Development." *Scientific American* 24 (3) ; 1963. p. 140.

[5] Abernathy, David and Coombe, Trevor. *op. cit.,* 35 (3) : 288. Summer 1965.

[6] Hanson, John W. and Brembeck, Cole S., editors. *Education and the Development of Nations.* New York: Holt, Rinehart and Winston, 1966.

[7] Humphrey, Richard A., editor. *Universities—and Development Assistance Abroad.* Washington, D.C.: American Council on Education. 1967. p. 9.

[8] Harrar, J. D. "AID Abroad: Some Principles and Their Latin American Practice." F. Emerson Andrews, editor. *Foundations—20 Viewpoints.* Russell Sage Foundation, 1965. pp. 42-43.

[9] Wood, Richard H. *U. S. Universities: Their Role in AID-Financed Technical Assistance Overseas.* New York: Education and World Affairs. 1968. p. 33.

[10] Humphrey, Richard A. *op. cit.,* p. 31.

[11] Cleveland, Harlan, Mangone, Gerard J., and Adams, John C. *The Overseas Americans.* New York: McGraw-Hill Book Co. 1960. p. 31.

[12] Enarson, Harold L. "The Successes and Failures of AID." *Phi Delta Kappan.* 47 (4) ; December 1965.

[13] Malik, Charles H. "The World Looks at the American Program." *Education and Training in the Developing Countries: The Role of U. S. Foreign Aid.* (Edited by William Y. Elliott.) New York: Praeger, 1966. p. 40.

[14] Leonard, J. Paul. "The Development of the National Institute of Education." (Unpublished.) New York: Teachers College, Columbia University, 1967. pp. 106-116.

[15] Bigelow, Karl S. "AID and Teacher Education in Nigeria." Report for Education and World Affairs, 1966. p. 24. (Mimeo.)

[16] Medina, Edward. Personal interview with Project Staff, August 1968.

[17] Lewis, W. Arthur. *Guidelines for the Planning of External AID Projects in Education.* New York: Education and World Affairs, 1967. p. 9.

[18] *Ibid.,* p. 10.

[19] Dart, Francis E. "The Rub of Cultures." *Foreign Affairs* 41: 360-68; January 1963.

[20] Butts, R. Freeman. *American Education in International Development.* New York: Harper and Row. 1963. p. 43.

[21] Beeby, C. E. *The Quality of Education in Developing Countries.* Cambridge, Mass.: Harvard University Press. 1965. pp. 58-82.

[22] Butts, R. Freeman, in *Education and the Development of Nations*. (Edited by John W. Hanson and Cole S. Brembeck.) New York: Holt, Rinehart and Winston, 1966. p. vi.

[23] Gardner, John W. *AID and the Universities*. New York: Education and World Affairs. 1964. p. 15.

[24] Frankel, Charles. *The Neglected Aspect of Foreign Affairs: American Educational and Cultural Policy Abroad*. Washington, D.C.: The Brookings Institution. 1966. p. 142.

[25] *Ibid.*, p. 133.

[26] Andrews, Stanley. "University Contracts: A Review and Comment on Selected University Contracts in Africa, the Middle East and Asia." Washington, D. C.: Technical Assistance Study Group, International Cooperation Administration, Department of State. 1960. pp. 14-17.

[27] Harbison, Frederick. "Development and Utilization of Human Resources; Building a System for Assistance Activities." in Shiver (ed.) *Higher Education and Public International Service*. Washington, D.C.: American Council on Education. 1967. p. 48.

[28] Brademas, John, chairman, *Task Force on International Education: Past, Present, Problems and Prospects*. Washington, D.C.: Government Printing Office, 1966. p. 281.

[29] Butts, R. Freeman. *American Education in International Development*. New York: Harper and Row. 1963. p. 39.

[30] Wood, Richard H. *op. cit.*, p. 54.

[31] Thompson, William N. *et al.* "AID—University Rural Development Contracts and U.S. Universities." (Unpublished.) Urbana, Ill.: University of Illinois, 1968. pp. 112-121.

[32] Liddle, Clifford. Personal interview with Project Staff. June 1968.

[33] Humphrey, Richard A. *op. cit.*, pp. 108-109.

[34] Wood, Richard H. *op. cit.*, p. 58.

[35] Harbison, Frederick, *op. cit.*, p. 64.

Chapter 4

Technical Assistance in Action

Section I
Variety and Diversity of Assistance Programs

Section II
Range of Assistance Programs

Chapter 4 is designed to provide a comprehensive survey of AID's involvement in technical assistance in the field of teacher education. Most of the projects are of recent origin and display the variety and diversity of America's response to the global needs of man for improved educational skills and services.

Institutions which have had little prior involvement in technical assistance in developing countries are sometimes called on to staff a new or on-going project. In such cases, it might be helpful to them to have case studies of actual projects available for study and reference. This information will also be useful for the orientation of new team members or for review in seminars concerned with technical assistance in teacher education.

The chapter reflects only a portion of the massive AID contribution to technical assistance overseas, even in the field of teacher education. Nevertheless the documentation is extensive and is therefore presented in two parts.

The first section describes projects that are illustrative of the range, variety, and diversity of technical assistance currently undertaken by AID. These case studies are not necessarily those that have proved to be most successful, but rather are indicative of the multifaceted approach by the American government and educational community to the unique problems, stages of development, and levels of aspirations facing educational planners in developing nations.

Examples are included from different kinds of contractors; the various levels and types of teacher preparation, in-service and preservice; institution building; program building; and national planning. Also included are programs which have unique or distinctive features. In each case, the objectives of the contract are stated and relevant background material and major activities are reported.

The second section provides additional examples as resource material and these, when added to the case studies of the first section, give some indication of the total contemporary contribution of American technical assistance to the improvement of teacher education and the teaching profession in the world.

Mass Training Program for Rural Teachers in Vietnam
AID/Direct Hire

This program was designed to assist the government of Vietnam provide teachers for a vastly expanded system of rural or hamlet schools.

Objectives

1. To provide a three-month training program for 11,500 teachers to staff additional classrooms and to replace teachers who have retired, died, or been drafted.
2. To initiate in 1968 an in-service education program for 5,000 hamlet school teachers in order to improve instruction in rural areas and for an additional 5,000 in 1969.

Background

In the early 1960's, the rural people of South Vietnam made known to the central government their urgent demand for education of their children. The hamlet school program, started in 1963, was the government's attempt to meet this demand and to win the loyalty of the rural population.

The program aimed at increasing the elementary school enrollment from 400,000 in 1962 to 2,000,000 by 1968. It was proposed in six years (1963-1968) to build 11,500 classrooms, each for 60 children, and to give 13,000 teachers a brief training course. By the end of 1966, over 6,500 classrooms had been built and 8,600 teachers trained, and plans were in hand to build 5,000 classrooms and train 6,500 teachers in 1967 and 1968.

By the end of 1967, it was reported that there were 1,700,000 students attending elementary schools in Vietnam, 370,000 in the secondary schools, and 32,000 in the universities. It was also reported that over 11,600 teachers had been trained in the 90-day intensive training courses and over 8,400 classrooms constructed. Another 2,800 classrooms had been built in the revolutionary Self-Help Program.

Major Activities

The program was administered by the provincial education authorities under the direction of the government of Vietnam and with the assistance of USAID technicians. The teaching was carried on by provincial teachers.

Three-Month Training Program

A three-month training program consisting of eight weeks of instruction and four weeks of on-the-job training was given to 11,600 teachers. It was designed to give a practical orientation to teaching in the hamlet schools.

71

It included some basic theory; a review of the subjects to be taught and methods of teaching them; and opportunities for observation and practice.

Local applicants with from five to eight grades of education received training at centers in each of the 45 provinces. In 1964, 85 percent of the trainees were men but, three years later, 95 percent were women. This was not only because military service had claimed the men, but also because the women were beginning to see teaching as an acceptable type of work for themselves.

In-service Training

During 1967, over 5,000 Vietnamese received some form of in-service training. This ranged from vacation courses three months in length to short workshops ten days long. Thirty-six hundred teachers, for example, participated in 32 workshops emphasizing the utilization of textbooks. They were taught by master teachers who themselves had received a three-month course in preparation. Other workshops were designed for ministry of education officials and inspectors so that they could understand and give assistance to the hamlet teachers. It was reported that, as a result of this, many inspectors were encouraged to get out of their offices and become actively involved in working with the teachers in their districts.

Participant Training

Over 90 ministry and provincial education officials were given a three-month study tour to the United States and Taiwan. This was divided between a specially-designed training program in a United States university, tours in the U.S. to observe community education in rural areas, and a tour in Taiwan to show progress in elementary education in that country.

Mobile Science Units for Elementary In-service Training
AID/International Voluntary Services

In 1963, International Voluntary Services received a contract from USAID to develop mobile science units for the improvement of science instruction in the elementary schools of Vietnam.

Objectives

1. To work with the Vietnamese in developing teaching methods which would be effective within the structure of the Vietnamese school system.

2. To make the teaching of science an exciting process so that science instruction could become more meaningful to the Vietnamese students.

Major Activities

The first mobile science unit was developed in Hue in the latter part of the 1963-1964 school year. It proved so successful that other units were added. By 1967, there were six units in various provinces and they had become a regular part of the International Voluntary Services program.

The science unit was usually carried in a panel truck. A typical tour took in some 15 to 30 schools. At each stop a demonstration was given to about 35 teachers who came from elementary schools in the area. There were usually about three lectures a week. In a four-week period, 14 demonstrations were given to 500 teachers from 63 schools. It was also reported that follow-up visits were made to help the teachers make some of the things demonstrated.

Vietnamese counterparts were trained in the operation of the mobile science units so that they could take over when the International Voluntary Services team moved out.

Assistance to Afghanistan's Teacher Education Program
AID/Teachers College, Columbia University

Since 1954, Teachers College, Columbia University, has provided technical assistance to the Afghanistan Ministry of Education in a program designed to improve teacher education at both the elementary and the secondary levels.

Objectives

The Teachers College technicians were asked to provide advisory and teaching assistance in developing staff and programs for the following:

Primary Teacher Education
1. An Emergency Teacher-Training Program operating at 29 middle schools (Grades 7-9) and 4 teacher-training schools to produce 800 primary teachers (Grade 10 graduates) a year by 1967.
2. Regular teacher-training programs at four teacher-training schools to produce 400 primary teachers (Grade 12 graduates) per year by 1966.

The Faculty of Education, Kabul University
1. Professional education programs with the faculties of letters and science for students preparing for secondary teaching.
2. Programs for teachers of professional education subjects at the secondary level and administrators for Afghanistan schools.

Establishment of English as the Major Foreign Language of Afghanistan
1. A program in the Department of English, faculty of education, to prepare English-language instructors.

2. Development of the English-Language Institute, Kabul University, to provide instruction in English for students in the 11 faculties at the university.

3. Development of a national supervisory organization to administer the English-language program on its own by 1967.

Science and Mathematics Program

Development of modern science and mathematics curricula and textbooks, and in-service training of teachers at two lycées as a demonstration school project. It was planned that the curricula and textbooks which were developed would be extended to other lycées to provide better qualified students to enter Kabul University.

Kabul University Administration

The establishment of an efficient centralized administration for Kabul University which had 3,000 students in 11 faculties in 1965.

Participant Training

Jointly with the dean of the faculty of education to select participants and plan for their training programs at Teachers College, Columbia University.

Major Activities

Faculty of Education

Seven members of the Teachers College team worked with the faculty of education. They introduced a degree curriculum in education, primarily designed for teachers of professional education courses and for school administrators. In the spring of 1967 there were 264 students enrolled in the faculty of education, 30 of whom were seniors. Of the 20 who graduated in 1966, the majority took positions in teacher-training schools.

The English teacher-training department developed a bachelor of arts program in the teaching of English, combining general education, a concentration in English, professional courses in education, and student teaching. By 1967, there were about 200 enrolled in the program and over the preceding seven years approximately 100 had graduated. The majority of these took positions as English teachers in the secondary schools.

It was decided by the university administration that the faculty of education would work with the other faculties in providing the professional courses and student teaching for prospective teachers in such fields as history, chemistry, and biology. Programs to do this were worked out and, by 1967, put into effect in agriculture and science.

Primary Teacher-Training Program

A team of Teachers College technicians assisted in the development of both regular and emergency primary teacher-training programs at the one initial teacher-training school in Kabul and in the five additional training schools developed between 1961 and 1967. They helped to develop the professional sequence of studies and to improve curricula in science, social studies, mathematics, and practical arts. They were also involved in preparing teaching materials and in the design, construction, and equipping of facilities such as laboratories.

All of these professional education texts were reviewed and, where necessary, were retranslated or revised. The Psychological Foundation texts, for example, all had to be retranslated because students found them too difficult to understand.

In-service seminars and workshops were conducted with the laboratory school teachers and the training school teachers and counterparts.

Textbooks on the teaching of agriculture, language arts, social studies, mathematics, and science were revised, used on an experimental basis, and prepared for translation into Pharsi and Pashto.

The number of students graduating from primary teacher-training programs was reported to have increased from 20, in 1956, to an estimated 950, in 1967, including both standard and emergency programs.

The responsibility for assisting in the training of primary teachers was transferred to UNESCO in July 1967.

Lycée Project in Mathematics and Science

The weakness of science instruction in Afghanistan is shown by the fact that in 1964 only two students out of the best lycée graduates were able to pass the science examination given by the American University of Beirut for admittance to its undergraduate college program. Reasons for this poor performance included the following: teachers were poorly prepared; teaching consisted largely of the dictation of notes; there were few textbooks; no science laboratories were being conducted; and attendance by teachers and students was poor. At the same time, as pointed out by the National Science Foundation Survey Team, 25 kits of German-made science instruction equipment and materials costing $250,000 remained unused, most of them still stored in their crates at the schools.

The Teachers College team concentrated its efforts on two lycées and attempted, by holding workshops each week for the 17 science teachers, to introduce laboratory instruction and to improve classroom teaching. Plans were laid for new science laboratories to be built; a start was made on preparing new textbooks; and science equipment and supplies were ordered.

Mathematics

A diagnostic testing program was administered at two lycées and revealed that students possessed only minimal knowledge. A re-instruction program was carried on in both schools, but only limited success was reported. New textbooks were prepared; equipment such as geometric models, logarithmic tables, and graph charts was secured; and a special math program was introduced for pre-engineering and pre-agriculture students.

A National Science Foundation Survey Team recommended, in 1966, that the scope of the pilot project be widened to include five additional lycées rather than undertake a nationwide series of vacation institutes.

Survey Team Recommendations

The National Science Foundation Survey Team recommended the following:

1. Expansion and improvement of counterpart involvement and training with at least one-half to be assigned for advanced study in institutions where the primary focus is on science-math *per se* but in a setting sympathetic to teacher needs.

2. Increase in the number of Afghans able to write textbooks and teaching materials, and increase in the number of United States technical advisors in order to produce higher quality materials than are presently being turned out.

3. Gradual expansion of the "pilot program," as indicated above, by initially enlarging from two to six or seven lycées (which would include about one-half of all science-math lycée teachers in the country), with the understanding that (a) all teachers in pilot lycées will be involved in the experimental program testing and using new materials, (b) all participating teachers will be given specialized instruction in math-science subject matter, and (c) emphasis also will be placed on the modern philosophy of science and mathematics education and practical experience in teaching new materials.

4. Establishment of a small center for the development of simple and inexpensive demonstration and laboratory materials.

Following the National Science Foundation report, the program was expanded to include six lycées and approximately half the secondary teachers in the country. Social studies were also added. Six specialists—three in science, two in mathematics, and one in social studies—were assigned to the project and four more pilot schools were added. New textbooks were introduced, and afternoon workshops were held to help the teachers understand the new materials and change their teaching techniques from a lecture activity to one of discussion and fact finding. A nine-week science institute was also held for 40 teachers in the Kabul area.

Participant Trainees

By 1967, 130 Afghan students had been sent to the United States for participant training. At that time, 23 were still on study leave, 43 were on the faculty of Kabul University, and the remainder were either in other schools or employed by the ministry.

In the early stages of the project, the majority of the participants studied in the field of education. Later, in response to the recommendations of a

National Science Foundation visiting team, the participants were encouraged to achieve a balance between content and professional education courses.

In view of the language difficulties experienced by many of the earlier participants, a new procedure was introduced. Those selected for participant training were sent to the American University of Beirut to take basic English courses and work in their content fields on a no-credit basis. When they achieved a suitable level of performance, they registered at a university in America. If they were unable to do this, they returned to Afghanistan. This avoided maintaining students at heavy expense in the United States mainly to study English.

Textbooks

A series of 12 textbooks was developed and distributed: *Afghans Learn English*. Through workshops and regional supervisors, a pattern was set up for in-service retraining of teachers in the provinces to use the new material.

Training of Teachers for Multipurpose High Schools in India
AID/Ohio State University

In 1956, Ohio State University began a long-range program to assist in the development of multipurpose or comprehensive high schools in India and to establish four regional colleges to train teachers for them. The program was organized in three phases with sharply modified objectives.

Phase I Objectives

The first phase of the project (1956-1958) focused on the in-service training of secondary school teachers through the establishment of extension training centers.

The Ohio State team was to assist the All-India Council for Secondary Education of the government of India in the following:

1. Improving secondary school teacher competence.
2. Introducing modern curriculum planning procedures.
3. Producing various types of curriculum materials.
4. Improving methods of examination and evaluation.

Phase II Objectives

The second phase of the project, which continued until 1961, was directed to the improvement of the vocational and practical arts curricula in the multipurpose secondary schools. After the completion of a survey of a number of multipurpose schools by the Ohio specialists, the following objectives were agreed upon:

1. Assist in the selection and development of 26 multipurpose schools throughout India as demonstration or model schools.

2. Assist in organizing and conducting workshops and seminars dealing with problems in vocational and practical arts.
3. Assist in establishing and organizing a curriculum aids laboratory.
4. Provide consultation services on problems of improving secondary education to the ministry of education.

Phase III Objectives

The third phase of the program (1962-1969) involved the creation of four regional colleges of education at Aymer, Bhopal, Bhubaneswar, and Mysore. Each of the colleges was to have its own demonstration school. The objective of the institutions was to train teachers for multipurpose schools. Training was to be in the fields of agriculture, commerce, home science, technology, crafts, and vocational guidance. The specific objectives of the project were:

1. To develop and demonstrate improved patterns for degree programs of teacher education, and produce teachers for secondary schools and specialized technical vocational institutions in the areas of science, commerce, agriculture, technology, crafts, English, home science, and fine arts.
2. To develop and demonstrate postgraduate degree programs for the preparation of qualified teacher educators for teacher-training institutions and other positions of leadership in selected aspects of education, with major emphasis on the secondary level.
3. To provide in-service education courses (non-degree) and extension field services for teachers in secondary and specialized post-secondary technical institutions.
4. To organize and develop four demonstration multipurpose secondary schools, one attached to each regional college, to serve as effective laboratories of teacher education and models of suitable programs and procedures for schools in the four regions.
5. To undertake pilot studies and research projects relating to problems in teacher education, secondary education, and post-secondary technical and vocational education.
6. To prepare and disseminate instructional materials for secondary schools and post-secondary vocational technical institutions.
7. To collaborate with other institutions and agencies in initiating and promoting improved educational programs.

Phase I Activities

A team of four education specialists spent two years, 1956 to 1958, working with the All-India Council. They participated in conferences, workshops, and seminars in 28 major cities and worked directly with an estimated 6,000 Indian educators. They assisted in the establishment of 31 extension centers and the improvement of 23 which were already in operation.

Phase II Activities

The original plan was for a team consisting of an agricultural, a commercial, and a technical education specialist to spend at least one month in each state working with two multipurpose schools and arranging for short-term seminars for practical arts teachers in the surrounding areas.

Due to delays in getting the program started, the seminars had to be omitted and the visits to the schools cut from four to ten days. Few schools were found with programs in all three streams, so the teams were split.

The visits appear to have been largely for "inspection," with reports being sent to the ministry of education. However, individual and group conferences were held with teachers on curriculum and methods of teaching. New equipment provided by USAID was assembled and demonstrated.

In-service Training

During this period, the number of extension training centers was increased to 74, and the new technical curricula were introduced to over 2,100 secondary schools.

Workshops from four days to two weeks in length were held for commercial and technical teachers. Seminars in guidance were also held for principals and counselors.

Materials of Instruction

In the summer of 1960, a workshop was organized to prepare handbooks for teachers of agriculture, commercial, and technical education. The materials which were produced were printed and distributed to all multipurpose high schools in India.

Assistance to the Ministry of Education

A number of reports were prepared at the request of the ministry of education examining the status of technical education in India, and making proposals for the further development of multipurpose high schools.

Phase III Activities

The Ohio State team members worked with the faculties of the four regional colleges at Aymer, Bhopal, Bhubaneswar, and Mysore to develop programs in commerce, industrial arts, agriculture, and science for teachers in multipurpose secondary schools. At first, four consultants were stationed at New Delhi and two at each of the four regional colleges. This was changed in 1965 to four at each of the colleges (one each in commerce, industrial arts, agriculture, and science), with a chief of party and education advisor at New Delhi.

With the assistance of the Ohio State University team, the four colleges were established with a combined enrollment of 3,000 students.

Preservice Programs

Ohio State staff assisted in developing four-year degree courses combining content and pedagogy in science, commerce, and technology. The degrees were granted by the particular university with which each college is affiliated. Plans for a four-year program in agriculture were formulated but not put into effect.

One-year curricula for candidates who already possessed a degree were developed in science, commerce, technology, and agriculture.

In-service Programs

A program combining summer school attendance with correspondence work was also developed to enable teachers to complete the requirements for the bachelor of education while continuing to teach. In 1966, about 500 teachers were enrolled. They attended two consecutive summer sessions. During the intervening school year, a combination of supervised field experience and correspondence work was planned.

The demonstration schools were developed and a beginning was made in their utilization as laboratories for the teacher-training program.

Summer workshops were held in agriculture, commerce, science, and technology.

Instructional Materials

It was reported that a modest beginning had been made in the preparation of instructional materials including handbooks, syllabi, and teachers manuals. A number of projects in science, commerce, and technology were reported. By way of example, a monograph, *Research Ideas for Science Projects,* especially suited to Indian schools, was prepared and illustrated. The first edition of 25,000 copies was so well received that an additional 50,000 were printed. Based on the monograph, a traveling science show was developed and presented before 50,000 science students and teachers.

Participant Training

Fifty Indian staff members received training in the United States for periods of from 3 to 12 months, most of them going to Ohio State University. By March 1967, 41 had returned, 37 of whom were reported to be on the staffs of the four regional colleges.

In-service Training for India's Science Teachers
AID/National Science Foundation

In 1963, the government of India requested USAID to assist in a program of summer science institutes to strengthen science teaching. The program has gone through three distinct phases. In the first phase, Teachers College, Columbia University, sponsored a pilot program to introduce high school teachers to the "new approach" in science education.

In the second phase, four universities cooperated in a greatly extended program. The University of Houston sponsored institutes for teacher training in technology; the University of Wisconsin, in engineering; Teachers College, Columbia University, in secondary school mathematics and science; and Ohio State University, in mathematics and science on the college and university level.

In the third phase, the government of India created a National Council for Science Education to develop a national program to improve science education throughout the country. In addition to sponsoring summer institutes, the new council was to provide for the indigenous development and production of inexpensive teaching, demonstration, and laboratory aids suitable to Indian situations; closer cooperation between college and school systems; and sustained year-round programs. Under an agreement between the government of India and USAID, the National Science Foundation assumed responsibility for advising the National Council for Science Education and coordinating United States contributions to the program.

Objectives of Summer Science Institutes

The purpose of the institutes was to bring together groups of science teachers for a period of from five to eight weeks and make available to them modern textbooks, improved techniques, and teaching aids. Specific objectives were to:

1. Establish channels of communication between schools and universities.

2. Improve the subject matter competence of participating teachers by acquainting them with recent developments in their subjects.

3. Enable teachers to develop a better understanding of the basic concepts of their field of specialization.

4. Enable teachers to conduct experiments with simple and improvised apparatus, and to encourage further experimentation along suggested lines leading to a consideration of theoretical ideas growing from experiments.

5. Strengthen the capacity of the teachers for motivating able students to develop an aptitude for research.

6. Stimulate interest in teachers by bringing them into contact with eminent men in their field study.

7. Enable teachers to exchange views with their colleagues in the profession and thus promote a greater understanding and appreciation of each other's teaching problems.

In 1966, the objectives were modified, and the National Science Foundation assumed responsibility for coordinating United States technical assistance in 1967. The program was now called *Science Education Improvement*, rather than Summer Science Institutes.

The new objective was to help India operate an effective program to improve science teaching without outside assistance. It was proposed to do this through the creation of a National Council for Science Education and national advisory panels on science education in mathematics, biology,

81

chemistry, physics, engineering, technology, and other disciplines as deemed necessary.

The National Council would be composed of Indian scientists and representatives of the various agencies concerned with science education. It would play a role in India comparable to that of the National Science Foundation in the United States. The following were given as objectives for the proposed National Council for Science Education:

1. Set goals and priorities for a national program of improving science education.

2. Have a permanent staff adequate to evaluate the strengths and weaknesses of the national program.

3. Continue and develop a program of improvement in science education to include:

   a. Centers in four disciplines working on the development of instructional materials.

   b. Cooperative university/college-school programs.

   c. College faculty development programs in six different disciplines.

   d. Continued program of short-term summer science institutes.

   e. A number of small, experimental projects.

Major Activities

In 1963, a physicist, mathematician, biologist, and chemist under the direction of the Teachers College, Columbia University team at New Delhi conducted a summer science institute on the "new approach" in science education for 160 high school teachers.

This project was so well received that it was included in more institutes. A comprehensive plan for summer science institutes was developed and carried on under the direction of the education division of AID, with the assistance of consultants from Teachers College, Columbia University; the University of Wisconsin; Houston University; and Ohio State University.

During the next three years, 236 institutes were held, and engineering and technology were included, in addition to the four original subject areas. Science teachers with a degree in a subject area and two years' teaching experience were eligible to attend. Separate institutes provided for the needs of different groups of teachers from secondary schools, pre-university and undergraduate institutions, and teacher-training colleges.

The National Council for Science Education was established in 1966 and began operation in 1967. A team of between 10 and 12 scientists selected by the National Science Foundation acted as advisors to the Council. The National Council has so far not manned a task force and so its activities have been mainly deliberative. Six national advisory panels on science education were established but had not, by the end of 1967, made any progress.

Summer science institutes were again held, however, and by the end of 1967 approximately 14,000 university, college, and high school teachers had taken part in 375 institutes over a five-year period. Many of the institutes conducted in 1967 were under the direction of Indian scientists and were held without United States aid.

The secondary institutes used the new materials developed for secondary schools in the United States. These included the Physical Science Study Committee course; the three versions of high school biology, prepared by the Biological Science Curriculum Study Group; the work of the Chemical Education Material Study Group; and the texts and commentaries of the School of Mathematics Study Group.

As a result of the program, Indian scientists had been brought into contact with the high school program; an impetus had been given to the improvement of science teaching in schools all over India; and a demand had been created on the part of Indian educators for more materials and improved curricula and syllabi.

Institute of Education and Research in East Pakistan
AID/Colorado State College

The project to assist the government of Pakistan in the development of an Institute of Education and Research at the University of Dacca was headed by a Colorado State College team from 1960 to the present.

Objectives

Objectives were to:

1. Promote and provide facilities for advanced study and research in education.

2. Provide teaching, training, and guidance in order to prepare candidates for M.Ed. and Ph.D. degrees in education at the university.

3. Promote courses for further study for those already qualified to engage in educational work.

4. Furnish services for those concerned with higher education in the university teaching departments and affiliated or constituent colleges.

Major Activities

The Institute of Education and Research began operations in 1960. A team of American consultants worked with the Pakistani staff. In 1966, for example, there were 9 specialists from Colorado State in various fields of education, and 41 Pakistani personnel. The chief of party served as director of the institute.

For the first six years of the project, the major efforts of the consultants were centered on training faculty, constructing and equipping facilities, developing teacher-training programs at the M.Ed. level, establishing a laboratory school, and starting a research center.

The return of participant trainees and the accomplishment of earlier objectives then permitted the team to turn to such activities as the development of a doctoral program; emphasis on research; and the development of a Testing and Guidance Center, and a Curriculum and Instructional Materials Center.

By 1967, the Institute of Education and Research had been established and was offering degree programs for college education teachers and school administrators. It had a Pakistani faculty of 49, an enrollment of over 300 students, and was financed by the Pakistani government. Of the eight departments, seven had Pakistani chairmen. The associate director was a Pakistani, and it was planned that a Pakistani would take over the directorship in the near future. Over 350 students had been graduated, the majority of whom were employed in some phase of education. About one-half were headmasters or teacher trainers.

Testing and Guidance Center

A Testing and Guidance Center was established to construct and validate scholastic aptitude and achievement tests for indigenous groups. Intelligence tests at the seventh-, ninth-, and eleventh-grade levels were prepared, validated, and printed. Other tests were prepared on a trial basis for use at the seventh-grade level in Bengali, Urdu, and English media schools. It was reported that the Pakistani government had authorized the institute to conduct a statewide testing program when they had instruments and trained personnel.

Educational Planning Services

The Department of Educational Administration organized an Educational Planning Service Center in order to augment the planning services of various governmental educational agencies and school districts. This center served as a depository for plans, materials, and equipment within the province, and acted as the focal point of in-service training for graduate students.

In-service Training

The Institute of Education offered short courses, workshops, and seminars for education officers and personnel of training institutes, training colleges, and institutes of higher education. Extension classes for teachers in the Dacca area, in-service workshops, and demonstrations were reported to reach approximately 1,000 teachers each year.

Graduate Curricula in Education

In 1960, a one-year M.Ed. program was offered to teachers and administrators who held a bachelor of education or equivalent degree. By 1967, over 600 teachers had enrolled, and 300 were graduated in primary or secondary education, counseling and guidance, or educational administration.

A two-year M.Ed. was developed in 1964 for persons with bachelor's or master's degrees in a teaching-subject field who had not had teacher training but wished to work toward an M.Ed. In 1966, about 150 students were enrolled in six areas of education. By 1967, it was reported that almost 60 students had been graduated.

A two-year work-study M.Ed. program was introduced in 1967 to provide specialized teacher training in English, mathematics, science, and commercial subjects for teachers in technical and commercial institutes. The plan enabled the student to study at the Institute of Education and Research for one year, teach for a year or more, and return to the institute for a final year of study.

A program of studies leading to the Ed.D. was introduced in 1967 with an enrollment of eight students. Major and minor specializations were offered in primary education, educational research and statistics, psychology and guidance, educational administration, secondary education, and business education.

Program for Industrial Arts Teachers

A bachelor of science program in industrial arts was initiated in 1967 for the purpose of training industrial arts teachers for secondary schools. Students were enrolled in both the faculty of science, where they studied physics, chemistry, and/or mathematics, and in the Institute of Education and Research, where they studied industrial arts.

Library

By 1967, the library had 25,000 volumes and 100 periodicals. These books were provided by funds from AID or from the Asia Foundation. In a six-month period in 1967, a circulation figure of over 25,000 was reported.

Educational Research Center

Faculties and students were encouraged to undertake research and an Educational Research Center was established to work on special projects.

Since 1961, a journal of research and education, *Teachers World*, has been published. Among the research topics reported were the following:

A study of types of errors made by students in English.

The construction and validation of individual performance tests. group verbal, and group nonverbal tests of mental ability.

A study of secondary school dropouts.

A major research activity in 1967 consisted of developing plans for a two-year study of the status of education in East Pakistan. Research and study plans and an instrument for the collection of data were completed. Eight hundred schools were selected for the sample and 20 field interviewers chosen.

Graduate training at Colorado State College was provided for 56 Pakistani educators in education and other subjects according to the applicant's needs. Forty-four of these registered for doctoral programs. By the close of 1967, returned participant trainees filled 26 of the 41 staff positions at the institute and 8 others were under appointment. The others were in teachers colleges or in other areas of education.

University Laboratory School

A laboratory school giving instruction in the first eight grades (kindergarten through seventh grade) was established. In 1967, it enrolled 280 students. Instructional materials for use in Pakistani elementary schools were developed and used on an experimental basis in the laboratory school. Experiments were carried out in the use of charts, flash cards, and supplementary reading materials.

A Regional Program for Teacher Training in East Africa
AID/Teachers College, Columbia University

Beginning in 1964, personnel were provided under a contract with Teachers College, Columbia University, to assist the governments of Kenya, Uganda, and Tanzania to achieve their goals in teacher education.

Objectives

The objectives of the program were stated as follows:

1. To provide preservice and in-service training for local teachers to meet the shortages that exist so that, eventually, external assistance in this field may be terminated in an orderly manner.
2. To assist in the consolidation and reform of the teacher-training colleges.
3. To assist in the radical expansion of programs for the production of nongraduate teachers for secondary schools and better-qualified teachers for primary schools.
4. To assist in the use of every possible means, including crash programs, for the production of graduate teachers for secondary schools.
5. To assist in the establishment and support of developing institutes of education.

Background

The project on Teacher Education in East Africa was an outgrowth of the Teachers-for-East-Africa program initiated in 1961, also by Teachers College, Columbia University, under a contract with AID.

The newly-developed nations of East Africa faced a critical shortage of trained personnel to maintain the functions of government. In consequence, there was a widespread transfer of secondary teachers to other government posts.

At the same time, they also faced increased demands from their peoples for education. In 1958, there were 1,356,000 pupils in the primary schools of East Africa. By 1962, this number had increased 35 percent to 1,832,-000. During the same five-year period, the number of students in second-ary schools had increased 147 percent, from 12,000 to 31,000. Not only was there a shortage of primary teachers, but the quality of many of those in service was also poor. It was estimated, for example, by Mr. Y. K. Lule, then acting vice chancellor of the University of East Africa, that 40 percent of the Ugandan primary teachers could not keep abreast of modern educa-tional ideas because they could not read English. He also estimated that 25 percent of the primary teachers in Kenya had only a primary education themselves, and that a large proportion of the Tanzanian primary teachers had no more than eight years plus professional training.

The shortage of teachers was aggravated by high dropout rates which in themselves reflected poor instruction. In Tanzania in 1960, for example, out of 1,000 students entering the first grade, it was estimated that 219 would enter the fifth grade; 100, the eighth grade; 40, Form I (ninth grade); 13, Form IV (twelfth grade); only 4, the Sixth Form, completion of which is required for university entrance.

The shortage of secondary teachers in East Africa was judged to be the most critical and, to help this, AID contracted with Teachers College to provide technical advice and assistance to the governments of Kenya, Uganda, Tanzania, and Zanzibar in developing programs to increase the number of East African secondary school teachers. They also recruited and selected 153 young Americans in 1961; 114 in 1962; 112 in 1963 and cooperated with Makerere College, in Uganda, to provide for their orienta-tion and training to fill existing vacancies in East Africa.

It was recognized that the United States could not attempt to supplement the supply of secondary teachers indefinitely. With the arrival of the fourth wave of teachers, it was decided that the secondary teacher supply func-tion should be transferred to the Peace Corps. AID efforts were then directed toward providing assistance in teacher training.

Major Activities

Tutors (Teachers) for the Teacher-Training Institutions

Tutors were assigned to 34 of the 84 teacher-training colleges in the three countries. They represented 9 out of a total of 35 in Kenya, 18 out of 26 in Uganda, and 7 out of 23 in Tanzania.

Experienced American teachers with at least five years' teaching experi-ence and an M.A., preferably in a discipline such as science, mathematics, English, or history, were assigned as tutors to those colleges for two-year periods of service.

In 1964, there were 22 tutors assigned to Kenya, Tanzania, and Uganda for a two-year term of service. In 1965, an additional 30 arrived, making a total of 52. In 1966, 25 were sent out, and in 1967 there were 43. They performed the following functions:

Taught a full load of regular classes, demonstrated modern teaching methods, and assisted in improving curricula in the teacher-training institution to which they were assigned. The tutors engaged in a variety of curriculum-building activities. Many specifics such as the following were reported: "wrote a home economics syllabus"; "developed a history syllabus"; "introduced a modern approach to mathematics teaching"; "helped students prepare and use visual aids in their student teaching."

Taught in-service courses designed to help inadequately qualified primary and secondary teachers. In 1967, for example, it was reported that 3,400 teachers attended in-service courses averaging three weeks in length, and covering the major subject areas taught in the teacher-training colleges.

Collaborated with the institutes of education and ministries of education in undertaking improvement of syllabi and teaching methods.

The local salaries and allowances of the tutors were paid by the respective African governments. AID provided teaching supplies and an addition to the African salary to make it feasible for American staff to participate in the program.

A six-week orientation program was held on Teachers College campus before the tutors embarked for Africa.

Annual Conferences on Teacher Education

Annual conferences on teacher education in East Africa brought together senior East African officials and donor representatives to focus on coordinated approaches to teacher education and to establish plans for future developments. In 1966, the conference at Dar es Salaam, for example, was attended by over 60 high-level representatives from the ministries of education of the three countries, the university colleges, teachers' organizations, USAID, the British Council, the Overseas Development Ministry, and Teachers College, Columbia University.

The 1964 conference was held at Mombasa, Kenya, and was directed to the need for institutes of education. It was proposed that the institutes be based at the university colleges of each country and provide leadership for teacher education in the particular country. A report was given on the effectiveness of similar institutes established in Ghana and Nigeria in 1950 and 1956.

The 1965 conference at Nairobi was on teacher education. Much of the time was devoted to the progress achieved by the institutes of education which had by then been established.

The 1966 conference at Dar es Salaam focused on the problems of the permanent staffing of teacher education institutions with qualified nationals. The urgency of the problem was shown by the fact that, in 1964, there were 910 tutors employed in the teacher-training colleges, of whom only 469 were nationals. Of the total, only 461 were qualified to teach students entering with the Cambridge Overseas School Certificate (twelfth grade-graduates) and, of these, only 49 were nationals.

Among the proposals to meet the staffing needs of the teacher education institutions, the following were reported as most likely to produce results:

Establish alternative avenues of entrance to the university, which would take into account the kind and amount of professional and academic training which teachers desiring to enter degree courses had received in primary and secondary teacher-training colleges.

Broaden the present teacher education programs at the university colleges to include a primary education option, which would make it possible to produce degree teachers with a primary bias who could be posted to teachers colleges.

The 1967 conference, held at Makerere University, lists over 80 representatives from the three countries, USAID, UNESCO, and Teachers College, Columbia University. The main topic of the conference was curriculum development and reform in East Africa, with particular emphasis on the role of the institutes of education. Much attention was also given to the exchange of information on curriculum projects being carried on in the three countries.

Institutes of Education

In the year which followed the conference on institutes at Mombasa, the three East African countries established institutes of education. Two of these were university-based, while the third was under the direction of the Kenya Ministry of Education. The main objectives of the institutes were reported to be the coordination and progressive improvement of teacher education at both primary and secondary levels, through and beyond present expansion and consolidation plans for the training colleges.

The proposed functions of the institute in Uganda are illustrative:

Constitute a focus for the study of education in Uganda, and a professional center for teachers and the training of teachers.

Provide facilities for research in cooperation with the East African Institute of Social Research, training schools, and colleges.

Provide library service for teachers in schools and training colleges.

Organize long- and short-term residential courses to supplement in-service training and also refresher courses for experienced teachers.

Without in any way interfering with the autonomy of training colleges, assist in achieving uniformity of standards in teacher training.

Assist in the preparation of syllabi for schools and colleges in collaboration with the institutions involved.

Act as a central source of advice and information to assist teachers in their work.

Education Specialists for Institutes

In 1965, eight education specialists were assigned, through Teachers College, Columbia University, to the three countries to assist in the development of the institutes. Three served at the Uganda institute at Makerere, three at the Tanzanian institute at Dar es Salaam, and two at the Kenya Curriculum Development and Research Center in Nairobi. In 1966, funds were made available for each technician to be used for the purchase or production of teaching aids. The specialists performed the following functions:

Served as consultants to curriculum groups to improve and adapt syllabi.

Taught in-service training and upgrading courses in teacher-training colleges.

Conducted demonstration classes.

Taught at teacher-training colleges.

Taught selected university-level classes.

In addition, a specialist in mathematics education and one in the teaching of science were assigned to the department of education of University College, Nairobi, to help staff a program directed at preparing Africans with bachelor degrees for secondary school teaching and to teach undergraduate education courses.

Somewhat different responsibilities were carried out by the institutes in the different countries. Among activities reported were:

Short weekend and vacation courses were held for secondary and teacher-training college teachers of English, of Swahili, and of geography. It was reported that the response by the teachers was enthusiastic, courses attracting up to 300 teachers in some centers.

Similar courses were given to primary teachers in such subjects as geography and general methods.

Panels of subject specialists were set up to work with the various subjects of the training curriculum.

Training college syllabi were reviewed and standardized by subject panels.

Seminars were held at regional levels to bring together education officers, inspectors, college tutors, and members of the teachers associations to discuss and solve common problems.

A one-year course for the further training of 30 college tutors was prepared.

In-service Training for Class C Teachers in Tanzania

Beginning in 1966, the Institute of Education at Dar es Salaam gave leadership to a program of in-service education for Class C teachers which would qualify them for Class A rank and salary.

Each year since 1966, 320 Class C teachers have been enrolled in a program which involves attendance at three successive sessions of vacation school. In the first session, six weeks long, instruction is given in Swahili and English. In the second, four weeks in length, mathematics and science are studied. And in the final session, six weeks in length, history and geography are taught. Courses stress increased depth of content as well as modern methods of teaching.

Members of the Teach Corps have taught English in the first phase of the program each year.

Degree Programs for Secondary School Teachers

In addition to offering the graduate diploma in education, Makerere University College in Uganda, in 1963, enrolled its first students for a three-year course leading to the bachelor of education degree. It was reported that 25 students were enrolled.

In 1964, a program was initiated at the University College of Dar es Salaam to combine education courses with a regular concentration of subject matter fields in a three-year degree curriculum. Fifty-seven students were enrolled in the 1964-65 school year, and it was expected that, by 1969, 125 graduate teachers would be trained each year. This foreshadowed a similar development a year later at University College, Nairobi.

It was reported that these developments would provide the foundations for self-sufficiency in secondary teachers to be achieved in the 1970's.

Participant Training

Funds were provided for six participant training grants for prospective staff replacements at the institutes of education. The host governments were reluctant to make these institute staff positions permanent, however. Under these circumstances, it was difficult to attract qualified Africans to undergo training without formal assurance of a position to which they could return. By 1967, these positions had been included in the table of organization, and the selection of participant trainees was feasible.

It was also reported, in 1966, that the shortage of trained manpower was so acute that the individuals qualified for counterpart training were already in posts of responsibility, and the ministries of education were unwilling to release them for overseas study at that time.

According to the latest available report, no participant trainees had been sent.

Consolidation of Teacher Education Institutions

Teachers College specialists assisted the ministries of education in the three countries in developing plans for reorganization of their elementary teacher-training programs. In 1966, the three governments reported firm plans for the consolidation of the 84 teacher education institutions by eliminating about half of the weaker colleges and strengthening the remainder.

91

Training Trade and Industrial Teachers at the
Bombay Central Training Institute

DUNWOODY INSTITUTE

Objectives

From 1960-1967, Dunwoody Industrial Institute assisted in the development and operation of the Central Training Institute, Bombay.

The objectives of the institute were as follows:

1. To provide instruction in various trades and in the art of teaching those trades.
2. To train the instructors required for the existing craft training institutes, and for those institutes to be established under the industrial development schemes of the country.
3. To provide refresher courses enabling previously trained instructors to keep informed of the newest techniques.

Background

After achieving independence in 1947, India recognized the need to train more skilled technical workers. Emphasis was placed on the development of technical-training institutes in the first three 5-year plans. At the end of the first 5-year plan, there were 52 industrial training institutes and, by the end of 1967, this number had been increased to approximately 350.

The Central Training Institute was first established in 1948 to train teachers for the industrial-training institutes, as well as to train higher-level technicians. The institute was later divided into seven separate institutions. One of these was established in Bombay in 1962, and the Dunwoody Institute was asked to assist in developing its program.

Major Activities

The Dunwoody team, consisting of from 5 to 9 specialists, worked with approximately 35 junior and senior teachers at the Bombay Central Training Institute each year. In 1967, the enrollment was 231, primarily from the Bombay area.

A one-year Technical Teacher-Training Program was developed. The students were mostly teachers from industrial-training institutes who were given a one-year leave to improve their teaching skills. Some were prospective teachers who had graduated from industrial-training institutes, and a few were sent from industrial employers to prepare for supervisory positions.

A model industrial-training institute, with an enrollment of about 200 students and a three-year curriculum, was set up on the same campus. It provided opportunities for directed teaching for the students at the Central Training Institute.

Instruction was given in the following trades: blacksmith, carpentry, mechanical drafting, civil drafting, electricity, fitting, grinding, instrument mechanics, machining, motor mechanics, moulding, painting and decorating, pattern-making, sheet metal, turning, welding, tool and die, and electronics.

Curriculum Development

In 1967, a Curriculum Development Committee was established for the purpose of developing high-quality instructional material, discussing problems arising in the development of written lesson material, and assisting the teachers in the development of course material.

The Dunwoody technicians worked with the teachers in the improvement of instructional practices. They demonstrated lessons and assisted in the preparation of lesson plans and tests. A Lesson Material Development Center was established, and each master teacher was required to submit monthly lesson plans. After approval by a committee, the materials were duplicated and made available to all teachers.

Participant Training

Participant trainees were sent to Dunwoody Institute for a period of six months to one year for advanced skill training and technical teacher training. They were given English-language training before leaving India.

Radio/Correspondence In-service Training in Kenya
AID/University of Wisconsin

The improvement of teacher education is one phase of a project to develop radio/correspondence courses for elementary school teachers.

Objectives

The specific teacher education objectives were to:
1. Upgrade unqualified teachers who are now part of the school system of Kenya.
2. Train headmasters and school teachers in the techniques of using radio and correspondence materials to improve classroom instruction.

Background

In 1964, 1965, and 1966, survey teams, at the request of the governments of Kenya, Uganda, and Tanzania, investigated the feasibility of using radio/correspondence for the training of teachers. Their recommendations were favorable. The government of Kenya was ready to go ahead, and it was hoped that the Kenya project would develop into a regional center for East Africa and would include television, as well as radio and correspondence.

It was proposed that correspondence courses would first be developed to prepare candidates for the Junior Secondary Leaving Examination (passing form, approximately tenth grade), which qualified candidates to become P3 (preparatory) teachers. This is the level of the main body of primary teachers. It was estimated by the ministry of education that there might be as many as 7,500 students who would enroll in the program by 1967, when it would be in full operation.

The urgency for some mass method of upgrading teacher preparation can be judged from the fact that, while 45 percent of school-age children are in school, 60 percent of primary teachers are substandard. They are being called upon to teach English, mathematics, and science with only minimal preparation. In addition, there are many *harambe* (freedom) schools established by local communities, most of whose teachers have no teacher training. As a result, in 1964, of 120,000 students who took the primary school leaving examination, only half passed and qualified for secondary school entrance.

Major Activities

The project was approved and, in April 1967, three technicians began work. Five radio/correspondence courses were written, in English, geography, history, Kiswahili, and math. In December 1967, 437 students were enrolled. The course enrollment was 1,417, since most students enrolled in more than one subject. One lecture was prepared for each assignment and broadcast twice a week, so that students missing the one presentation could listen to the second. Each technician worked with and trained an African counterpart.

The Faculty of Education, Haile Selassie I University, Ethiopia
AID/University of Utah

In 1959, the government of Ethiopia requested the assistance of the Ford Foundation in examining the structure of higher education in the country. A survey team from the University of Utah conducted the study. The focus of its report was that the various colleges in the country should be consolidated into one university, under a central administration. It was also recommended that, in view of the fact that only 300,000 of the 5 million children of school age were in school, emphasis should be placed on the establishment of a faculty of education, with responsibility for the preparation of secondary teachers, elementary teacher trainers, and supervisory personnel.

The report was accepted, and the University of Utah was asked by AID to supply a president and a team of technicians to help establish the new institution to be called the Haile Selassie I University.

Objectives

The objectives, so far as teacher education was concerned, were:

1. To develop a college of education within the framework of the Haile Selassie I University.
2. To define programs for training teachers at every level within the jurisdiction of the university.
3. To participate with the faculty of education in planning, teaching, and developing programs for training secondary teachers, teachers for elementary school teacher-training institutions, and school administrators for the schools in Ethiopia.

4. To develop a program of research and experimentation in the teacher-training centers of the university and in the government schools.
5. To render special advice and assistance toward the improvement of education extension programs in the secondary-level schools.
6. To develop a university campus demonstration school to be used as a basic part of the teacher-training program.
7. To prepare curriculum materials, including textbooks and visual aids.

Objectives in Vocational and Technical Teacher Training

In 1966, a further task was added: To aid in the development of a national program in vocational and technical education to meet the estimated need for 2,000 skilled workers and 6,000 semi-skilled workers each year in the areas of agriculture, industry, and commerce. These objectives were stated as follows:

1. To establish, by 1972, a four-year degree program of instruction to prepare high school graduates for vocational training.
2. To establish, by 1968, a program of short-term courses for vocational arts teachers.
3. To establish, by 1972, an Ethiopian cadre of 20 trained vocational officers, with the capability to administer an expanding vocational arts education program.

Major Activities

The University of Utah contract team, which was at first 5 in number and later increased to 16, began its work in 1962. The major assignment was to work with Ethiopian colleagues in creating a faculty of education out of a small department within the faculty of arts.

Faculty (College) of Education

By 1967, the faculty of education had been established with an enrollment of 900 students, a faculty of over 70, and Ethiopians in seven of the eight administrative positions.

Technicians in the basic teacher education program had been phased down to three. In addition, there were seven technicians in the technical and vocational program which had been established the year before.

Curricula in Elementary Education

Two four-year programs leading to a bachelor of arts degree in education were developed. One was designed to prepare instructors for the secondary level in elementary teacher-training institutions; the second was to prepare elementary school directors and supervisors. Both programs consisted of general education, a professional major, an academic minor, and electives. Academic minors were offered in English, Amharic, history, geography, mathematics, and geology.

A one-year diploma program was developed to prepare elementary directors and supervisors, and 120 elementary teachers were selected for the first class. A similar program to be carried out over four summers was also introduced, and about 280 teachers enrolled the first summer. A follow-up study of the success of graduates of the diploma course was carried out by the ministry of education. Widespread evidence of improved practices, and increased dedication to their task on the part of those participating in the program, was reported.

Secondary Education Curricula

In secondary education, degree curricula were developed, combining general education, professional education, a teaching major, and a teaching minor. Teaching majors and minors were offered in Amharic, English, geography, history, biology, chemistry, physics, and mathematics. An additional teaching minor was available in library science.

Technical Teacher Education

Beginning in 1967, two-year diploma programs were introduced to train teachers in business (accounting, typewriting, shorthand, etc.), home economics, and industrial education (auto mechanics, electricity-electronics, metal working, and woodworking) in the junior-secondary, senior-secondary, and technical schools of Ethiopia. It was reported that there were 60 students enrolled in the first class beginning in the fall of 1967, and almost 300 applications for 100 places in the following year.

Plans were also being developed to introduce degree programs in the 1969-1970 school year.

Demonstration School

The Bede Mariam Library School was established in 1962. In addition to being a demonstration school and laboratory, it served as a feeder for the secondary education department at the university. It was reported, in 1967, that it was providing about 200 new students, or 90 percent of the secondary trainees, per year. Due to financial problems, however, the administration of the university was considering closing down all but the twelfth grade.

Consultant Service to the Ministry of Education

The members of the University of Utah team were used extensively in an advisory capacity by the ministry of education. It was reported that they had assisted in virtually every phase of the development of all education programs in the country.

Preparation of Curriculum Materials

Syllabi and courses of study were prepared for the various courses. In addition, two textbooks, one in educational psychology and one in secondary school methods, were written by the Utah team members.

While there was no participant training clause in the Utah contract, team members were involved in screening and selecting candidates for participant training who were designated to join the faculty of education. By 1967, 16 participants had received advanced training in the United States, and others were planned for, especially in technical education.

In-service Training

Assistance was given in developing in-service programs for both elementary and secondary teachers. In 1962, for example, 150 secondary teachers attended a workshop in English, educational psychology, and secondary methods.

An eight-week program was conducted for elementary teachers in the summers. Instruction was offered in the teaching of various elementary school subjects. In 1966 and 1967, it was reported that 900 elementary teachers participated.

Research and Experimentation

It was reported that only minor accomplishments had been made in the area of research, due to the demands made by the rapid expansion of teacher-training program staff.

The National Teacher Education Center in Somalia
AID/Eastern Michigan University

The Eastern Michigan University contract was an integral part of an AID activity which provided for the construction and equipping of a teacher-training institute in Somalia and the provision of teacher/advisory assistance for a six-year period.

Objectives

Major responsibilities of the contract group were:

1. Developing a preservice teacher education program at the National Teacher Education Center.
2. Providing an in-service teacher education program at the National Teacher Education Center.
3. Improving instruction (including demonstration teaching), organizing departments, streamlining the administration, and developing specialists in teaching at the Teacher-Training Institute of Afgoi.
4. Training a qualified staff of counterparts and instilling in them high standards of performance.
5. Assisting in developing a professional laboratory experience in demonstration, observation, and practice teaching in off-campus schools.
6. Assisting in the technical supervision, planning, and implementation to improve teacher education principles and practices.

7. Advising the ministry of education, through USAID, on the qualitative and quantitative improvement of teacher education.
8. Advising USAID on the development and implementation of a participant training program to provide a sufficient number of qualified teachers and administrators to assure the successful, continued operation of the institute at the termination of the contract.
9. Advising on procurement of needed supplies and equipment.
10. Producing syllabi for teacher education, for elementary and intermediate education, and assisting in the production of teaching materials.
11. Providing training in English for selected participants and government officials for further study in all areas.
12. Providing course studies for the improvement of English teachers throughout the country.
13. Improving women's education.
14. Providing general curriculum consultation through school visitation and conferences with teachers and administrators, particularly with graduates of the National Teacher Education Center.

Background

With the gaining of independence and the union of former British and Italian Somalilands, the government of the new Republic of Somalia found itself with a serious lack of educational facilities and with virtually no national program for education and the training of teachers. In 1960, in its five-year plan, the government of Somalia decided to place major emphasis on education. It was decided that the best place to start was through a sound teacher education program.

The difference in educational philosophies and languages between North and South added complexity to the problems faced by Eastern Michigan University in establishing a National Teacher Education Center. The one language common to the whole country, Somali, has no commonly accepted written form. Arabic has been used for instruction in the first four grades, since many Somali parents want their children to be familiar with the Koran. Most children attend a preschool Koranic school where the Koran is memorized in Arabic and the rudiments of the Arabic language are learned. Thus the typical child starts his education in a school in which his mother tongue is of no use as a basis for teaching and reading. Then, after four years of Arabic, the child is expected to learn a foreign language —either English or Italian.

Major Activities

The first responsibility of the Eastern Michigan team was to get the National Teacher Education Center operational. This was done in temporary quarters during the first year, while the new buildings were being constructed. In the first two years, most of the teaching was done by the team members because of the scarcity of qualified Somali faculty members.

As the program continued, Somali counterparts were given "on-the-job training" and this was coordinated with participant training, so that Somalis could take over complete responsibility for the institution.

Teacher Education Curriculum

A basic three-year program for elementary teachers was developed and put into operation. The first class of 57 graduated from this program in 1966 and the second, numbering 98, in 1967. A four-year curriculum was also developed, looking forward to the adoption of the recommendation of the Eastern Michigan team that a four-year program be the minimum preparation for teachers of Grades 1-8.

Based on the informal comments of principals and government officials, it was reported that the first group of National Teacher Education Center graduates had established a good reputation for the school after their first year of teaching.

In-service Training

Workshops of from four to eight weeks' duration were held each summer for about 40 teachers. These included some work in all the subject fields, with special emphasis on improving the teacher's own mastery of English.

There were so many primary teachers with very little training—a few months—or even none, that the Eastern Michigan University team felt that the summer workshops were inadequate as the sole means of training and should be supplemented by assistance during the school year. An English and science-mathematics in-service workshop for 32 teachers was conducted during May and June 1966.

The workshop staff was at first concerned with the irregular class attendance and low interest shown by Somali teachers returning from in-service education. However, once the teachers saw what could be done, enthusiasm grew. In October 1967, a workshop was held in which materials were produced in the afternoon, and then used in active teaching the following morning, under supervision and observation of the workshop instructors. The increased enthusiasm and evidence of change in teaching techniques, as the workshop proceeded, encouraged the Eastern Michigan University staff to plan similar workshops for the future.

Curriculum Development

The National Teacher Education Center staff members were involved in a number of projects for the development of curriculum guides and teaching materials for the Somali public schools. They participated in the revision of the syllabi for the primary grades. They produced, in cooperation with Peace Corps volunteers, three reading pre-primers. They were also responsible for a teachers guide for oral English instruction, three science handbooks, and a textbook of Somali history. They also developed many other publications and items of curriculum materials.

In March 1966, the team produced a comprehensive fifty-page report, for consideration by the Somali Ministry of Education, entitled *A Rationale for Curriculum Development in Teacher Education in Somalia*. This report was intended to provide guidelines for the continuous study and improvement of teacher education curricula, so that they would be directly related to Somalia's needs, and not transplanted imports from other countries. A careful attempt was made to demonstrate the relationship which should exist between the different aspects of the National Teacher Education Program and the unique conditions and purposes of the country. Twenty of the specific recommendations of the report were restated in summary form as follows:

1. Identify national goals which have the most relevancy for Somali teacher education. This would be done by the ministry of education.

2. Plan educational goals which reflect national goals and interests, but which also allow some provision for individual interests and goals.

3. Work toward development of teacher education programs which are uniquely suited in form and characteristics to Somalia.

4. Give teacher education programs equal status with the highest level of education offered in the country. This can be done through the type of program established, through use of appropriate student admissions policies, through proper placement of graduates, and through determination of suitable salary schedules. An immediate step in this direction would be to increase the duration of teacher education programs from three to four years.

5. Consider making the general education portion of secondary schools, and of teacher education institutions, comparable. One approach to accomplishing this would be to make the first two years of schooling in both secondary education and teacher education a general education program, and to use most of the latter two years for specialization in teacher preparation or in given subject fields.

6. Transfer teacher preparation programs to the university level when such an institution comes into being.

7. Discontinue use of "leaving examinations" or any other national tests for purpose of determining student graduation or promotion. Base student placement, promotion, and graduation on a variety of tests and evaluation activities.

8. Evaluate all of the teacher education goals regularly through a variety of means.

9. Use available relevant research findings from other countries, but begin a systematic program of research geared to Somalia's educational needs.

10. Develop a working relationship between teacher education institutions and the Department of Inspection and Planning, emphasizing regular ongoing assistance to teachers who have had up to three years of teaching experience.

11. Establish a minimum level of certification standards for all teachers, and offer an in-service education program that will enable teachers to meet the standards as rapidly as possible.
12. Consider in-service education as an integral and major part of teacher education for both present and future planning. Assign specific responsibility for short-range and long-range planning in this area.
13. Broaden and strengthen student teaching experiences in teacher education.
14. Recognize individual differences through individualization of instruction. Offer breadth and depth in methods and materials used.
15. Develop comprehensive guidance and counseling programs in teacher education that involve all staff members.
16. Organize *what* is to be learned in ways which are both psychologically and logically sound for Somalia. This may lead to approaches which are not used in other countries.
17. Organize the curriculum of teacher education so as to promote curriculum integration and staff unity.
18. Conduct studies to determine strengths and weaknesses of the teacher education program. This would be done with both present students and graduates.
19. Use teacher-training institutions as centers for development and revision of syllabi and other teachers guidebooks for use in the primary, intermediate and, eventually, secondary schools.
20. Involve staff of teacher-training institutions in development of textbooks and other teaching aids for use in the public schools.

Participant Training

Each year, between 4 and 12 Somalis were selected for two years of training in the United States. The majority of them were enrolled at Eastern Michigan University so that their programs could be supervised and they could get the preparation they needed in science, mathematics, English, and other subjects to become counterpart teachers at the National Teacher Education Center on their return. They received a two-month orientation, including intense study of English, before going to the United States. Inasmuch as the majority of the participants had no prior college education, and many of them had little secondary education, their course work at Eastern Michigan University was intended to be primarily oriented to content preparation, with lesser emphasis on methods courses. The participants were enrolled in degree programs, and the majority of them proved themselves academically.

After teaching at the institute for two years, a number were sent to the United States for another two years so that they could obtain a degree. By 1967, over 50 individuals had received participant training or were currently in the United States. Of those who had returned, the majority were employed in the field of education either at the National Teacher Education Center or in some other position.

101

Degree Programs for Secondary Teachers in Sierra Leone
AID/University of Illinois

At the request of the Sierra Leone government, USAID contracted with the University of Illinois to assist in the creation of an agriculturally- and educationally-oriented university college at Njala, a rural location 125 miles from Freetown, in the southwestern part of the country.

Objectives

The original objective in teacher education was to conduct programs for preparing the following:

1. Secondary teachers of vocational agriculture.
2. Teachers in the biological and physical sciences.
3. Teachers of vocational courses of an industrial nature.
4. Teachers of home economics.
5. Leaders for extension services in agriculture.
6. Primary teachers.
7. Secondary teachers.

Investigation by Illinois team members into the educational backgrounds of prospective students revealed serious deficiencies in the sciences and a total lack of previous agriculture training. They decided, therefore, that they should redefine their task to one of preparing secondary teachers with emphasis on science. It was felt that this would also enable Njala University College to complement existing teacher education programs at Fourah Bay College and Milton Margai Training College.

Background

The plans for economic development of the newly-formed government of Sierra Leone were hampered by the low literacy level of its population, particularly in the rural areas. In its development plan, the government proposed to double the primary enrollment to 191,000 and triple the secondary enrollment to 27,000 by 1970.

This called for sharp expansion of the facilities for training teachers. At the secondary level, the teacher shortage was accentuated because the government wished to replace expatriate teachers, who composed 40 percent of the secondary teaching staff, with qualified Sierra Leoneans. Of the Sierra Leonean staff, only 15 percent were considered qualified.

Nearly 90 percent of the provincial population existed through subsistence farming. A second goal of the government was, therefore, to raise the level of agricultural practice from a subsistence structure to intensive commercial farming, both to improve the inadequate domestic food supply and to provide raw materials for basic industries. This pointed up the need for agricultural research and a training program for agriculture teachers.

To help solve these problems, the government decided to combine an agriculture research station and a small primary teacher-training college in a rural area 125 miles from Freetown into one institution, patterned on the American land-grant college.

The new institution, called Njala University College, was opened in October 1964 and, in 1966, together with Fourah Bay College, became a constituent member of the newly-formed University of Sierra Leone.

Major Activities in Teacher Education

A team of 10 technicians from the University of Illinois joined the staff of the newly-formed Njala University College in 1964 and 1965. This number was later increased to 13, but not all were directly involved in the teacher education program. The others were engaged in training agricultural technicians and conducting four-year degree programs in agriculture.

Development of Njala University College

The Njala University College was opened in September 1964 with 101 students. By 1967, enrollment was over 300. Of these, approximately 200 enrolled in the four-year curriculum leading to a degree, and the majority of the others in a three-year certificate course. Eight students were in a one-year intensive course in agricultural education. About half the students were in agriculture and half were in various teacher-training curricula. These included majors or areas of emphasis in biology, agricultural education, home economics, English, and geography.

In 1967, there were 60 faculty members on the senior staff, about half of whom were Sierra Leonean. This represented a student-faculty ratio of five to one, which was regarded as excessive in view of financial limitations and manpower needs. A rapid expansion of the student body to correct this was not regarded as feasible from several points of view: the availability of secondary school graduates with the capacity for degree work; the capacity of the country to absorb the graduates, particularly in agriculture; and the capacity of the country to finance the increased costs necessary to support a much larger student body.

Degree and Certificate Curricula

Four-year curricula combining subject matter and professional teacher education courses were developed with emphasis in biological science, agriculture, English, and home economics. Three-year curricula were also developed leading to the higher teacher certificate.

Work Experience Program

A work experience program requiring students to work six hours a week was instituted in an effort to instill in prospective students a favorable attitude toward useful, productive work. In spite of careful planning to ensure that the work would be useful, the student reaction and the quality of work produced were discouraging to the faculty.

Agricultural Education

The agricultural education department developed a land laboratory, a pilot teaching center in cooperation with the Taioma Secondary School, and a research program to aid in training agricultural teachers.

Science Curriculum Center

A Science Curriculum Center was established with a seven-member staff including a Peace Corps volunteer, a University of Illinois technician, and a science educator supplied by the Educational Development Center of the ministry of education. It devolped teaching units and materials, directly related to student experiences in Sierra Leone and oriented toward the idea of basic scientific concept formation. By way of illustration, one project consisted of 25 study units prepared to enable teachers with little science background to introduce problem-solving techniques. Each unit was trial-taught by a staff member, revised and tried by classroom teachers, and again revised before being published by the Njala University College Press.

In coordination with the department of education, the teacher-training colleges, the Board of Teacher Training Colleges and Fourah Bay University College, the center conducted extensive preservice and in-service teacher-training programs in many areas of Sierra Leone. It was reported that 2,700 teachers and headmasters had been reached with materials, demonstrations, and evaluation.

One indication of the effectiveness of the program is the fact that the Board of Teacher Training Colleges has assigned to the center the responsibility of setting all future examinations in science and science teaching, and determining the content and method for all future in-service programs for elementary science teachers in Sierra Leone.

Participant Training

Fourteen Sierra Leoneans were sent to the United States for training, most of them working for advanced degrees. By 1967, three had returned and joined the Njala faculty. It was reported that the number would have been greater had it not been for the inability of the university to spare staff members for such training.

Founding a Multipurpose Teacher-Training College in Nigeria
AID/Ohio University

Beginning in 1961, Ohio University accepted the task of assisting the Northern Region of Nigeria to develop a teacher education program at Kano.

Objectives

The objectives of the program were modified as the project developed. As finally written they were to:

1. Develop a five-year program for primary school teachers, and a three-year advanced program for secondary teachers and primary teacher-training college tutors at the Kano Teacher Training College.

2. Create and develop curricula, courses of study, lesson plans, and materials for both the five-year and the three-year training programs.
3. Provide a staff for classroom teaching, when necessary, until counterparts can assume such teaching duties.
4. Develop a program of counterpart and participant training, leading to a total Nigerian staff of 31 tutors by 1969.
5. Develop an in-service program in the Kano area for the training of uncertified and Grade II teachers.
6. Establish an instructional materials center including closed-circuit educational television for Kano and the adjoining areas.
7. Initiate a follow-up program for the graduates to give guidance during their early teaching experience.
8. Develop a language laboratory to improve English usage.
9. Assist in planning for a new physical plant during 1965-1966.

Background

In 1961, the government of Northern Nigeria faced the fact that the education system in the North was much less developed than in the other regions. Only 14 percent of Northern region children of primary school age were in school, as compared with an average of 80 percent in Eastern and Western Nigeria. In addition, 90 percent of the primary school teachers were untrained or inadequately qualified.

The government's plan called for a school enrollment of 25 percent of the school-age population by 1970, the training of 13,000 new teachers, and the upgrading of 10,000 unqualified teachers.

This required additional teacher-training facilities, and the United States was approached for assistance. It was proposed, with AID support, to develop a teacher-training college at Kano as a high-priority impact project. At first, the Kano Teacher Training College prepared students for Grade II (primary teacher) positions. In 1965, a three-year advanced program, leading to the Nigerian certificate in education and preparing secondary teachers and teacher-training tutors, was added.

It was also proposed that the Kano Teacher Training College would assist in:
1. The in-service training of teachers.
2. The development and use of instructional materials, including educational radio and television.
3. The development of courses of study for other teacher-training colleges.
4. The development of a laboratory school as a proving ground for curriculum materials for use in the primary school system.

Major Activities

The contract team began its work in temporary quarters in 1961. At the height of the project, 19 Ohio specialists were involved. By 1967, the college was finally established in its new site and was fully operational. It had an enrollment of about 400 students in a five-year program for Grade II primary teachers, and over 300 students in the three-year program for secondary teachers and tutors for Grade II teachers colleges.

During this period the Ohio team was involved in many activities in the immediate task of developing a multipurpose college and in programs for the upgrading of primary teaching in Northern Nigeria.

Curriculum Development

Curricula and course syllabi were developed for three programs. The first was the five-year program for Grade II primary teachers, planned for students who had completed elementary school. The second was a three-year program leading to the Nigerian certificate in education, which accepted students who had completed secondary school. Its graduates were prepared to be secondary teachers and tutors for Grade II (primary) teachers colleges. The third program consisted of a two-year course to prepare students who completed secondary school to be Grade II primary teachers.

These materials were tried out in class by the Ohio team members, along with their Nigerian counterparts, and modified as the project proceeded. The findings from experimental courses in English, arithmetic, and science were also incorporated into the curriculum.

A major contribution was the development of a general education or core curriculum for students working for the Nigerian certificate in education.

Production of Textbook and Syllabi

Teaching materials in English and arithmetic were produced for in-service teachers working to attain higher certificates. A general science syllabus and curriculum guide was prepared for tutors working with students preparing for the Grade II teaching certificate. The concepts, discussion questions, laboratory activities, and test items for the five years of the program were tried out in the classroom, before being revised and put into printed form. A manual, *Educational Principles and Learning Activities*, was developed for the use of elementary school teachers.

In-service Training

In-service activities included correspondence courses, vacation classes, three in-service centers in the Kano area, and the preparation of radio tapes. It was reported that the different activities were providing assistance to several thousand Northern Nigerian teachers each year.

Correspondence Courses

Materials for Northern Nigerian correspondence courses were developed. The English course consisted of 120 lessons and was designed to cover four years of work. The mathematics course was designed to cover four years work in arithmetical processes and required the use of a standard British text. Both courses were taken by several thousand teachers in preparation for the Grade II examination. In 1966 alone, it was reported that 3,500 in-service teachers were enrolled in the program. A fifth-year arithmetic course was also written for Grade III teachers, and was tested out in the Kano Teacher Training College.

In connection with the English correspondence courses, a series of radio programs were produced to help students learn English as a second language. These included two sets of 30 lessons each.

Evening and Vacation Courses

Each year, between 15 and 50 courses were held for teachers, headmasters, and librarians in the Kano area. They were developed to meet the needs of the participants and were held in the evenings, on weekends, or during vacation times as was found convenient.

The subjects taught varied from course to course and included English, arithmetic, geography, history, science, classroom management, and teaching methods. The impact of the program is illustrated by the fact that in one project, carried out in 40 centers with the assistance of Peace Corps volunteers, about 3,000 Grade III primary teachers were enrolled for in-service courses.

In-service Centers

Three teachers' in-service centers were developed in the Kano area. They were supplied with a library of 5,000 books and facilities for the production of teaching aids. A technician was regularly on hand to assist teachers. Educational films were also shown.

Counterpart and Participant Training

From the beginning of the program, the Ohio University staff both taught and worked with Nigerian faculty members. As the project developed, some of the counterparts were selected for further education in the United States. By December 1967, 18 participants had been sent to the United States for study. Of these, five were still studying at Athens, Ohio. With one exception, the remainder had returned to the Advanced Teachers College at Kano. One of these had become the principal.

Research and Publications

Beginning in 1966, research activities were conducted in a number of areas, such as the following:

A follow-up study of the success of Grade III teachers graduating from the college.

A survey of primary teacher-training college curricula in arithmetic and mathematics.

A study of correspondence course effectiveness. It was found, for example, that students who took the correspondence course had a better chance of passing the Grade II examination in English and arithmetic than students who studied on their own.

By 1967, 16 textbooks had been written, and over 60 articles had been published in professional journals by Ohio faculty members of either the Kano or the Ibadan project.

Library

A library with over 8,000 volumes and 8 periodicals was organized. The use of the library is shown by the fact that, in one six-month period, over 4,000 books were used. A large increase in the use of reserve books and materials was also reported.

Film Library

A film library of over 700 films and film strips was developed and made available to teacher-training colleges throughout the North.

Language Laboratory and Closed-Circuit Television

A language laboratory and closed-circuit television for use over a 30-mile radius were planned and installed in the new plant. During the latter part of 1967, a number of programs were produced. They included a 20-show science series, for seventh- through twelfth-grade students; a 10-show series in English; and a pilot history series.

Laboratory School

An operational program was developed for the new laboratory school.

Program Building in Northern Nigeria
AID/University of Wisconsin

In 1962, at the request of the Northern Nigerian government, AID sent a three-man team from the University of Wisconsin to study the status of education and make recommendations. It was particularly concerned with the development of programs for preparing primary teachers and with the expansion of primary education within teachers' colleges.

Based on the recommendations of the study, a joint agreement was reached between the Northern Nigerian government, Ford Foundation, USAID, and the University of Wisconsin. The Ford Foundation provided $2.2 million for 32 advisors from the University of Wisconsin for two years. In 1966, AID took over the responsibility for the financial support of the Wisconsin team. A development loan of $3.8 million was also proposed to finance the construction of four new colleges and the improvement of a number of others.

Objectives

During the first two years, the goals of the project were to increase the number of primary teachers and, at the same time, to improve the quality of teacher education. Specifically the objectives were to demonstrate, test, adopt, and refine new content and materials of instruction, programmed learning, language laboratories, and other audiovisual aids for the preparation of teachers.

Revised Objectives

In 1966, when AID took over the financial support of technical assistance, the objectives were stated as follows:

1. Assist in improving primary education in the areas of English, mathematics, geography, history, science, and principles and practices of education, with special attention to:

    a. Development of new and improved course syllabi and materials and methods to teach them.

    b. More efficient use of teacher-training college staff members in team teaching, large-group instruction, and individualized instruction.

    c. Provision of professional assistance in an in-service program for teacher-training college staff members.

2. Assist the ministry of education in developing materials and techniques for the preparation of primary teachers.

3. Assist the institute of education in field testing new materials by providing support to research activities.

4. Train key Nigerian staff through counterpart and participant training so that they can assume full responsibility for carrying on the improved programs developed by this project.

Background

In 1960, a commission headed by Sir Eric Ashby made a broad and sweeping survey of education in Nigeria. It proposed that the percentage of children in primary school be raised from 11 percent to 25 percent by 1970; that secondary education be provided for at least 10 percent of the primary school graduates; and that 30 percent of those completing the school certificate course go on for higher education, including degree courses.

These goals were accepted by the Northern Nigerian government and, in 1962, a team from the University of Wisconsin was asked to survey the educational system of the country and make proposals for an overall program.

The Wisconsin Survey Report gave detailed information as to the status of education in Northern Nigeria, including teacher training. It projected future teacher needs and the expansion of teacher-training facilities. It made estimates of the cost involved, and it developed criteria and specifications for the planning and construction of teacher-training colleges.

Following the report, the government of Nigeria requested the University of Wisconsin to provide consultant services for the expansion and improvement of primary teaching.

Major Activities

In 1964, a planning team of three members arrived in Northern Nigeria to prepare for the arrival of the main Wisconsin team. Early the following year, 28 additional consultants arrived and were assigned to seven of the larger Grade II (primary) teacher-training institutions distributed over Northern Nigeria. These institutions typically enrolled 4 streams of 30 students in a five-year curriculum. Entrance to the program required the successful completion of elementary school. At the beginning of the project, the elementary school curriculum required seven years but was recently reduced to six.

Program Building

A team of four Wisconsin faculty members with expertise in English, mathematics, geography and history, and principles of education worked in each of the seven colleges. They taught a full load of classes and, in addition, worked with their counterparts on the faculty in restructuring procedures and developing new materials and methods. As one example, team teaching was introduced for certain classes where facilities were available. In this way, not only was a new technique making use of specific areas of expertise introduced, but it was also possible for consultants and counterparts to work together and compare notes.

The Wisconsin team recognized that program building is a long-term type of activity. In consequence, they planned a two-phased approach by which the seven project institutions would be used as prototype or starter colleges in which new ideas could be tried out. Then, when they had been modified and proved successful, they could be introduced into the 47 smaller primary teacher-training colleges in Northern Nigeria. It was also felt that a team, working together with counterparts in a particular college, would have greater success in introducing problem-solving and discussion techniques than a single teacher.

Phase I

In Phase I, materials already available were accepted, such as *English 900*, prepared for adult students of English as a second language,* and the Entebbe mathematics program. These were used in an exploratory way to try out a number of innovative approaches. A series of conferences was held to share experiences. In some of these, the members of the seven teams, together with their building principals, met together in subject groups. As a result, materials which seemed useful were selected for modification.

Phase II

In the second phase, those materials which seemed promising were selected for modification in terms of the needs of the country. For example, a version of *English 900* especially suited, in structure, content, and illustrative materials, to Northern Nigeria was prepared.

---

* Prepared by English Language Services, Inc., Washington, D.C.

110

A special mathematics methods course was developed on an experimental basis in several of the project colleges. The course was designed to help the teacher trainees develop basic mathematics concepts so that they could, in turn, teach them in the primary schools. Through the subject matter work conferences which were held twice a year, information and ideas were exchanged leading to the development of a syllabus and textbook materials for all Grade II colleges.

Units of work, to be used in the seven primary grades, were developed around major related themes in history and geography.

Counterpart and Participant Training

Over 50 Northern Nigerians were involved in a counterpart relationship with the Wisconsin team. Five of these were selected for participant training in the United States in 1967, and an additional five were planned for 1968. It was reported that the counterparts were frequently transferred or promoted which added to the problems of the project, but was not all loss, inasmuch as the basic concepts of the program became more widely known throughout Northern Nigeria.

A Program of Reform in Peruvian Education
AID/Teachers College, Columbia University

Teacher education projects were part of an overall program of assistance to basic education reform and development. In 1963, Teachers College signed a contract with AID to provide professional consultants to assist the ministry of education to develop and implement a program to expand and improve the educational system in Peru.

Objectives

The original contract and early amendments provided that Teachers College was to provide technical advisory services to the ministry of education in the following areas:

1. Educational planning and organization.
2. In-service and preservice training for teachers.
3. Curriculum and teaching materials.
4. Technical and vocational education.
5. Construction and equipment of primary schools in rural areas.
6. Relating education programs to overall economic development.
7. Providing participant training for Peruvian educators.

Background

In 1964, nearly a million children out of a school-age population of 2.8 million did not attend school. Facilities for the remainder were often limited, with poorly trained or untrained teachers, few if any textbooks and educational materials, poor classroom facilities, and a teaching system poorly designed for the needs of a modern nation in the 20th century.

Of those entering elementary school, only 30 percent finished Grade 5 and only 8 percent graduated from high school. Over half of the primary school teachers had had little or no training, and only 38 percent had graduated from regular teacher-training programs.

In the urgently necessary area of technical training, there were also serious problems. It was estimated that less than 10 percent of those who attended technical secondary schools succeeded in graduating, and less than 20 percent of the graduates were able to find jobs in industry commensurate with their training.

Peru, like many other Latin American countries, was attempting to achieve the education goals proposed in the *Charter of Punta del Esté* under the Alliance for Progress:

> *To eliminate adult illiteracy and by 1970 to assure, as a minimum, access to six years of primary education for each school-age child in Latin America; to modernize and expand vocational, technical secondary, and higher educational and training facilities; to strengthen the capacity for basic and applied research; and to provide the competent personnel required in rapidly growing societies.*

Major Activities

A contract team started to arrive in November 1963 and was at full strength (10 members) by August 1964. It included specialists in evaluation, educational administration, fundamental (adult) education, teacher education, technical education, vocational education, and primary school curricula.

In the beginning, due in part, to a series of changes among ministry officials, it was difficult for the Teachers College team to know just how they could best provide consultant services to the ministry of education that would be accepted, and would have some chance of being implemented. They were nevertheless involved in assisting in the development of a Five-Year Plan for Improving Education in Peru and in developing detailed plans for its proposed implementation.

As the project developed, greater demands were made for their services and they became involved in an increasing number of activities.

Planning an Educational Program for Peru

A Teachers College economist worked with the ministry of education and the Institute of National Planning to identify crucial manpower needs projected to 1980. This would enable the ministry of education to define manpower needs, equate them with educational goals, and plan the efficient organization of Peru's educational resources.

Improvement of the Administrative Structure and Procedures of the Ministry of Education

Teachers College technicians provided guidance in a program to reorganize the ministry of education and regionalize many of its administrative functions. Team members assisted in a conference of regional directors, the preparation of a statement of the rationale for decentralization, a survey of the operation of the regional offices, and the development of a step-by-step program for their reorganization. A training program was developed for officials in eight regional offices in Peru. This program was extended through a participant training program at the University of Puerto Rico.

Development of Regional Normal Schools

They assisted in planning for the consolidation of many small normal schools, the development of regional normal schools, and in preparing a request for an AID loan to help construct and equip the first four schools as centers of excellence, or models for the later development of other consolidated normal schools.

Normal School Curriculum

From the beginning, the Teachers College team took a strong interest in the normal school curriculum, working with committees to improve individual courses and syllabi and to strive for a better selection of courses with improved balance and sequence. Teachers College pushed, too, to help ministry officials re-introduce innovations that had failed in 1957. In these efforts, work groups recognized, as they had not in 1957, that normal school administrators and professors must be involved in the planning if the changes were to succeed.

In 1965, a national conference on teacher education was organized and held at Huampanf, outside Lima, to permit normal school administrators and professors to meet with ministry officials to discuss the possibilities for upgrading the normal school curriculum. At that conference, commissions worked toward selecting courses and co-curricular activities for a four-year program of quality education. Also, the necessity for curriculum flexibility and a new philosophy of teaching, learning, and evaluation received much comment and consideration. Conference delegates requested that the Division of Teacher Education proceed with plans for a new curriculum, a system of credits to permit curriculum flexibility, and a new system of student evaluation to emphasize activity and inquiry. Teachers College technicians helped organize and direct the conference and secured funds from the United States Information Service to finance it.

The ministry organized and sponsored a second national teacher education conference at Huampanf the following year (1966), with financial aid from UNESCO and the United States Information Service. Purpose of the conference was to discuss progress that had been made in planning the new curriculum and its adjuncts, and to attempt to foresee problems that might arise in the implementation of the plans.

In 1967, final touches were put on the four-year curriculum, the credit system, and the evaluation scheme. These completed plans were discussed again in detail with normal school representatives at five regional symposia, conducted late in 1967. Thus, after two years of joint planning, the stage was set for implementing the changes. Further, and most important, personnel of all the normal schools knew the details of the plans; had participated, through delegates, in their formulation; and had given tacit approval to their introduction into the normals.

Rural School Training Centers

The Teachers College team assisted in planning and developing training centers for teachers in "nucleo" (central or consolidated) schools in the rural areas of Peru. Three training centers for community education were planned. One was completed in 1965 near Cuzco, and Teachers College advisors provided guidance to the faculty in establishing the program.

Secondary and Post-Secondary Vocational Education

Technical and vocational education specialists worked with the Division of Technical Education to evaluate the existing program, develop an improved curriculum, and establish adequate programs of vocational-teacher education. They also assisted in designing five polytechnical high schools, and in preparing applications for a World Bank loan to construct and equip them.

CRECER—Action Research Program

They worked with CRECER, the nationwide action research program, in which teachers studied their school communities and tried to link educational development to social, cultural, and economic development. Among 30 activities reported were such programs as the introduction of special counseling services and the use of teacher teams to prepare their fellow teachers for more effective work in their school communities. A four-week seminar was held in 1966 for 200 in-service elementary teachers and, in 1967, for 200 normal school professors.

In-service Training in Supervision

In 1965, Teachers College team members participated in a six-week course in supervision and curriculum development given to 60 national and regional supervisors. In this course, supervision was presented as professional assistance to teachers rather than mere inspection and fault-finding.

Participant Training

By 1967, 105 participant trainees had been sent to the United States, Puerto Rico, Mexico, Brazil, and Colombia for study in the fields of technical-vocational education, teacher education, rural education, and administration. Problems due to lack of competency in English were substantially met by developing individual programs of study and internship at the University of Puerto Rico and the State Department of Education of Puerto Rico.

An In-service Program for Guatemalan Science Teachers
AID/Texas Education Agency

In 1966, the Texas Education Agency undertook a pilot program to train science teachers. Arrangements were made for a group of 10 Guatemalan science teachers to go to Texas for training, and observation of natural science teaching techniques used in the Texas state school system. The head of science education of the Texas Education Agency then went to Guatemala to work with his Guatemalan counterpart in developing a plan to equip two model science laboratories. In the summer of 1968, it was planned that 10 Texas science teachers go to Guatemala to work with their counterparts in conducting a series of in-service training seminars for Guatemalan science teachers. If the program proved successful, it was proposed to extend it to include mathematics and language teaching.

Study Tours for Brazilian Elementary Educators
AID/University of Wisconsin-Milwaukee

A nine-month program, including study, observation, and internship experiences in elementary education, was provided for 25 educators from Northeast Brazil in 1966. Another 22 participated in a similar program in 1967. The nine-month program, in the latter case, was preceded by three months of intensive study of English at Georgetown University, Washington, D.C.

Objectives

The general goal of the project was to assist in the expansion and improvement of the Brazilian system of elementary education, with particular reference to the Northeast section of the country.

It was planned that the visiting educators would have opportunity to observe and participate in American life, with emphasis on cultural values and English-language practice. The contract stipulated that the following areas and activities would be developed for the Brazilian educators:

1. Curriculum development in elementary education, with participation in seminars, university classes, and on-going school curriculum development programs.
2. Principles and programs of administration and supervision in elementary education.
3. Principles and practices in adult education, including university seminars, and participation in community development and literary

115

programs. Special attention was given to school-community activities for the underprivileged and the school's role in community change.

4. Professional organizations related to education, including national, state, subject area, community, and service organizations.
5. Programs of teacher education, including both preservice and in-service programs.
6. Field experiences, including extended internship-type participation in selected elementary schools.
7. Attendance at one major national professional convention or conference.

Major Aspects of the Nine-Month Program

The plan for the nine months of study was divided into four phases. The weekly periods below were taken from the 1966 program (which was modified somewhat in 1967):

1. Orientation—four weeks.
2. Academic course work—18 weeks.
3. Field experiences—nine weeks.
4. Culminating activities—five weeks.

Phase I—Orientation

The first four weeks of the program were for general orientation which was planned to provide background for later course work and field work in elementary schools. The schedule consisted of lectures on education in the United States and visits to state education offices, to schools, and to various institutions related to education. Both urban and rural schools were visited, and the various levels of education were explained. Each aspect of the educational system discussed in a lecture was illustrated by a visit; thus, an overview from historical development through modern programs was presented. Discussion and evaluation sessions were planned to interpret and clarify the observations.

Phase II—Academic Work

The course work was organized around a series of seminars dealing with major aspects of elementary curriculum and administration. Opportunity was given to the participants to attend regular courses in areas of individual concern.

Phase III—Field Experiences or Internship

In 1966, the participants were divided into three groups for the field experience: (1) those largely concerned with state-wide or area planning, (2) those who supervised instructional programs, and (3) those who administered one school building. In 1967, the organization was between (1) those responsible for preservice training and (2) those oriented toward in-service training. Participants were placed in schools or with supervisors where their particular interests could best be met.

Phase IV—Culminating Activities

In the fourth phase, the group returned to the Milwaukee campus for a variety of short-term activities, including a series of evaluation sessions.

Training Elementary Teachers in the Use of New Textbooks
AID/Contract Technicians

An in-service training program was initiated to orient teachers in the use of new textbooks prepared under the ROCAP textbook program. With USAID assistance, 24 out of a projected total of 33 textbooks in the fundamental elementary school subjects had been printed in 1967. Complementing the book distribution, a training program was carried on for 140 teachers in several different areas of the country. These teachers were utilized in 126 short training courses, and about 5,000 teachers were trained in the use of the new textbooks.

KENYA
Vocational Agriculture Education
AID/West Virginia University

Objectives

1. To provide technical advice and assistance in setting up a program of vocational agriculture at the Agriculture Diploma College at Edgerton.
2. To aid in the development of courses in vocational agriculture for six rural secondary schools in Kenya.

Activities

During the first four years of the program, a team of six agricultural specialists from West Virginia University set up a demonstration vocational agriculture program at the Agriculture Diploma College at Edgerton. By 1967, the number of programs had increased to 12. A teacher education program was to be introduced as soon as the vocational agriculture curriculum had become firmly established, and the government of Kenya was ready to proceed with the introduction of courses in vocational agriculture in the rural secondary schools of Kenya.

Present Status

A specialist in secondary school agriculture arrived at Edgerton in 1967, and a program was designed to produce qualified teachers of agriculture at the secondary level.

Plans for training African teachers to take over the roles of the advisors were initiated. A systematic course for training counterparts was approved by the ministry of education, and three Kenyan counterparts were trained in a degree program in the U.S.

English-Language Training Project
AID/National Education Association

Objectives

The National Education Association provided 8 primary school specialists, later increased to 12, to assist in introducing a new primary curriculum, involving instruction in English, starting at the first grade. It was called the "new primary approach." Their assigned task was to train the following:

1. Elementary teachers scheduled to use English as the language of instruction.
2. Elementary teachers already using the new primary approach.
3. Education officers working with the new primary approach.

It was estimated that assistance would be needed for six years, so that the program could become self-sustaining and capable of continued expansion, without further technical assistance from the U.S. government.

Background

The new primary approach was first tried out in 1958, with financial support from a Ford Foundation grant. By 1963, when the AID/NEA project was initiated, over 200 African schools had already been introduced to the new medium. Also, beginning in 1963, the teacher-training colleges for primary school teachers had introduced the "PEAK" (Primary Education for Africans in Kenya) methods and materials published by the Oxford University Press.

Prior to this, Kenyan primary school children studied in the vernacular or in Swahili through Standard IV (Grade 4). From then on, their subjects were taught in English. English was thus a book subject, and mastery of the language was rare and deficiency in English at the secondary level was so great, it was estimatesd that over 75 percent of failures in the school certificate examination (Grade 12) were due to poor English.

Instruction in English was very popular with the African people, and demand for the introduction of the new program was so widespread that the original target was increased from 2,000 to 3,350 of the 5,350 primary schools. As a result of this rapid expansion, the English medium was used by a large number of very poorly-qualified teachers. There was, therefore, a critical need for both the preservice and in-service English instruction for primary teachers.

Major Activities

The NEA primary school specialists were sent to the different regions in Kenya to work directly with the school districts under the direction of the chief inspector of the schools. They then became involved in the direct supervision of schools and on-the-job training of counterpart assistant education officers.

The technicians visited the schools, gave demonstrations, conducted in-service workshops with classroom teachers, and held conferences with assistant education officers. In the later stages of the project, some members were asked to work with the staff of the Curriculum Development and Research Center in Nairobi.

Some indication of how extensive these duties were can be seen from the fact that the service area of 200 schools for one technician was not uncommon.

Because a number of other groups were also involved in some aspect of the new primary approach program, it is difficult to identify the specific contribution of the NEA specialists. The Kenya Inspectorate worked through model schools, teacher-training institutes, and the school syllabus. The Curriculum Development and Research Center produced new materials and curriculum programs. The Institute of Education coordinated the many in-service programs. A Canadian government team also performed in-service duties. There were personnel from the British Overseas Development Ministry. The Ford Foundation provided materials and funds toward operating costs. The Teach Corps also sent two teams of five primary teachers who assisted in summer workshops in 1965 and 1966.

As a result of these combined efforts, the materials and procedures developed at the various experimental centers were introduced to the teachers in the field and to the assistant education officers.

LIBERIA
Rural Teacher-Training Institutes
AID/Tuskegee Institute

Tuskegee Institute contracted with AID to provide technical assistance for the operation of teacher-training institutes which would meet the needs of Liberia's expanding rural school development programs. Two 3-year institutes, with a combined capacity of 375 students, were constructed with AID assistance. The first of these, at Zorzor, was opened in 1961; and the second, at Kakata, in 1964.

Objectives

The specific objectives of Tuskegee assistance were to:

1. Provide personnel in advising and/or operational roles, as required, for assisting Liberians in developing the knowledge and skills necessary to operate the two rural teacher-training institutions effectively.

2. Train in-service and preservice teachers through the regular and special programs of the two institutes.

3. Develop a program of education for rural school teachers in Liberia based on the needs of the students and their communities.

4. Develop textbooks and other instructional materials for use in the rural teacher-training institutes, subject to the approval of the department of education.

Background

In a survey conducted by two members of the Tuskegee Institute, it was reported that, of the estimated 250,000 school-age children in Liberia, only 21 percent were in schools, and 70 percent of these were in primary grades (kindergareten through third grade), with 50 to 60 pupils of several grades under one teacher. For the 626 schools of the nation, it was reported by the Secretary of Public Instruction that there were 300 qualified teachers, of whom anly 150 could be considered adequate. (Ninety percent of these were foreigners teaching in the mission schools.) Since 95 percent of Liberians live in the rural area, it was felt by the Liberian government that AID could make its greatest impact by assisting in the training of teachers who would not only teach in the rural areas but also serve as leaders for the communities.

Major Activities

In the first phase of the program (1961), the Tuskegee team consisted of five members who carried most of the responsibility for teaching and administration at the Zorzor institute. By 1962, the team increased to eight. They included specialists in language arts, mathematics and science, health and vocational education, and curriculum and methods. With the opening of the Kakata institute in 1964, this number was increased to 11. As the project progressed, the team members gradually shifted to an advisory role and, by May 1967, had reduced their numbers to seven, and were preparing for the phase-out of the program in 1969.

Establishment of Rural Teacher-Training Institutes

The first task of the Tuskegee team members was to make the institute at Zorzor operational, then to put the one at Kakata into operation. This meant developing curricula, teaching classes, and carrying on all the duties involved in the running of a college.

By 1967, the two institutes were operating at full capacity and had produced 261 teachers, of whom 244 were teaching and 15 pursuing higher degrees. At that same time, both teaching and administrative positions were held by 27 Liberians, who had received training in the United States under the participant training program.

Curriculum

A program of instruction was developed using the required high school curriculum, supplemented with professional education courses, to enable students to fulfill the requirements for Class C teaching certificates. The curriculum was three years in length and required completion of the ninth Grade for entrance.

A variety of instructional materials was produced. This included manuals, handbooks, guides, syllabi, workbooks, and course outlines.

The Liberian staff was involved in a team approach to the preparation of curriculum guides, course outlines, evaluation techniques, and the use of instructional aids made from indigenous materials.

Progress was made at each institute in the establishment of libraries as aids to the instructional process.

Participant Training

Thirty-three Liberians were sent for training to the United States for periods of 9 months to 48 months; the majority stayed 12 months. Of these, 25 had returned by the end of 1967 and were filling positions in the two institutes.

In-service Training Program

Beginning in 1963, vacation schools were held each year for teachers and principals. By 1967, over 1,000 had attended. During the same period, in-service training programs were held for institute faculty and maintenance staff.

Student Teaching

In cooperation with rural teacher-training institute supervisors a student teaching program was initiated that involved critic teachers from 35 primary schools.

Sixty-two Liberians were engaged in off-campus student teaching assignments and workshops for faculty and staff in 1966. In addition, the institutes provided in-country training workshops for Peace Corps volunteers.

NEA Teach Corps

Plans were made for six Teach Corps team members to conduct summer teacher workshops in three schools in 1967.

Work Experience

A work experience program was introduced. In 1965, for example, over 300 students worked for two to four hours a week without pay under faculty supervision. They worked in such places as the library, cafeteria, and dormitories, and as assistants to the instructors in nonteaching duties.

Student Admission and Follow-Up

Admission and placement instruments were developed for screening applicants, the number of whom had risen to 500 for 125 places by 1966.

A follow-up study of 113 graduates of the two institutes was carried out by Pearl W. Head, a member of the Tuskegee team. It was found that 98 percent were teaching in government schools in their home districts.

MALI

Pedagogic Institute
AID/Southern Illinois University

The original plan called for a contract team of nine Southern Illinois faculty members to develop a Pedagogic Institute as the research arm of a proposed Higher Teacher-Training College. The Pedagogic Institute, an essentially French type of institution, has no exact parallel in the United States. It was to have two major purposes:

1. To serve as a functional adjunct to the Higher Teacher-Training College, providing a library, an instructional materials and audio-visual equipment center, a student counseling service, and a body of special lecturers.
2. To provide a general research and advisory service to the ministry of education.

Unfortunately, there was a delay in securing a loan for the construction of facilities for the Higher Teacher-Training College. It also took three years before Southern Illinois University was able to field a team. During this period, the government of Mali created an independent National Pedagogic Institute, located it in the ministry of education, and staffed it with French and Malian personnel.

Thus, upon arrival in Mali in 1965, the United States contract team found that the Higher Teacher-Training College was not built, and that a new institute, the National Pedagogic Institute, was operating with almost a full staff of Malian and French technicians. During the first two years of operation it became clear that some of the objectives of the Southern Illinois University contract were no longer pertinent. The Malian government was not interested in a fundamental reexamination of the curriculum; it lacked the funds to develop libraries in the secondary schools; and textbook writing was retained in the hands of French personnel. This called for a reassessment of the role of Southern Illinois University and its Pedagogic Institute.

Objectives

As revised and narrowed down in 1967, the objectives of the Southern Illinois team were as follows:

1. To conduct in-service training courses for teachers and administrators.
2. To prepare textbooks and other teaching materials for English-language teaching.
3. To assist the ministry of education in adapting the English-language curriculum to reflect an oral approach to teaching.
4. To provide vocational guidance, including educational testing and evaluation, for pupils in the fundamental (elementary) and secondary schools.
5. To develop and equip a demonstration audiovisual center whereby a limited number of teaching aids could be produced and used in the fundamental schools. This included a lithoprinting center for the production of textbooks.

Background

When Mali became an independent republic within the French community in 1958, less than 10 percent of school-age children were in school. The new government set free compulsory education for all children as one of its high-priority goals. While the system remains basically French, modifications are being made by using ideas gleaned from American, English, Czechoslovakian, and other educational systems. At the same time, it was made clear that it had already chosen its social-democratic, political, and economic form of organization, and did not look to the United States for a philosophy.

United States technical assistance was requested in establishing a Pedagogic Institute as an integral but separate part of the UNESCO-sponsored Higher Teacher-Training Center in Bamako. The University of Pittsburgh sent a survey team which recommended the project as feasible and worthwhile, but decided that they lacked qualified French-speaking personnel. The contract was then accepted by Southern Illinois University.

Major Activities

The Southern Illinois University team, in cooperation with Malian educators, established the organizational framework for an in-service training program for English teachers. It provided for a maximum of six summer courses after which the candidates were to be examined and, if successful, would be awarded a teaching certificate.

An English-language textbook adapted to Francophone West Africa was prepared.

The basic organizational framework of a vocational guidance testing program was developed, and a seminar for administrators and inspectors held.

An audiovisual center was established in the institute.

Four Malians have received training at Southern Illinois University, two in library science and textbook preparation, and two in the teaching of English as a foreign language.

A library was established at the institute, a cataloguing system initiated, and a Malian trained to maintain it.

NIGERIA

University of Nigeria, Nsukka and Enugu
AID/Michigan State University

The major purpose of the project was to assist the government of Eastern Nigeria to develop a university based on the land-grant philosophy, and tailored to the economic, social, and intellectual needs of Nigeria.

Assistance was to be given in planning the organizational structure, administration, facilities, curricula, equipment requirements, and staff training requirements necessary for the orderly expansion of the University of Nigeria, at Enugu and Nsukka, to a peak enrollment of 6,000 by 1972. Particular attention was to be given to a continuing education center, an economic development institute, general studies, a faculty of education, a faculty of engineering, and a faculty of agriculture.

Objectives

A comprehensive *Plan for the Development of the College of Education*, drawn up in 1961, listed priorities in teaching, research, and service functions as follows:

Teaching

1. Development of a degree program in education at the university to provide graduate teachers for the teacher-training colleges and secondary schools.

2. Provision for short institutes and workshops for teachers already in service in such areas as the teaching of English as a second language, and the teaching of science in secondary schools and teacher-training colleges.

3. Development of postgraduate courses leading to a certificate of education for graduates with subject matter degrees who wish to teach in the higher forms of the secondary schools.

4. Establishment of a center of international study, which would sponsor projects such as comparative education tours of other countries for leaders in Nigerian education.

Research

It was proposed that, for the immediate future, research be focused on problems of immediate relevance to Nigerian education. Three areas were pointed out as being of pressing need:

1. Child growth and development in West African societies.
2. Problems of selection and evaluation of students, particularly selection and guidance for study in appropriate higher educational curricula.
3. Methodology in the various teaching areas.

Service Activities

It was proposed that priority be given service activities which: (a) were designed to help people help themselves; (b) met with eagerness to respond on the part of teachers and school administrators; and (c) gave promise of feeding back new knowledge to teaching or research programs.

Among those suggested were:

1. An instructional materials development center with a mobile unit.
2. A demonstration school library.
3. A center for adult education and community development.
4. Short institutes and workshops.
5. The publication of professional materials for teachers at all levels.
6. Advisory functions to such bodies as the ministry of education; the Nigerian Union of Teachers; specialized teaching groups, such as the Association of Teachers of Science; and the teacher-training colleges.

Background

The need for a sharp expansion of university-level educational opportunities was emphasized in a report of the International Bank Mission on the Economic Development of Nigeria in 1954. It pointed out that Nigeria had less than one student in college for every 70,000 people, while India, by comparison, had one for every 1,400. A later survey by the Ashby Commission, published in 1960, stated that Nigeria's educational system needed to produce 80,000 people with post-secondary education over the following 10 years.

In 1958, paralleling the Ashby Commission Survey, President John Hannah and Dean Glenn Taggart of Michigan State University and James Cook of Exeter University were invited to make an educational-economic survey of Eastern Nigeria. Their report advocated the establishment of a University of Nigeria in the Eastern region.

The recommendations of both surveys were approved by the government of Eastern Nigeria, and USAID negotiated with Michigan State University to assist in the development of the University of Nigeria with campuses at Nsukka and at Enugu. It was to be dedicated to the principle that the total program should grow out of the demonstrated needs of Nigeria.

The rapid growth of the University of Nigeria can only be understood in the context of the political-social climate of Eastern Nigeria. A major factor lay in the nature of the dominant Ibo tribe. They prided themselves as being aggressive and go-ahead, and readily accepted education as a way of advancing their children and, consequently, their family position.

In the 1950's, there had been a primary school explosion in Eastern Nigeria. By the late 1950's, pressures had developed for a comparable secondary school and university explosion. Assistance in the education of a promising member of the family was seen as a sound investment which would repay the family many times over. By 1960, it was realized that primary education alone did not really help an individual to improve his economic position. This led to an increasing demand for more opportunities for children to attend advanced schools, and to an interest in technical schools.

An increasing number of Eastern Nigerians, who had received their education in the United States, were eager to give direction to this popular demand. Prominent among these was Dr. Azikwe, leader of the dominant political party of Eastern Nigeria, who had been the first president of the Republic of Nigeria. He was very critical of the rate of growth, limited enrollment, and traditional academic orientation of British education, as represented by the University College, Ibadan, which had been created as the university-level institution in Nigeria. He gave powerful support to the establishment and financing of the university and its development along American "practical" lines.

Major Activities

Three members of the Michigan State team, which totaled approximately 30, had responsibilities in the field of education. Their work was designed to be advisory in nature. In the early stages of the program, however, they found themselves combining administrative and advisory roles. For the first two years, by way of example, one of the team members acted as chairman of the College of Education. A Nigerian counterpart then assumed this responsibility, and the Americans continued in an advisory role.

Degree Programs in Education

The Michigan State advisors worked with the Nigerian faculty of the College of Education to develop a four-year program leading to a bachelor's degree in education. It combined general education and professional work in education with sufficient courses in two subjects to prepare for teaching at the secondary level.

126

Vocational Education

A three-year program leading to the Nigerian certificate in education was developed to prepare vocational teachers for the new junior high schools. Degree curricula were developed and syllabi prepared in industrial, agricultural, business, and home economics education to prepare teachers for secondary schools and teacher-training schools.

Vacation Schools

Beginning with the summer of 1962, vacation schools were held for over 500 qualified teachers to enable them to obtain teaching certificates. This program was carried out in cooperation with the Nigeria Union of Teachers, with additional staff provided by the Canadian Federation of Teachers and the Peace Corps. The program was continued until 1964 and has been requested annually by the Nigeria Union of Teachers, although the university found it impossible to staff the program after 1964.

Continuing Education Centers

Short courses and workshops were given either on campus or in 37 provincial continuing education centers. A program of off-campus credit courses for teachers was also started. By 1967, it was reported that over 10,000 adults had participated, but there was no information as to how many were teachers.

Science Seminar

A science seminar was held in 1965 to make a comprehensive assessment of the development of the university in the science fields. Among the areas considered were: curriculum development, teaching materials and equipment, and relationship of science to teacher training and to graduate study.

Institute of Education

An Institute of Education was established in 1963. It engaged in a program of mutual consultation and curriculum development with the 52 higher elementary teacher-training colleges. Extramural conferences were held under the sponsorship of the Institute of Education for such groups as school principals, mathematics tutors, English teachers, and elementary science teachers. In 1964, an Advanced Teacher-Training College in Owerri was established with formal links to the university through the institute.

Center of International Study

Beginning in 1962, with USAID assistance, comparative education tours were sponsored for Nigerian educators. Included were tours through European countries, the United States, and French West Africa. A proposed tour of East African states was interrupted by hostilities.

Research

Research projects were carried out in such topics as:

Reconstruction in Nigerian education.

Methods of teaching science in Nigerian primary schools.

Intellectual abilities of Eastern Nigerian children.

The economics of education in Nigeria.

In 1967, 34 Nigerians had returned to the faculty with advanced degrees. Thirty were studying in the U.S. and 26, scheduled to depart in September, were unable to go because of the hostilities. There was no information as to how many of these were specifically involved in teacher training.

University Forced to Close

In 1966, because of the critical relations between Eastern Nigeria and the central government, all students from other regions were repatriated. The following year, when hostilities broke out, the university was forced to close. It was reported that a number of campus buildings had been destroyed in the fighting.

At that time, the university had an enrollment of 3,000 students, of whom over 400 were enrolled in the faculty of education. Eight hundred graduates from the colleges of education and science and engineering had been employed by the ministry of education, most of them teaching in secondary schools or teacher-training colleges. The university was administered and staffed by Nigerians. The vice chancellor was a Nigerian, as were 90 percent of the deans and department heads, and 80 percent of the 448-member faculty. Of the latter, 37 were on the faculty of education.

NIGERIA
Federal Advanced Teachers College, Lagos
AID/University of California at Los Angeles

In 1961, AID, UNESCO, and the Ford Foundation assisted the government of Nigeria in the construction of a Federal Advanced Teachers College in Lagos which was merged in April 1967 with the University of Lagos. Seven technicians from the University of California at Los Angeles, with eight from UNESCO, formed the instructional staff for the new college, which opened in November 1962, with 146 students.

Objectives

The specific objectives of the University of California at Los Angeles team were:

1. To increase both the quantity and quality of Nigerian teachers for the secondary schools and teacher-training colleges.

2. To develop and administer a program for in-service education in the Federation.

3. To prepare Nigerians, through both participation and counterpart programs, to be able to staff the college in administrative and academic roles by 1965.

4. To graduate, by the summer of 1965, at least 150 students with the award of the Nigerian certificate of education.

5. To develop a demonstration laboratory school, as part of the program of the college.

6. To develop an institution, unique in type, which would serve the needs of the Federation as a whole and would influence a unified approach to country-wide educational practices.

Background

In 1960, the government of Nigeria recognized the need for a sharp increase in the supply of qualified nongraduate teachers for the secondary schools and also for more trained primary teachers. The need was pointed out by the Ashby Report, *Investment in Education,* and the subsequent White Paper of the government of Nigeria, *Educational Development 1960-1970.* The Ashby Commission reported that approximately 90 percent of the primary teachers were insufficiently trained and revealed that the output of the educational system of Nigeria, in relation to her needs in skilled manpower, was critically inadequate. Illustrative of the poor level of qualification of Nigerian teachers was a report published in 1963 by the ministry of education entitled *Characteristics of Teachers in Primary Schools in Northern Nigeria.* It stated that the typical teacher in the North in 1963 had only two years of education beyond the primary school level.

In its plans for the 1960-1970 decade, Nigeria assigned high priority to increasing the supply of qualified secondary teachers and providing in-service programs for the upgrading of primary teachers.

Major Activities

Over a six-year period, the University of California at Los Angeles team worked with Nigerian and UNESCO staff members to develop the Federal Advanced Teachers College as a fully-operational institution for the preparation of secondary teachers, with a three-year curriculum leading to the Nigerian certificate in education.

The institution opened in 1962 with a class of 139, and the first graduating class three years later numbered 135. In 1967, the college merged with the University of Lagos and became the School of Education.

In addition to teaching their classes, California team members reported the following activities:

Curriculum Development

A three-year program leading to the Nigerian certificate in education was developed for students who had either passed the West African school certificate examination (Grade 12) or were certified Grade II teachers.

Approximately two-thirds of the curriculum was devoted to two major disciplines and one-third to professional preparation. The combinations of majors were: English-French, English-mathematics, mathematics-physics, mathematics-geography, physics-chemistry, chemistry-biology. Syllabi were developed for the various courses in the program.

In 1967, the University of California at Los Angeles team proposed curriculum revisions to permit the graduates of the Federal Advanced Teachers College to enter the second year of the university program and qualify for degrees after two years teaching experience.

A student-teaching program, developed under the supervision of both academic and education departments, consisted of four weeks in the second year and six weeks in the final year.

Library and Communications Center

A Communications Media Center was established. Teaching materials, including maps, charts, posters, transparencies, drill games, and film strips, were prepared. A 16mm film library was established. Teacher trainees were given instructions in audiovisual techniques, and made use of the center in connection with their practice teaching.

The library building was completed with a total of 17,000 books. By 1967, 14,000 of them had been processed and were available for distribution. A library handbook, manual, and workbook had been written and an orientation course given to each first-year student. Newspapers and periodicals were available for students and faculty, and microfilm had been purchased.

In-service Training

In-service courses were conducted for both elementary and secondary teachers in instructional materials, tests and measurements, and communications media. In 1963, 60 teachers enrolled in a two-month in-service program. By 1967, the enrollment was reduced to 29.

Participant Training

Between 1961 and 1967, six Nigerian staff members received overseas participant training. Four joined the faculty of the Federal Advanced Teachers College.

Research

In the later phases of the program, team members carried on a variety of research activities. The following are illustrative:

Follow-up study of 1965 graduates.

Evaluation of English-language skills of first-year students.

Comparison of British and American systems in spelling and pronunciation.

Development of extensive reading lists for Nigerian secondary schools and colleges.

Evaluation of academic achievement of high anxious and low anxious students.

Evaluation of academic achievement of Grade II teachers compared with holders of the West African school certificate.

Study of the development of library services in Nigeria.

Survey of student teaching practices in Nigeria.

A follow-up study was carried out on the first class of students which was graduated in July 1965. Out of a total of one hundred thirty-five, 123 were working in education, the great majority as classroom teachers. Interviews were held with 61 administrators who supervised 80 of the teachers. There was general agreement that the Federal Advanced Teachers College was producing teachers of high standards, who knew their subject matter as well as how to teach it.

NIGERIA

Advanced Teachers College of Education, Ibadan Branch
AID/Ohio University

Objectives

The objective of the Ohio program was to assist Western Nigeria in training teachers, both by preservice and in-service programs. The overall goals, as they were finally formulated, were:

1. Develop an advanced-level teacher-training program, qualifying teachers for secondary schools and teacher-training colleges, or to continue their education at a degree-granting institution.

2. Develop a commercial teacher-training program, and assist the ministry of education in the supervision and curriculum development of business education in secondary schools.

3. Develop an in-service program for tutors, headmasters and principals, and teachers of different levels.

Specific activities to achieve these goals were to:

1. Develop entrance examinations, syllabi, and curricula for the college, reviewing them with other institutions in the region in order to maintain consistent standards.

2. Develop a well-qualified Nigerian staff through counterpart, on-the-job, and participant training.

3. Develop textbooks and teaching materials specifically for use in Nigeria.

4. Assist in conducting research in teacher education.

5. Establish a follow-up program to provide support to graduates.

6. Assist in the development and staffing of an in-service program, including short courses, workshops, and seminars, and train counterparts so that the Nigerian staff might be in complete charge by 1968.

7. Assist in the establishment of instructional materials departments in a number of in-service centers, and offer guidance in the preparation of materials.

Background

In 1958, Ohio University, under a contract with ICA, the forerunner of AID, provided assistance to Western Nigeria in improving the quality and number of its teachers. The first project was the development of a one-year program at the Government Teacher-Training College at Ibadan for upgrading tutors employed in Grade III teacher-training colleges.

This phase of the program was completed in 1962, at which time the Government Teacher-Training College was strengthened and renamed the Olunloyo College of Education. It offered a three-year course of study leading to the Nigerian certificate in education, the highest non-degree certificate obtainable. In April 1965, Olunloyo College of Education and Ransome Koti College were combined and called the Advanced Teachers College of Education, Ibadan Branch. A further merger with the Advanced Teachers College at Ondo, which had been developed with British and UNESCO technical assistance, took place in January 1968. The Advanced Teachers College is now located at Ondo and is receiving assistance from the British and from UNESCO.

Major Activities

The Ohio team, which averaged between 12 and 15 members, had as its first task the development of a one-year in-service program for assisting tutors in Grade III teacher-training colleges to improve their qualifications. This project was completed in 1962, and the main thrust of the program was directed to the development of a three-year curriculum leading to the Nigerian certificate in education; a program for the training of commercial teachers; and the development of in-service centers throughout Western Nigeria.

Advanced Teachers College of Education

A three-year advanced-level teacher-training program for secondary teachers, leading to the Nigerian certificate in education, was developed and put into operation at the Olunloyo College of Education which was successively merged with two other colleges to become the Advanced Teachers College of Education at Ondo. The three-year curriculum provided students with the necessary academic background and professional teacher training to teach their major subjects in the secondary schools to the level of the West African school certificate (Grade 12) and to teach in Grade II teacher-training colleges.

The Ohio staff worked with Nigerian expatriate faculty members in teaching classes and developing course outlines, syllabi, teaching materials, science laboratories, and a library.

By 1967, the college was operating under the direction of a Nigerian principal and vice-principal and had 24 Nigerians on its faculty, over half of whom had received participant training in the U.S. In addition, there were seven other staff members, including Peace Corps volunteers and expatriate teachers and 16 members of the Ohio team.

Curriculum for Secondary Commercial Teachers

A program for the preparation of commercial teachers was introduced. Graduates of this program were responsible for introducing commercial subjects into the secondary schools of Western Nigeria. In 1966, the responsibility for this program was transferred to the Western Michigan Technical Education Project, also located in Ibadan.

In-service Training Program

In-service training was provided for primary teachers in 34 centers and reached thousands of teachers. Four Ohio team members were assigned to develop the program. In 1962, 2,000 teachers were enrolled in 26 centers. The number climbed steadily until 1967, when 7,000 teachers registered. The effectiveness of the in-service program was increased by the active cooperation of the ministry of education, and also by the fact that successful participants were awarded teaching certificates.

Curriculum materials and teaching aids were made available in 19 major centers, and 18 library centers were established for the distribution of books.

Nigerians were trained to take over the responsibility for running the centers, and it was reported that they would be ready to staff the program when the Ohio contract terminated in 1968.

Teachers In-service Centers

Centers were established to make available books, audiovisual equipment, instructional programs, guest speakers, film shows, and facilities for construction of teaching aids. In 1967, there were 26 centers servicing approximately 15,000 teachers. Their programs were planned by advisory committees, which included local teachers and headmasters, as well as local education officers. During 1967, for example, it was reported that 12,000 teachers made use of the in-service centers.

Production of Teaching Aids

One-hour video tapes in eight subject matter areas were prepared for the in-service training of 7,000 unqualified Grade III teachers in the Western region.

The team members worked with Nigerian educators to produce syllabi and teaching materials in science, social studies, arithmetic, and English. In the preparation of the science program, for example, 60 primary teachers were involved in a workshop to study a syllabus and teaching aids, which were then tried out in a pilot project in 10 schools.

Textbooks were published in physical education, art, and business practices; manuscripts were ready for publication in commercial education, general science, and guidance in December 1967.

Research and Publication

The Ohio staff members were able to become more involved in research and textbook writing as the project continued. Together with their colleagues in the Kano project, they had written 16 textbooks and had had over 60 articles published in professional journals by 1967.

Eighteen participants were sent to the United States for periods of 6 to 36 months. In December 1967, all but one of these had returned and, with exceptions, were employed in some phase of education in Western Nigeria.

SUDAN
Khartoum Senior Trade School
AID/Dunwoody Industrial Institute

Teacher education was one phase of a project in which the Dunwoody Industrial Institute undertook to provide technical assistance to the Khartoum Senior Trade School. In 1963, a 16-member team was sent out to assist in developing the school as a demonstration center and central institution to train skilled workmen and technical teachers for the Republic of Sudan. Enrollment was to be limited to secondary school graduates from either academic or technical schools.

Objectives

Objectives so far as teacher education is concerned were:

1. To assist in developing a teacher-training program for the Khartoum Senior Trade School which would include the teaching of the various trade skills, as well as methods of teaching, shop organization and management, and the preparation of teaching materials.

2. To assist in planning in-service programs for the staff of Khartoum Senior Trade School, as well as the staffs of the intermediate technical and post-intermediate technical schools.

3. To produce approximately 100 new teachers each year.

Background

Both the government of the Sudan and the USAID Mission recognized that the lack of trained Sudanese personnel in the various occupations was a major handicap. To help remedy this, a technical education program was established in 1958 by the United States in cooperation with the government of the Republic of Sudan. It was designed to increase the number of intermediate technical schools, from 11, in 1959, to 40, in 1970, with a total enrollment of 6,400 students; to increase the number of post-intermediate and technical schools from 4 to 17, with an enrollment of 4,000; and to establish a new terminal senior trade training center in Khartoum for Grades 12 and 13, which would include a comprehensive trade teacher-training program.

Major Activities

It is difficult to separate teacher training from the rest of the program. Only those activities directly related to the preparation of teachers have been included in this report.

Teacher-Training Program

In 1966, 18 trainees were enrolled for the first time in a one-year program of teacher training. Two earlier attempts to initiate a teacher-training program, in 1964 and 1965, had failed because of administrative indecision and lack of support on the part of the ministry of education, student resistance, and lack of interest on the part of the Sudanese staff. The teacher trainees represented six trade areas and spent half a day in skill improvement, in addition to half a day in teacher preparation. The teacher trainees were most reluctant to take seriously the continued emphasis on the development of skills. It was reported that they did not complete or, in some cases, attempt to perform shop work which was an integral part of the program. No use of student teaching was reported.

In-service Training

The Dunwoody teacher-trainer advisor was active in conducting seminars and workshops to meet the need for in-service training. In 1963, teacher-training courses were held at the Khartoum Technical Institute for two groups of intermediate and post-intermediate teachers and graduates.

In 1964, a series of seminars was conducted for headmasters and selected teachers. The purpose of this was to discuss, modify, and review the syllabi of various trade courses; prepare sample lesson plans; and review and make recommendations that would help implement the new syllabi. Each seminar continued for ten days, and five different groups were served. In 1965 and 1966, a two-week course was conducted for assistant headmasters of the post-intermediate trade schools.

A series of short courses, six weeks in length, was given in the teaching of the various trades to approximately 100 teachers.

Participant Training

Seventeen participant trainees were sent to Dunwoody Institute. Most of these spent two years in advanced skill training in specific areas and technical teacher training. They all had experience as teachers in intermediate or post-intermediate schools. Fifteen returned to teaching positions at the Khartoum Senior Trade School.

End of Project

The project came to an end with the breaking of diplomatic relations with the United States by the government of Sudan in June 1967 as a consequence of the Israeli-Egyptian conflict.

LAOS

Teacher Training: Ecole Supérieure de Pédagogie et Ecoles Normales des Instituteurs AID/International Voluntary Services

The contract of the International Voluntary Services in Laos was modified a number of times as the project developed.

Objectives

As stated in 1966, the objectives of the program were:

1. To provide technical assistance and advice for developing and strengthening the preservice and in-service teacher-training programs for elementary and secondary teachers at the Ecole Supérieure de Pédagogie (national education center) near Vientiane and at designated affiliated village laboratory centers.

2. To assist in establishing and developing facilities and training programs at the Ecoles Normales des Instituteurs (regional training centers) at Luang Prabang and Pakse, and in other places as mutually agreed on.

Background

When Laos gained its independence from the French, the country possessed great natural resources, but there was a critical shortage of trained people among its 2,500,000 citizens. With United States assistance, the number of children in school was increased from 20,000 to nearly 200,000 in 1967.

To prepare the teachers made necessary by this expansion, the Ecole Supérieure de Pédagogie was established in 1959 on a location which is planned some day to become the site of a university.

The school has an enrollment of 1,400 students, all of them training to be teachers. Students enter the school after six years of previous schooling and stay from two to nine years. Two-year graduates can teach in Grades 1-3 and nine-year graduates in Grades 9-10. The majority of the students received this instruction in French. In 1967, for example, 180 were taught in English and 400 in Lao, the remainder being taught in French. During the same year, there were 51 French faculty members, 30 from the United States (most of whom were members of the International Voluntary Services) 25 Lao, and 16 from six other countries. All students sign a contract to teach in Laos for 10 years after graduation. Otherwise, they must pay for their board. There is no tuition. Only three percent paid their own expenses in 1967.

The Ecole Supérieure de Pédagogie is under the supervision of the ministry of education. The school administrators are Lao, and the French and English sections each have a head staff as liaison between their teachers and the administration.

In 1961, two ecoles normales des instituteurs were built at Luang Prabang and Pakse to train teachers for village schools being built with USAID assistance. The program, which was in the beginning a one-year "crash" program, was later extended to two years and, in addition, a four-year program was added. The curriculum, in addition to the basic subjects, emphasized such things as community health and improved farming techniques, which it was hoped the teachers would take back to the rural communities.

136

Major Activities

Ecole Supérieure de Pédagogie

The education team of the International Voluntary Services in Laos grew from 8 in 1959 to 40 in 1967. The original group consisted primarily of practical arts teachers, and much of their work was to keep the physical facilities of the school operating. As the program grew and Lao staff became available, more emphasis was placed on training counterparts to construct and maintain the facilities. Counterparts were also trained to take over most of the teaching in home economics, practical arts, and agriculture.

The activities of the volunteers were then expanded to include more teaching in the academic classrooms. After a University of Michigan contract in the teaching of English was phased out, the volunteers filled most of the teaching assignments in that area. In 1967, they taught English, economics, government, history, geography, mathematics, general science, biology, physics, home economics, electricity, woodworking, motor maintenance, and agriculture.

Ecoles Normales des Instituteurs

A volunteer was assigned to each of the Ecoles Normales des Instituteurs. In addition to teaching various courses, they were active in the entire life of the schools.

Among the different projects reported were: working with the agriculture program, developing school libraries, working on curriculum development, building a language laboratory and a science laboratory, establishing a teaching aids center, and writing a history textbook for primary teachers.

By 1966, over 1,600 students were enrolled in the various teacher-training programs, and there was an annual graduating class of about 300, all of whom were qualified to teach in the elementary schools of Laos.

Participant Training

Between 1964 and 1966, over 50 participant trainees were sent abroad for further education.

LAOS

Education Development (Secondary Education) AID/University of Hawaii

Following a survey in 1965, the University of Hawaii agreed to assist the ministry of education in establishing a comprehensive Lao secondary school as a pilot for the improvement of the secondary school program.

Objectives

1. Development of a curriculum for Grades 7-10 comprehensive secondary school offering courses in practical and vocational subjects, including agriculture, as well as academic secondary subjects.
2. Performance of such teaching duties as may be necessary, putting

emphasis upon training of Lao teachers assigned to the school, and enabling them to carry out all teaching and administrative duties at the earliest feasible time without foreign assistance.

3. Training of Lao teachers temporarily attached to the school for in-service education.

4. Development of textbooks and other instructional material in the Lao language, for publication by the ministry's Material Production Center.

Background

Beginning in 1956, support to teacher education played a dominant role in United States assistance programs to Laos. In the early years, this assistance was directed to developing a system of teacher-training institutions for the country's elementary schools. While much was accomplished, the problems in education facing the country were still staggering. A UNESCO report in 1964, for example, concluded that "almost all the problems besetting Laos, except the major one of war, are educational problems and the country is thus in need of a marked expansion in education." In 1964, it was reported that only 143,000 children, out of an elementary school-age population of 835,000, were in school and that only one out of 10 of those who started the elementary grades finished.

One reason for the heavy dropout at the elementary level was the fact that all instruction was in French. Consequently, the students were forced to study all subjects in a language not their mother tongue. As a result, few passed the qualifying examination admitting them to the secondary level (Grades 6-13). To remedy this, the Education Reform Act of 1962 provided for the use of Lao in the school system. It was stated that this was to be done gradually and completed by 1980.

At the secondary level the acute nature of the problem became very clear. In 1964, about 900 students were enrolled in secondary school and less than 100 were graduated. The curriculum was based on the French lycée and had little relevance to the needs of Laos. How critical the situation was can be judged from the fact that it was estimated that only one of the 500 children entering the first grade succeeded in graduating from the secondary school. This means that the secondary school system, as then organized, was totally inadequate to provide the trained leaders and the vocational specialists desperately needed for national development.

In their book, *Education, Manpower and Economic Growth,* Harbison and Myers made two points about education in the developing countries which appear to have special relevance to Laos. The first was that "deficiencies in secondary education are even more serious than in primary; in part because governments have given first priority to the building of primary schools and the next priority to the development of universities. There is strong political pressure for primary education and universities are symbols of prestige and national grandeur. Secondary education, upon

138

which the real success of both primary and higher education depend, is commonly given the lowest priority."[1]

They also pointed out that the traditional orientation of secondary education needs to be changed: "Its purpose should be to provide a fundamental and broad education, including adequate exposure to science and mathematics, for students planning to take jobs directly; to become technicians or school teachers; or enter the universities. Therefore, the emphasis should be on multipurpose secondary schools, with the various choices for specialization, whose major function would be to produce well-educated people who can later be trained either in employment or in higher education institutions for a wide variety of occupations in the high-level manpower category. This is certainly the most economical means of increasing both the quantity, quality and flexibility of output of secondary schools."[2]

By 1965, there was growing conviction that study should be given to the type of teacher training necessary to implement an elementary-secondary school program containing instruction in academic and vocational areas. The University of Hawaii was requested to conduct a survey of education in Laos and recommend a program of action.

Recommendations of Survey Team

The survey team recommended that the University of Hawaii could best help the development of education in Laos in the following ways:

1. Plan, develop, and operate a comprehensive secondary school for 900 students as a pilot school. The school would emphasize English as a strong second language, thereby opening the door to able Lao students who might desire to study abroad in English-language countries. It would emphasize the vocational and technical fields, providing greater opportunity for the Lao to find gainful employment and enabling training to be given in areas that will be useful in the development of Laos.

2. Assist the ministry of education in further developing its secondary and teacher education programs.

3. Conduct research with emphasis on areas that would contribute to the further betterment of the Lao system of education.

Major Activities

In 1967, a complex of 12 buildings was constructed on the outskirts of Vientiane to house the comprehensive secondary school. The school was unique in that it used the Lao language as its medium of instruction. The classes were taught by Lao teachers with the assistance of four staff members from the University of Hawaii.

Curriculum

A program and schedule for the first year of instruction, beginning with the seventh grade, was developed by the University of Hawaii team. A school year consisting of four eight-week sessions was planned to include both academic and pre-vocational education, with tracks in agriculture, home economics, and industrial arts. The following courses were offered: Lao language and literature, practical arts, arithmetic, science, social studies, French, English, health and physical education, vocational guidance, student government, and interest clubs.

Student Recruitment

A comprehensive examination was given to 800 applicants, and 100 were selected for admittance in 1967.

Equipment and Supplies

Administrative office supplies and equipment were purchased by the University of Hawaii team and the Laotian counterpart.

THAILAND

Vocational Education Project
AID/California State Polytechnic College
Oklahoma University

Objectives

The objectives of AID assistance to the Vocational Education Project so far as teacher education is concerned were:

1. A senior advisor was to assist the director general of vocational education in developing a program of vocational education for the whole country.

2. A team of six trade and industry specialists, provided through a contract with Oklahoma University, was to assist in the improvement of instruction and facilities at Thewes Vocational Teacher Training College and its 14 project secondary schools.

3. A team of five agriculture specialists, provided through a contract with California State Polytechnic College, was to assist in the improvement of instruction and facilities at the Bangpra Agricultural Teachers College and its nine project secondary schools.

4. Participant training for 12 individuals in trade and industry and 10 in agriculture was proposed to ensure the effective operation of the program after the phasing out of the AID technicians.

Background

In an endeavor to improve and extend vocational training in Thailand, the government, aided by a $6 million loan from the International Bank for Reconstruction and Development, embarked on a five-year program for the expansion of vocational secondary schools and colleges.

It was planned that craft skills such as welding, auto-mechanics, electronics, industrial electricity, machine shop, and buidling construction be taught at 14 project schools and that industrial teachers be trained at

Thewes College. Agriculture was to be taught at nine project schools and agriculture teachers were to be trained at Bangpra College.

A condition of the International Bank loan was that competent technical assistance be secured to carry out the project.

AID, therefore, agreed to provide 11 technicians for a period of five years to assist in the development of the program and also to provide participant training for 22 Thai personnel.

Major Activities

Oklahoma University Team

No reports were available in February 1968 as to progress of the Oklahoma team.

California State Polytechnic College Team

The primary assignment of the five members of the California State Polytechnic team was to develop a three-year certificate curriculum at Bangpra College. The first two years would be shared with students training to be agricultural technicians, and the third year would be devoted to teacher training. It was decided that the initial thrust should emphasize technical skills and, in consequence, the first team was composed of secondary school agriculture teachers with the dean of the school of agriculture as chief of party.

For the first eight months, the team members were primarily active in working through Thai counterparts with the faculty of the Bangpra Agricultural Teachers College and visiting the nine project secondary schools.

The California team also worked with the best of the secondary agriculture schools to develop proposals by which their graduates could enter the department of agriculture of the University of Thailand.

Participant Training

Three participant trainees were already on the California State Polytechnic campus by the end of 1967. A program combining technical skills and professional courses leading to an M.A. in education, with a concentration in agriculture, was arranged to suit the individual needs of each student.

VIETNAM
Elementary Teacher Training
AID/Southern Illinois University

Objectives

Southern Illinois University contracted with AID to provide a team of elementary teacher education specialists to carry out the following activities:

1. Assist in the improvement and development of administration, organization, and procedures in normal schools and elementary schools.

2. Assist in the improvement and development of curricula, course content, and instructional materials.

3. Assist in the improvement and modernization of teaching methods and procedures.

4. Assist in the improvement and development of in-service training programs.

5. Advise and give assistance to USAID in the selection and development of training programs for participants directly related to the normal schools, demonstration schools, and allied institutions.

Background

In 1960, Southern Illinois University conducted a survey of the conditions and potentials of the elementary education schools and elementary teacher education program in Vietnam. It was reported that the chief aim of the education program in 1960 was to produce an educated élite, who would lead the majority of the people. Over one-third of all elementary-age children had no opportunity to attend either public or private school, and the schools which existed were overcrowded, understaffed, provided inadequate teaching materials, and were unable to cope with the problems of maintenance and repair. The majority of the people had only five years of elementary schooling. Few persons in governmental positions considered elementary education important and, as a result, teacher status was low.

At the start of the 1961-62 school year, there were three normal schools in South Vietnam with an enrollment of 894. In December 1961, one new normal school began operation with an enrollment of 291. The 1961-62 school year enrollment thus became 1,185. In October 1962, a second new normal school began operation with an enrollment of 616. Enrollment for the 1962-63 school year was therefore 2,211. A total of 1,111 students graduated in the spring of 1963.

At the start of the 1966-67 school year, five normal schools were in operation, with a combined enrollment of 2,916. A total of 1,314 students graduated in the spring of 1967.

The 1967-68 school year started in September with a combined enrollment of 3,078.

At the time of the last report, plans had been completed and construction begun on one more school. This was to be a replacement for one of the oldest of the five schools, the one for the training of Montagnard teachers.

The 1972-73 target set by the ministry of education is an annual graduating class of 2,800.

Major Activities

The Southern Illinois team, which by 1967 numbered 15, worked with the normal school faculties in developing curricula, preparing teaching materials, and assisting with in-service programs.

142

Normal Schools

The normal school curriculum was lengthened from a one-year to a two-year program and included more attention to methods of teaching and more practice teaching. Admission requirements were also raised, and applicants for all but one of the normal schools had to have the first Baccalaureate (the equivalent of 11 years of formal education).

Five normal schools with an enrollment of over 3,000 were staffed and administered by Vietnamese personnel, the Southern Illinois team providing advisory services.

Demonstration Laboratory School

In 1962, a demonstration laboratory school was built for the Saigon Normal School to enable students to have more opportunity for observation and instruction in teaching, through demonstration and practice teaching.

In 1965, a second demonstration laboratory school was completed in Qui Nhon and began operation in the 1965-66 school year.

In-service Training

An in-service elementary teacher education center was opened in 1962, and provided training for almost 2,000 elementary principals, inspectors, and teachers. A nucleus of master teachers was given special instruction to help them assist in in-service training programs with the rural teachers.

In June 1967, the normal schools held three weeks of in-service training with over 300 teachers participating.

In 1967, a five-day seminar for directors of normal schools was held. Among the more significant topics of discussion were: problems of the student teachers, teaching assignments after graduation, criteria for selection of candidates for the normal school teacher-training courses, and in-service centers at normal schools.

Textbooks and Reference Materials

The Southern Illinois University team worked with textbook writing committees in the areas of reading, civics, geography, health, science, physical education, and mathematics.

Much attention was given to securing books on teaching, teacher training, psychology, pedagogy, and the subject matter areas. Many books were secured from the United States and the Asia Foundation. The team also assisted in the selection of films, worth $75,000, which were donated by the Encyclopedia Britannica Education Corporation to the elementary teacher education program.

The Southern Illinois team aided in the establishment of an educational materials and project exhibit in 1965 which was attended by over 15,000 citizens, teachers, students, and officials.

Lecture and Demonstration Series

The Southern Illinois team conducted or participated in lectures, demonstrations, and seminars. Among those reported in 1965 were the following:

1. Operation and use of audiovisual equipment.

143

2. Evaluative guide for teacher education.
3. Guide for evaluating normal schools.
4. Organization and use of library.

Participant Training

In 1967, it was reported that 67 trainees had worked or were working in the United States for advanced degrees in elementary education. Twenty had returned and had been assigned positions. An additional 40 had been approved and were waiting for final arrangements to be made.

Course for Normal School Professors

In September 1967, the University of Saigon began a new course in the faculty of pedagogy to prepare professors specifically for the normal schools. A modest first year group of 40 was selected. Attrition reduced the number to 26. The course was conceived as a full 12-month preparation, with emphasis upon child psychology, teaching methods, evaluation of learning, community education, methodology of teaching in elementary schools and in normal schools, and practice teaching in normal schools.

VIETNAM
Secondary Teacher Training
AID/Ohio University

The Ohio University contract provided for a team of six specialists, later increased to 16, to assist in the development of preservice and in-service training programs for secondary school teachers. They were to be assigned as follows:

1. In the faculty of pedagogy, University of Saigon, and the attached secondary school.
2. In the faculty of pedagogy, University of Hue, and the attached secondary school.
3. In such other teacher-training institutions as were mutually agreeable.

Objectives

The objectives of the project were to:
1. Assist in the modification of administrative organization and practices.
2. Assist in the development and modification of curricula, course content, and instructional materials.
3. Assist in the development and modification of teaching methods, practices, and techniques.
4. Assist USAID in the development of training programs for participants.
5. Assist in the development of comprehensive secondary curricula at two high schools as a pilot project. (This was included in 1967, when an additional five advisors were added.)

Background

Between 1955 and 1960 no significant progress took place in the secondary education program in Vietnam. Enrollment increased somewhat, but this was made possible through private institutions which provided secondary education for two-thirds of the secondary enrollment. In 1962, a contract team from Ohio University arrived to work with the faculties of pedagogy in Saigon and Hue to improve the quality of secondary instruction.

Major Activities

The Ohio technicians served in an advisory capacity in secondary education to the national ministry of education, the faculties of pedagogy, and secondary teachers employed in the two demonstration schools.

A demonstration high school was established at the University of Saigon that was used for educational research and the demonstration of teaching methods. It also provided facilities for teaching interns.

The philosophy and objectives of the demonstration school at Thu Duc illustrate the purpose of the program: "It shall be the philosophy of the Thu Duc Demonstration High School to provide a secondary education for all of its students, consistent with their individual interests and abilities, so that they can rightfully assume their roles as contributing members in a free, democratic, Vietnamese society.

"To develop a new secondary high school curriculum, a new system of school administration, a new concept of teaching and learning that will be gradually implemented throughout the many secondary schools in Vietnam.

"To provide a laboratory for the student teachers of the faculty of pedagogy in order that they might observe, practice teach, and discuss new educational trends and developments.

"To provide an environment of learning in which the value of the Vietnamese cultural heritage is highly appreciated.

"To serve as a center for experimentation and research in secondary education in aspects of curriculum, methods of teaching, evaluation, counseling, administrative organization, and public relations.

"To serve as a pattern of education for future Vietnamese secondary schools."[3]

Comprehensive High School Curriculum

A curriculum for the proposed comprehensive high school was developed by the Ohio team with the assistance of their Vietnamese colleagues. It attempted to expand the original curriculum, largely patterned on the French lycée, to one based on the needs of Vietnamese society and the characteristics of Vietnamese youth. Secondary education in Vietnam is structured in two cycles following the completion of five years of elementary school. The first cycle consists of four years and the second, three. Programs were developed for students planning to enter an occupation or trade, as well as those continuing on into higher education. Proposed curricula included concentrations in sciences, foreign languages, history, mathematics, business education, agriculture, home economics, and industrial arts. Provision was also made for electives in art, music, home economics, business, and industrial arts.

Over a period of four years, this program was put into effect in the first cycle (Grades 7-10) of the demonstration school at the University of Saigon, and plans were developed for its introduction into the second cycle (Grades 11-12).

Participant Training

Twenty-four teachers had received training in the United States under the participant program and were teaching on the faculty of pedagogy in Saigon or in the demonstration schools by July 1967. Ninety were studying in the United States at that time, and 25 had been nominated for the 1967-68 school year.

The majority enrolled in programs for advanced degrees in the major content and professional areas necessary to staff a secondary teacher-training program.

In addition, members of the ministry of education and principals of the pilot schools made a three-month tour of comprehensive high schools in the United States.

Teacher-Training Curricula

Three-year curricula for secondary teachers were developed. They were comprised of general education, concentration in a specialized subject area, and professional education, including student teaching. In addition to the more traditional subjects, curricula were developed in business education, home economics, industrial arts, and library science. It was proposed to use these new programs to train staff for the pilot comprehensive high school.

Workshops

Four workshops were held for teachers in the pilot demonstration schools and other secondary schools in the areas of guidance, home economics, biological science, and science education.

Instructional Materials

Instructional materials, including textbooks, courses of study, lesson plans, and resource units, were developed for the secondary curricula in business education, home economics, industrial arts, and science education. These were available for introduction into 12 comprehensive pilot schools when they were built.

Provincial High Schools

The team members worked with the faculties of 12 provincial high schools in pilot programs to introduce the methods and materials developed in the Thu Duc demonstration school at Saigon.

146

INDIA
National Institute of Education
AID/Teachers College, Columbia University

The National Institute of Education was established by the government of India in 1961 as the principal agent of the newly-formed National Council of Educational Research and Training. It brought under one organization six earlier institutes, all of which were concerned with various aspects of education. It was, in effect, to be a graduate professional university discharging three functions:

1. Training for leadership positions through postgraduate degree programs and advanced in-service seminars.
2. Conducting and sponsoring research of national importance.
3. Extending its influence throughout India by publications (textbooks, research, and creative writing) and by developing working relations with state departments of education and other colleges and universities.

Objectives

The objective of the Teachers College project, as stated in the 1966 contract, was to provide advice and assistance to the National Institute of Education in the following ways:

1. To train the faculty for teaching the graduate courses in the National Institute of Education.
2. To engage in research projects.
3. To teach and offer courses in research methods to the faculty and research staff.
4. To engage in examination reform projects with the secondary examination boards of four Indian states.
5. To work with 94 extension centers in secondary teacher-training colleges for the in-service training of teachers.
6. To develop programs and projects for the improvement of teacher education.
7. To build model syllabi and prepare textbooks for the elementary and secondary schools in reading, science, and social studies.
8. To act as consultants to the Education Commission and its task forces and participate in conferences and seminars held throughout India under the auspices of the National Institute of Education.

Background

From the time of its independence in 1947, the government of India faced serious problems in endeavoring to develop a clear national concept of the goals of education for the country.

For one thing, each of the 17 states was responsible for its own educational program. Each developed its own syllabi, textbooks, and examination

147

system and decided on the language of instruction, usually the language of the region. There had been little progress in any of the states in relating education to the problems of a developing technological society.

Then, too, in spite of the fact that elementary and secondary school enrollments rose from 18 million to 56 million in the period between 1950 and 1965, the number of illiterates increased each year. This was because of the increase in population and the large dropout rate, 65 percent, between Grades 1-5. It was estimated that, unless this trend could be reversed, between one-half and two-thirds of the population would be too illiterate to participate effectively in the economic or social development of India.

There were also problems at the secondary level. There had been a rapid increase in enrollment but the "élite" pursued an arts curriculum. Few enrolled in vocational classes, science education was most inadequate, and the failure rate was high. As a result, the schools were failing to produce the trained manpower needed for agricultural and industrial development.

The status of teachers was extremely low. Salaries were unattractive and teaching was selected as a profession by far too many students whose own educational qualifications were marginal. In 1960, 64 percent of the lower primary teachers (Grades 1-5) and 50 percent of the teachers in the middle schools (Grades 6-8) had not even completed Grade 10, and 50 percent of the higher secondary school teachers (Grade 11) lacked a degree.

Teacher-training institutions were small in size, rarely exceeding an enrollment of 100, and were severely criticized by the Indians themselves as being of poor quality in staff and equipment, and failing to make any impact on the improvement of education.

Beginning in 1948, the Central Ministry of Education set up 17 All-India Advisory Committees to help solve these various problems. It also established a number of institutes to conduct research in such areas as curriculum and textbooks, guidance, basic education, fundamental (adult) education, and audiovisual education.

After a number of years it was realized that these different agencies were concentrating on specialized areas and neglecting the total pattern of educational reconstruction in India. In 1958-59, R. Freeman Butts of Teachers College studied both the teacher-training institutes and the special institutes. From this study came recommendations for developing a national center for leadership training which would combine research, teaching, and extension services and would incorporate some of the existing agencies.

This led to the establishment of the National Institute of Education by the National Council of Educational Research and Training. USAID was asked to supply technical assistance and Teachers College, Columbia University, took on the task, beginning in September 1959.

Major Activities

Over a six-year period, 30 consultants from Teachers College, Columbia University, worked with their Indian colleagues to develop the National

Institute of Education. By 1967, the institute had been established with a permanent staff, and a number of its buildings were completed. The following major activities were reported:

School Curricula and Instructional Materials

Members of the institute staff and a Teachers College consultant worked with the Education Commission to develop a school curriculum for the lower primary stage (Grades 1-4), the higher primary stage (Grades 5-7), and the lower secondary stage (Grades 8-10).

As they worked with the syllabi it became clear that textbooks would also have to be prepared. The textbooks were out-of-date, contained many errors, and, in addition, had been written by subject matter specialists with no attempt to take into consideration the background and reading ability of the children who would use them. It was decided that textbooks, complete with teacher's manuals, should be prepared to demonstrate what could be done.

The procedure used in social studies is an example of how this project was handled. An analysis of the syllabi for the Indian states was first made. Then, between 1963 and 1965, a series of work conferences for school administrators and training college and university teachers of social studies was scheduled in five different locations to pool ideas and check on the progress to date. Between meetings, the National Institute of Education staff worked on the proposals and carried them step-by-step from a set of objectives for social studies at the different grade levels to a draft syllabus for Grades 1-11 with sample units, textbooks, and teachers handbooks.

Five thousand copies of each of three textbooks for Grades 3, 4, and 5 were printed and several others were in preparation in 1967. Five of the states had already adopted the syllabus or one based on it.

The reading project in Hindi began with a careful study of children's spoken and hearing vocabulary, sentence patterns, and reading and spelling difficulties. Based on this research, a series of textbooks, workbooks for pupils, and teachers manuals were then prepared. They covered from primer level to the fifth reader. Indian stories were used and concepts in agriculture, industry, and health were included to reinforce ideas for the improvement of Indian life and the achievement of national goals.

The books were adopted by the states of Delhi and Bihar. Over two million copies of each were printed. Before the new books were introduced to the schools, workshops for inspectors (supervisors) and teacher trainers were held in Delhi so they could train their teachers. A similar program was planned in Bihar.

A general science syllabus for Grades 1-8 was prepared, together with three activity handbooks. The purpose of the handbooks was to help the teacher who was inexperienced in science teaching to use the children's experiences and everyday materials to teach scientific principles.

At the secondary level a plan was developed to prepare a national unified program in science from Grades 5-11, including the production of syllabi, curriculum guides, textbooks, and teachers manuals. A textbook in biology was prepared and adopted by the Central Board of Secondary Education.

In-service Training

A major activity of the institute consisted of the staffing of workshops, seminars, and short in-service training courses. In six years the institute was involved in 400 such courses, attended by over 12,000 teachers and educational leaders. The wide scope of the courses is seen by the fact that they were offered by the following departments: administration, adult education, audiovisual education, basic education, curriculum and evaluation, field service, psychological foundations, science education, and teacher education.

Examination Reform

The National Institute of Education staff devoted considerable effort to examination reform in an effort to shift the emphasis from memorization to reasoning and problem solving and to supplement the external final examination with periodic testing. Workshops and conferences were held for examiners and members of examination boards. Approximately 10,000 paper setters and readers attended training sessions.

By 1967, 14 states were moving to modify their examination system to test reasoning and problem solving, as well as memory. Objective examinations were being introduced as part of the final external examination; internal examinations were added to supplement the external final; and periodic examinations were being introduced throughout the curriculum.

Graduate Curricula in Education

Three graduate curricula were developed: a one-year M.Ed. program for holders of a B.Ed., primarily for those planning to teach in the primary teaching institutions; a two-year M.Ed. program, for holders of an M.A. in a content area who wished to teach in a secondary teacher-training college or to become an inspector or administrator; and a Ph.D. program.

By 1965, a faculty of about 350 had been developed in the various departments adequate to introduce the graduate programs, and, by 1966, four buildings had been completed on a 72-acre plot in New Delhi. Nine-month certificate courses were offered in research methodology, audiovisual education, child study, and teacher education. At the time Teachers College assistance was phased out, the graduate degree program had not been started.

The Central Institute of Education, established in 1947, which was affiliated with Delhi University and considered a part of the National Institute of Education, continued to train about 120 B.Ed. and 20 M.Ed candidates and one Ph.D. candidate each year.

Summer Institutes

In 1963, the National Institute of Education initiated the summer science institute program for college and secondary school science teachers. In that year, four institutes—each for about 40 teachers—were held in biology, chemistry, physics, and mathematics. The program was so successful that it was expanded with the assistance of scientists from a number of universities and the National Science Foundation. By 1967, 375 institutes had been conducted and over 14,000 high school and college teachers had attended.

The National Institute of Education also cooperated in staffing and organizing eight English-language institutes carried on by the British Council in 1965, and by the British Council and Teachers College in 1966.

Research

The training of National Institute of Education staff in research was an important responsibility of the Teachers College team. Under its direction, over 150 research projects were carried on by staff members. Of these, 90 had been completed by 1967. A central research laboratory, with data processing equipment, was established with Ford Foundation and USAID assistance to facilitate the research program. It was reported that, between 1961 and 1966, there was considerable improvement in the selection and design of studies, in the use of appropriate techniques, and in the ability of the staff to analyze data and report findings.

In 1964, the Indian Ministry of Education requested the National Institute of Education to conduct a comprehensive review of education in India and set up plans for the direction of education in the country for the next 20 years. The study was carried on by institute staff members, assisted by the Teachers College team over the following two years, and formed the initial working paper for the Indian International Education Commission. The Commission's final report was subtitled *Education and National Development*.

Publications

The publication program of the institute included textbooks and related instructional material; periodicals; yearbooks of the National Council of Educational Research and Training; an educational encyclopedia; research monographs; and reports, surveys, miscellaneous brochures and pamphlets, posters, and charts.

By 1967, 250 different manuscripts had been published and almost one million copies of various publications had been sold. One state government had arranged to print 1,700,000 primary reading books developed by the institute.

Six periodicals published by the institute were consolidated into three journals: *School Science, The NIE Journal* (general articles of interest to educators), and *Indian Education Review* (research reports).

A series of yearbooks was also planned and the first two, *A Review of Education in India, 1947-1961 and Elementary Education,* were published. Two additional volumes, *Secondary Education* and *Educational Research,* were in the process of publication in 1967.

Participant Training

A program of participant training was established, and 48 selected personnel on the institute staff were sent to the United States for graduate study. A program was developed by Teachers College for each participant according to individual needs. Programs varied. In some cases, they consisted of full-time study at Teachers College or some other university; in other cases, they alternated between field visitation and campus study. Of the 48, ten studied for M.A.'s and two completed work for the Ed.D. In 1967, 33 of the 48 were on the staff of the National Institute of Education and 11 had been assigned to other educational posts in India.

NEPAL

Secondary Education-National Vocational Training Center
AID/Southern Illinois University

The principal objective of the original Southern Illinois University contract was "to advise in the preparation, operation, and administration of the National Vocational Training Center located at Sano Thimi in the Kathmandu Valley." The N.V.T.C. physical plant was in the final stages of construction and consisted of a multipurpose high school for Grades 6 through 10; and a technical institute building complex designed for agriculture, business and secretarial science, home economics, trades and industries; and classrooms for supporting subjects such as mathematics and science. An Educational Materials Center for housing audiovisual services and a printing plant, although not a part of N.V.T.C., was located adjacent to these facilities.

Objectives

The contract team was to provide advisory services in:

1. Administration of technical education teacher-training programs.
2. Teacher-training programs in vocational education, mathematics and science; industrial arts programs in building trades, woodworking, basic electricity, drafting, and applied science; business programs in secretarial science (typing, stenography, general business practice).
3. Agricultural programs in agronomy, horticulture, and applied science.
4. Home economics programs and women's affairs programs for training teachers and rural women workers.

The following year the scope of the contract was broadened to include participant training and assistance in "the preparation, operation, and administration of the College of Education, affiliated with Tribhuvan University" and to advise "in the development and upgrading of elementary and secondary education materials prepared by the Education Materials Center."

This amendment charged the S.I.U. team as follows:

The primary purpose of this activity is to improve teacher training in Nepal by developing a cooperative and effective interchange among three national institutions, the National Vocational Training Center, the

152

Education Materials Center and the College of Education. To achieve this purpose the contract team will:

1. Place on an operational basis a central training facility which will develop a wide range of vocational, technical, and educational skills. In addition to providing actual skill training, its purposes will include the training of new teachers for service in secondary education in the applied fields of vocational work and the upgrading of existing secondary school staff; a basic concern will be evolving techniques for teaching mathematics and science in such a way as to instill the observational and experimental approach to learning of both teachers and students.

2. Make effective use of the facilities of the Education Materials Center by developing and upgrading elementary and secondary education materials and accompanying teachers guides. Teachers involved in teacher training also will be assisted in developing techniques in the utilization of educational materials.

3. Assist with the development of the primary teacher-training program at the College of Education through materials development, instruction and demonstration of effective teaching techniques, and supervision of teacher-training activities. In addition, the contract team will provide expert guidance to the administration of the College of Education for the operation of an effective program of instruction, demonstration, and research in the elementary and secondary laboratory school program. As a part of the overall responsibility for assistance the contract team will aid in the development of utilization of appropriate testing and measurement materials and techniques pertinent to the various other aspects of the teacher education program.

Background

In 1960, the government of Nepal decided to build, with AID assistance, a National Vocational Training Center at Kathmandu. Its primary purpose was to be the preparation of teachers and instructional materials for industrial arts, secretarial science, home economics, agriculture, mathematics, and science for multipurpose secondary schools.

By the time the Vocational Training Center had been constructed, five years later, the educational scene had changed. King Mahendra had declared a need for educational reform to bring education in line with actual needs in Nepal.

Questions had also arisen as to the role and future of the multipurpose secondary schools—their cost, their impact in furthering vocational aims, and the possible need for other kinds of vocational training institutions. There was, therefore, a need for a review of the function of the Vocational Training Center in preparing teachers for such schools.

In consequence, the role of the Southern Illinois team at the Vocational Training Center was broadened to include the whole area of elementary and secondary education, including the training of teachers and the development of instructional materials.

Major Activities

In 1967, there were 10 advisors from Southern Illinois University at the Vocational Training Center. They were active in planning curricula, working with the Nepali staff to equip the National Vocational Training Center, and assisting with the in-service teacher-training program.

In-service Training

In 1966, and again in 1967, workshops were held for about 80 teachers in multipurpose schools. The workshops, which ranged from three to nine months, were designed to give technical instruction to the teacher who would be responsible for vocational courses.

Two-Year Diploma Program

A program was developed for a two-year diploma course to train skilled technicians in home science, agriculture, business, and trade and industry. This program was designed to open in 1968 with an enrollment of 120 students, selected from over 400 applicants.

Degree Program for Vocational Teachers

A cooperative program was set up with the College of Education at Tribhuvan University in which prospective vocational teachers would receive a B.Ed. degree from the College of Education and would gain their practical experience, including student teaching, at the National Vocational Training Center. In 1967, about 35 students were enrolled in home economics, agriculture, and trade and industry.

Participant Training

Seven participants were sent to Southern Illinois University for a period of between six months and one year for training in educational administration and vocational education.

Task Force Concept

A special feature of the program was the proposed use of special task forces for specific short-term tasks related to project implementation. It was envisioned that they could be either advanced students under a faculty advisor or senior specialists, depending on the particular need.

EAST PAKISTAN

Summer Science Institutes
AID/Institute of International Education

In 1966, the Institute of International Education accepted a contract with AID to organize, in East Pakistan, a program of summer science institutes similar to the one which had proved successful in India.

Objectives

As stated in the contract, the objectives of the program were as follows:

1. To introduce modern approaches, instructional innovations, and subject matter in the teaching of science in Pakistan.

2. To explore through laboratory-lecture experience how modern instructional techniques and advanced subject matter content could be used in Pakistan's courses of study.

3. To instruct Pakistani educators to analyze and reevaluate their present math-science curricula and syllabi.

Major Activities

Four institutes were conducted in 1966. Fourteen scientists taught five-week courses in mathematics and physics to high school and college teachers. The institutes were well received, and it was decided that the project should be continued in 1967, and that the number of participants in each workshop could be increased.

In 1967, ten United States specialists, in combination with five Pakistani scientists, conducted five institutes, six weeks in length, for college teachers. At the University of Dacca, institutes were held in mathematics, chemistry, and physics; and at Rajshahi University, in mathematics and physics. About 120 teachers participated. New concepts, teaching materials, and methods of testing were introduced. The teachers attended lectures for half the day and worked in the laboratories half the day.

It was decided to add biology to the 1968 institute program. Plans were also made by the Pakistan Ministry of Education, with the advice of the contract team, to establish an East Pakistan Institute for Science Education as a semi-autonomous body to provide leadership in science education. It would also develop a follow-up program, plan revised curricula, and recommend books.

Difficulties Reported

Following the 1967 institutes, it was agreed that there should have been 50 percent more teachers in attendance.

Because of the limited amount of time allowed for planning for both the Teachers College faculty and its Pakistani counterparts, lectures and laboratory experiences were not coordinated as well as they might have been.

Too many seminars, lectures, and topics were introduced to participants whose previous background and experience were limited and, as a result, much of the program was not particularly effective.

It was felt by the team that the institutes could not have a major effect on the upgrading of science education without a strong follow-up program.

It was reported that much of the material presented in the chemistry institute assumed that the participants had an M.Sc. in chemistry, but this was not so and the material was, in consequence, too difficult for many of them.

Much of the laboratory equipment needed for the institute did not arrive in time to be used.

Commercial Institute in East Pakistan
AID/Colorado State College

Objectives

The objectives of the Colorado State College project were:

1. To assist in the establishment of educational training institutes to train in clerical skills.
2. To train administrators and instructors for commercial institutes engaged in training clerical workers in East Pakistan.
3. To institutionalize a system under which diploma holders majoring in commercial subjects could continue their education toward the attainment of a teaching certificate in commercial subjects.

Background

In 1966, AID agreed to assist the government of East Pakistan in the development and staffing of 14 commercial institutes for the training of clerical and business personnel.

In 1967, Colorado State College was asked to supply technicians for this project, and a contract was signed to aid and assist in the establishment of 16, instead of 14, institutes.

Major Activities

It was reported that 14 institutes were in operation in December 1967. As it was a new project, no information was available as to the activities of the contract team.

TURKEY

Technical and Vocational Education
AID/American Vocational Association

The purpose of the American Vocational Association contract was to provide assistance to the ministry of education in developing a system of education to meet Turkey's needs for qualified technical manpower.

The proposed approach fell into three stages:

Stage 1. A two-man contract team to determine the scope of work, objectives, and suggestions for carrying out the contract.

Stage 2. The development of a modern and practical system of technical and vocational education at the Men's Technical Teacher-Training College, which was responsible for training teachers for all the secondary

156

technical and vocational schools in Turkey. It was also proposed to establish demonstration programs at the two Ankara vocational schools.

Stage 3. The extension of the localized activities to technical and vocational schools throughout the country.

Objectives

In 1966, after the two-man team had made its report, the objectives of the project were stated as follows:

1. The development of a modern, practical system of technical and vocational teacher education in order to help satisfy the critical manpower requirements for skilled workers and middle-level technicians in Turkey's modern economy.

2. The development and introduction of new curricula, textbooks, teaching methods, and teaching materials at Men's Technical Teacher-Training College in Ankara, at two Ankara technical schools, and at the Ankara Vocational Center.

3. Special emphasis on developing trade standards, job analyses, testing materials, and teacher work experience.

Major Activities

Specialists in shop organization, vocational education, curriculum development, the preparation of instructional materials, and vocational teacher education arrived at the Men's Technical Teacher-Training College during 1966.

A series of workshops was planned to introduce new curricula to the Men's Technical Teacher-Training College and to the technical and vocational schools.

Two courses in occupational analysis and shop organization and management were introduced and taught by team members in cooperation with the training college staff.

The content of a number of courses, including machine shop practice, tests and measurements, instructional aids, and teaching methods, was revised.

Four seminars, two weeks in length, were held in vocational and technical research techniques, occupational analysis, course construction, programmed learning, and shop organization and management. The participants were vocational and technical teachers and administrators throughout Turkey and were selected by the Ministry of Education.

A program for translating and printing technical books in Turkish was developed. Approximately 50 titles were selected, and by June 1967, 17 of these books were either printed or in the process of being printed.

A paper on the purpose, function, and method of operation of advisory committees was prepared for translation.

Preliminary study was given to a program for two projected pilot technical schools. It was proposed that they be planned for from 500 to 700 students, and offer instruction in electricity, electronics, machine shop, woodworking, and blacksmithing.

Plans were developed for the establishment of a National Advisory Committee to give leadership to the development of vocational education in Turkey.

An evaluation took place in May 1968, to determine if basic and significant changes had been established sufficient to warrant continuation of the project. The evaluation was favorable but the contract was not renewed.

BRAZIL
Elementary and Secondary Education
State University of New York
AID/San Diego State College Foundation

In 1966, it was decided by USAID that technical assistance should be given to the government of Brazil and to the state governments in their efforts to develop coordinated plans for education in the nation. San Diego State College was asked to work at the secondary level, and the State University of New York at the elementary level.

State University of New York

The objectives of the State University of New York contract team were:

1. To assess, on a national and regional basis, the quality and effectiveness of elementary education, and to develop and implement a specific plan for improving the flow of pupils through the elementary school system.
2. To develop plans to better relate elementary, secondary, and higher education.
3. To improve national and regional services to state councils, and to state secretariats of education, in the development and implementation of effective elementary education programs.
4. To train a corps of at least six Brazilian planners for elementary education at the national level, who will be able to provide assistance to regions on a continuing basis, and who will train key personnel at the state level in techniques of planning, implementation, evaluation, and administration of elementary education.

Major Activities

The State University of New York contract team, together with Brazilian educators, assisted in the development of plans for upgrading teacher training in the nine Northeastern states and revising the teacher-training curriculum.

They also developed an analysis of Brazilian primary education and a model plan designed to reduce the number of dropouts and grade repeaters.

Considerable interest was shown in the study by federal and state educational leaders, but no plans to implement it had been reported by December

1967. Because of the limited progress of the project and limitations of funds, it was decided to phase out the project in January 1968.

San Diego State College Team

In 1966, a team of four specialists from San Diego State College, and four Brazilian counterpart educators, initiated a program to provide advisory services to the states in the area of secondary education. It was proposed that secondary education programs, that met state and national requirements, be planned and implemented in order to serve as models for other states.

By September 1967, preliminary data gathering and analysis of information had taken place in seven states, and efforts were being made to provide for full-time planning teams in four states.

At that time, it was decided by USAID and the government of Brazil to combine planning for elementary and secondary education and work for better articulation between the elementary and the secondary curriculum. Plans were made for a sociologist to be added to the team to analyze current research on socio-economic factors affecting elementary and secondary education in Brazil.

The revised and expanded set of objectives stated that the San Diego team members were to work with a team of Brazilian educators sponsored by the ministry of education in order to:

1. Develop elementary and secondary education plans for such states as designated by AID which would serve as models to other states.
2. Train state organizational staff members in the process of elementary and secondary education planning.
3. Train a corps of Federal Ministry of Education officials, responsible for the nationwide educational system, in the process of assisting states in their planning procedures.

DOMINICAN REPUBLIC

Teacher Education
AID/San Jose State College Foundation

In 1966, San Jose State College was invited by AID to provide technical assistance to the Dominican Ministry of Education in the improvement of in-service and preservice programs for elementary and secondary teachers.

Objectives

The objectives of the program were:

1. To improve the quality of the ministry of education and field supervisory staff personnel.
2. To improve in-service and preservice teacher education programs for the normal and secondary schools.
3. To put primary emphasis on the development and proper usage of instructional materials and equipment.

4. To collabroate with the Planning Commission of the ministry of education to improve education without conflict or duplication of programs by such groups as UNESCO, the Peace Corps, the Teach Corps, St. Louis University, or Texas Agricultural and Mechanical University.

5. To reorganize the normal school curriculum.

Major Activities

During the first year, the nine members of the San Jose State team visited high schools and normal schools and worked with nine Dominican counterparts to plan curricula, prepare instructional materials, and organize in-service workshops. By the second year of the contract, the major emphasis of the project was directed to planning for the opening of two comprehensive high schools. The following major activities were reported:

Summer Workshops

A three-week workshop was held for secondary teachers in science, mathematics, social science, and audiovisual materials to enable them to be guide or supervisory teachers in their local areas.

In cooperation with the Teach Corps, a five-week workshop was conducted for 180 normal secondary school teachers in science, mathematics, English, and social science. A number of the previously-trained guide teachers were involved in this project.

A four-week workshop for approximately 125 primary school inspectors was conducted in six subject areas.

Assistance was given to the Teach Corps and UNESCO in conducting a five-week workshop for approximately 125 elementary master teachers whom the ministry of education planned to use in connection with in-service programs for the 8,000 elementary teachers with only eight years of formal education. The participants were divided into three groups and worked on the use of modern methods and teaching materials in language arts, science, and mathematics.

The San Jose State team also served as consultants to the Peace Corps in carrying out workshops for approximately 700 non-certified primary teachers during the summer of 1967. It had been planned to continue in-service programs with these teachers during the school year, but this had to be given up when the emphasis of the project shifted to the comprehensive high school.

Professional Journal

A professional journal, *Al Professorado Dominicano*, was developed for teachers, the secretariat, and other educational personnel. Eleven thousand copies of four issues had been published by the end of 1967.

Comprehensive High Schools

The ministry of education decided to convert the curriculum at two secondary schools from their traditional programs to those of comprehensive high schools, as a pilot program, preparatory to establishing such schools in 17 areas throughout the country. They were to offer programs in commercial, industrial, agricultural, and primary teacher education in addition to the earlier university preparatory curriculum.

The San Jose team and their counterparts worked with the teachers and administrators at the two schools in developing curricula, planning units of work, preparing instructional aids, and getting ready for registration. Almost 3,000 students enrolled in the two schools, the great majority in the new curricula. Approximately 350 entered the primary-teacher training program.

Participant Training

The contract provided for 25 Dominican teachers to come to the United States for participant training. It was reported that almost none of those recommended had sufficient command of English to carry the work required at a university in the United States. The chief of party was investigating the possibility of sending them to Puerto Rico or Mexico.

JAMAICA

Teacher Training in Human Resources Development
AID/San Diego State College Foundation

USAID agreed to provide technical assistance to the government of Jamaica in the program of secondary school expansion which was financed by the International Bank of Reconstruction and Development. San Diego State College Foundation accepted the contract. Following a year's work by a team of 11 advisors and short-term consultants, an evaluation was conducted by AID/Washington.

Objectives

Following its report, the objectives of the program were narrowed down to providing technical assistance to the government of Jamaica in the development of the senior secondary schools.

The contract team's objectives were to assist the government of Jamaica in:

1. A re-examination of the philosophy, purposes, and objectives of the junior secondary schools.

2. The development of the administrative organization of the junior secondary schools.

3. The development of the overall educational program of the junior secondary schools, in the areas of new concepts, methods, or content in subject matter fields.

4. The development, production, and proper utilization of instructional materials for the junior secondary schools.

161

5. The development of a teacher-training program designed specifically for preparing teachers for the junior secondary schools.

6. The development of an internship program for the junior secondary school teacher trainees.

7. The extension and improvement of the in-service education available to teachers.

Background

In Jamaica, as in many other countries, it was difficult for the country to provide sufficient additional facilities to keep up with the growth rate, let alone make improvements.

While 75 percent of Jamaican children of primary school age were reported to be in school, overcrowding was severe. Some classes exceeded 100 pupils, the average was one teacher to 57 pupils. The level of teacher training was equally poor. Almost half the teachers had no professional preparation at all, and the annual turnover was extremely high—above 50 percent in 1966, for example. At the secondary level, the picture was in sharp contrast. The quality of instruction was high, but only 10 percent of the relevant age group was enrolled in school.

In 1963, the government's Five-Year Independence Plan emphasized the increase of elementary school facilities and the provision of more trained teachers. Following a survey of education in the country by UNESCO, the government decided that the point of greatest urgency was at the secondary level.

The World Bank granted a loan of about $3,400,000 for the construction of over 40 junior secondary schools, the expansion of space at teacher-training institutions, and the development of other specialized educational institutions.

One of the conditions of the loan was that the government of Jamaica negotiate a technical assistance program which would help the ministry of education to organize itself for its expanded responsibilities and, to facilitate the changes in curriculum, methodology, and materials which would prepare teachers to work effectively in a new type of school program. USAID agreed to provide this assistance through a contract with the California State College System.

Major Activities

By December 1967, the contract team reported having participated in the following activities:

Teacher-Training Colleges

In addition to teaching in the regular classes, team members reported introducing such subjects as remedial and developmental reading, team teaching, and programmed instruction.

162

Teaching Internship Program

As an economy measure, the elementary teacher-training college curriculum was changed from three years to a program providing two years on campus and a year of internship. The San Diego team assisted in the change-over and organized the placing of 600 interns in Jamaican schools.

Assistance to the Ministry of Education

Consultative assistance was given to the ministry of education in school plant planning, and conversion of the educational testing program to objective machine-scored tests.

Junior Secondary (Grades 7-9) Curriculum

Assistance was given to curriculum planning for the junior secondary schools. A series of seminars for junior secondary school teachers, principals, and education officers was held at which curricular changes in mathematics, reading, and art were introduced.

Teach Corps Workshop

In 1967, in cooperation with the San Diego team, seven Teach Corps volunteers held a four-week workshop on the campus of the University of the West Indies for teachers and principals of junior secondary schools. Altogether, 275 participated in the workshops: 150 in social studies, 80 in science, and 45 in school administration.

VENEZUELA

National Manpower Training and Development
AID/University of Wisconsin-Milwaukee

AID provided technical assistance to the government of Venezuela in national manpower training and development. Teacher education was one aspect of the program, which placed emphasis on technical training, labor development, and education.

Objectives

The objectives of the program as they related to teacher education were:

1. To make a survey of the national education system for the purpose of determining the level of competency; identifying needs for changes in structure, content, and methods of procedures; and determining the most effective means for developing a system of continuous evaluation, planning, and research.

2. To develop an effective guidance service within the national education system.

3. To restructure the components of the secondary education system and generally upgrade the capability of the professional personnel in

order to provide a more adequate education system to support government plans for economic and social development.

4. To provide free textbooks, teachers manuals, and instructional materials to both public and private tuition-free schools in Venezuela.

5. To provide assistance to the Experimental Pedagogical Institute of the Barquisimeto Vocational Teacher Training Institute, in developing curricula and training counterparts.

Major Activities

The major efforts of the University were focused on three types of activity: participant training, consultant help, and intensive study tours.

Participant Training

Between 1962 and 1964, 84 professional personnel from the Venezuelan Ministry of Education were sent to the United States for a ten-month non-credit course organized by the University. They studied the comprehensive high school curriculum and vocational education. Their work was focused on reorganizing Venezuelan secondary education and developing ways of integrating technical training with college preparatory curricula.

In 1965, it was decided to shift from a non-credit to an M.A. program. Thirty-one Venezuelans were selected for two years of study in vocational education. The majority studied at the University of Wisconsin and Stout State Vocational College, and the remainder in Puerto Rico. The program was coordinated by The University of Wisconsin-Milwaukee.

A unique feature of the program was that the Venezuelan Vice Minister of Education was resident at the Milwaukee campus for one year during the project.

It was reported that, by December 1967, almost all of those who had received participant training were in the ministry of education in responsible positions.

Consultant Help

Short-term and long-term consultant services were given to a number of projects.

For example, the coordinator of the participant training program at Milwaukee was sent to be resident advisor at Caracas. One technician spent a year assisting in the area of curriculum materials. Another spent three years working in vocational technical education. A specialist in teacher training spent nine months helping to develop a student teaching program. Another spent eight months working with in-service training programs.

Four technicians were sent to the Barquisimeto Vocational Teacher Training Institute to help initiate a program of training secondary vocational teachers in agricultural, commercial, and vocational technical subjects. They assisted in developing curricula and training counterparts.

164

For shorter periods ranging from three to five months, assistance was given in such areas as science education, guidance and counseling systems, vocational guidance, and rural education.

Intensive Study Tours

Between 1964 and 1966, six-week study tours were set up for senior educational personnel who couldn't be spared for longer periods. They were directed to such fields as elementary education, vocational education, secondary education, and teacher education.

FOOTNOTES

[1] Harbison, Frederick and Myers, Charles A. *Education, Manpower and Economic Growth*. New York: McGraw-Hill Book Co., 1964. p. 81.

[2] *Ibid.*, p. 97.

[3] "Faculty Handbook, Thu Duc Demonstration Secondary School, Faculty of Pedagogy, University of Saigon."

APPENDIXES

Table 1
AID INVOLVEMENT IN TECHNICAL ASSISTANCE, 1967*

| | Countries Receiving Technical Assistance | | |
	All Forms	Education	Teacher Education
FAR EAST AND VIETNAM	6	6	4
NEAR EAST AND SOUTH ASIA	9	6	6
AFRICA	34	18	14
LATIN AMERICA	20	17	16
Totals:	69	47	40

* Data from *Foreign Assistance Program 1967* and *A Survey of AID International Cooperation in Developing Countries, 1967.*

Table 2
AID PROJECTS IN TEACHER EDUCATION, 1967*

Project	Contractor	Date Started	Estimated Total Cost
FAR EAST			
Korea			
Education Policy and Planning	Direct Hire	1967	$ 35,000
Vocational, Technical In-Service Training	Direct Hire	1956	3,142,000
Laos			
Community Development Teacher Training	International Vol. Services	1956	1,567,000
Education Development (Community Education)	Direct Hire	1964	1,146,000
Education Development (Secondary Education)	U. of Hawaii	1967	10,000
Thailand			
Vocational Education	Calif. State Poly.	1967	56,000
Vietnam			
Hamlet Schools	Southern Illinois U.	1958	1,076,000
Elementary Teacher Training			
Vocational Education	Direct Hire	1955	2,232,000
Secondary Education	Ohio U.	1962	3,662,000
Mobile Science Unit	International Vol. Services	1963	....
			$12,926,000

* Data are from *A Survey of AID Educational Cooperation in Developing Countries, 1967* when available, otherwise from Survey, 1966.

Project	Contractor	Date Started	Estimated Total Cost

NEAR EAST AND SOUTH ASIA

Afghanistan

Elementary and Secondary Education	Teachers College, Columbia U.	1952	$10,546,000

India

National Institute	Teachers College, Columbia U.	1960	2,150,000
Multipurpose Secondary Education	Ohio State U.	1956	3,272,000
Science Education Improvement	National Science Foundation	1965	2,408,000
Bombay Central T. Institute	Dunwoody Ind. Institute	*	1,057,000

Nepal

Teacher and Tech. Ed. (Teach Corps included)	Southern Illinois U. Nat. Ed. Assoc.	1963	729,000

Pakistan

Teacher Training Inst.	Col. State U.	1959	3,824,000
Summer Science Inst.	Inst. of Int. Education	1967	78,000
Commercial Institutes East Pakistan	Col. State U.	1967	*

Turkey

Technical and Voc. Education	Am. Voc. Assoc.	1962	665,000

Regional

AUB Regional Training (Est. for Teacher Education)	American U.	1951	7,000,000
			$31,729,000

AFRICA

Cameroon

Secondary and Tech. Education	Teach Corps	1965	*

Congo

National Pedagogic Inst. (Teacher Training)	Direct Hire	1967	31,000

Ethiopia

U. Col. of Education (includes technical)	U. of Utah	1960	1,835,000

Kenya

Voc. Agriculture Education	West Virginia U.	1964	477,000
English Language Teacher Training	Nat. Ed. Assoc.	1963	385,000
Radio/Correspondence Education	U. of Wisconsin	1967	20,000

* Data available.

Project	Contractor	Date Started	Estimated Total Cost
Liberia			
Teacher Training, Institutional, Development and Support	Tuskegee Inst.	1958	$3,849,000
Rural Education Develop.	Direct Hire	1956	2,928,000
Malawi			
Soche Hill	U. of S. California	1966	34,000
Mali			
Higher Teacher Training College	U. of Southern Illinois	1962	831,000
Nigeria			
N. Nigerian Teacher Education*	U. of Wisconsin	1962	242,000
University of Nigeria (Nsukka)	Michigan State U.	1960	7,979,000
Federal Advanced Teachers Col. (Lagos)	U. Calif., Los Angeles	1961	1,796,000
Adv. Teachers Col. of Ed., Ibadan Branch	Ohio U.	1960	3,629,000
Kano Teacher-Training	Ohio U.	1963	2,372,000
Sierra Leone			
Rural Ed. Improvement	Nat. Ed. Assoc.	1961	1,431,000
Njala U. College	U. of Illinois	1963	1,484,000
Somali			
Nat. Teacher Ed. Center	Eastern Mich. U.	1961	2,280,000
Sudan			
Technical Education	Dunwoody Ind. Inst.	1958	7,177,000
Tanzania			
Education Materials and Advisory Services	Nat. Ed. Assoc.	1965	151,000
Zambia			
Educational Develop. Support	Direct Hire, Ed. Services, Inc.	1962	307,000
East Africa Regional			
Teacher Ed. in East Africa	Teachers College, Columbia U.	1964	1,616,000
			$40,854,000

LATIN AMERICA

Bolivia			
Human Resources Survey	Ohio State	1962	$ 515,000
Teacher Training	Direct Hire	1966	109,000
Brazil			
Elementary and Basic Education	State Univ. of N.Y. U. of Wisconsin	1963	4,030,000

*Supported by Ford Foundation for two years.

Project	Contractor	Date Started	Estimated Total Cost
Secondary and Ind. Ed.	San Diego State College Foundation	1964	$1,506,000
Chile			
Education Sector Loan		1967	*
Colombia			
National Ed. Planning	Direct Hire	1964	136,000
Costa Rica			
General Assistance to Education	Direct Hire, Nat. Ed. Assoc.	1965	144,000
Dominican Republic			
Teacher Education	San Jose State College Foundation	1963	1,157,000
Ecuador			
Secondary Education	Direct Hire	1968	*
El Salvador			
Ed. Planning and Normal School Development	Nat. Ed. Assoc.	1967	305,000
Guatemala			
Development of Educational Policies and Priorities	Direct Hire, Texas Ed. Agency	1964	885,000
Honduras			
Educational Development	Direct Hire, Nat. Ed. Assoc.	1965	618,000
Jamaica			
Human Resources (Teacher Training)	San Diego State College Foundation	1965	459,000
Nicaragua			
Ed. Planning and Development	Direct Hire	1955	1,884,000
Paraguay			
Rural Ed. Development	Direct Hire	1962	2,904,000
Peru			
Public Education	Teachers College, Columbia U.	1962	2,091,000
Uruguay			
Human Resources Develop.		1967	22,000
Venezuela			
National Manpower Training and Develop.	U. of Wisconsin	1962	2,638,000
			$19,403,000

INTERNATIONAL

Teach Corps	Nat. Ed. Assoc.	(included in separate countries)	
Administrative Internships	A.A.C.T.E.		
	Total		$104,912,000

* Data available.

172

American Educators, Including University Contract Personnel Overseas

American Vocational Association

HOYT TURNER, staff associate

California State College

RALPH EVANS, Chief of Party, California State Colleges Project

Colorado State College

JACK G. BLENDINGER, contract instructor, campus coordinator, AID/East Pakistan Projects

GILBERT J. HAUSE, professor of College Student Personnel Work

JACK SHAW, professor of educational psychology and guidance, Chief of Party, AID/ East Pakistan Project (Institute of Education and Research, University of Dacca, East Pakistan)

Dunwoody Industrial Institute

LYNDON BERG, assistant coordinator, International Services Division (member of contract team, Sudan Industrial Institute)

ROBERT R. MINARIK, coordinator, International Services Division, campus coordinator, India and Sudan Projects

T. C. OLIVO, director, Division of Industrial Education, Vocational Survey, AID consultant, Bolivia

JOHN R. WALSH, president

Eastern Michigan University

STANLEY GEX, dean for the Center for International Studies, professor of education, campus coordinator, AID/Somalia Project

SCOTT STREET, Chief of Party (1965-67), AID/Somalia Project

Ford Foundation

THERESE E. NADEAU, assistant program officer, Middle East and Africa

V. R. PLUMB, education consultant, Kathmandu, Nepal

HANS SIMONE, program officer, Caribbean and Latin America

Institute of International Education

JOHN S. H. RUSSEL, program administrator, AID/Pakistan Education Project

International Voluntary Services

CLIFFORD DOKES, program officer

RICHARD PETERS, assistant program officer

Michigan State University

IRVING WYETH, campus coordinator, AID/Nigerian Project

National Education Association

C. C. AXVALL, acting chief, National Education Association Teach Corps

ELIZABETH B. YATES, program coordinator, Africa and Asia, National Education Association Teach Corps

National Science Foundation

MAX HELMAN, head, Cooperative Science Activities, Office of International Science Activities

Ohio State University

DONALD P. SANDERS, assistant professor of education and economics, campus coordinator, AID/Bolivia Project

D. ALEXANDER SEVERINO, associate dean of the College of Education, professor of fine arts, campus coordinator, AID/India Project

Ohio University

JOHN R. BOONE, television producer/director (1966-68), AID/Nigerian Project (Kano Teacher Training College)

WILLIAM H. COOPER, assistant professor of education, consultant (1958-60), AID/Nigerian Project (Federal Advanced Teachers College—Ibadan Branch)

GILFORD W. CROWELL, professor of education, dean—College of Education, Chief of Party (1960-62), AID/Nigerian Project (Advanced Teachers College of Education)

LOUIS D. DEPRIN, Deputy Chief of Party

MAX R. EVANS, Chief of Party, AID/Nigerian Project (Kano Teacher Training College)

DONALD A. GREEN, associate professor of education, Chief of Party (1962-64), AID/Nigerian Project (Advanced Teachers College of Education—Ibadan Branch)

LUTHER HASELEY, associate professor of education, Deputy Chief of Party, Nigerian Project, campus coordinator, AID/Nigerian Project (Advanced Teachers College of Education and Kano Teacher Training College)

EDWARD P. LYNN, assistant professor of education, education advisor (1966), AID/Vietnam Project.

RUSSEL A. MILLIKEN, associate professor of education, director of International Education Institute, Chief of Party, AID/Nigerian Project (Kano Teacher Training College)

LESTER MILLS, assistant professor of education, science advisor (1964-66), AID/Vietnam Project

MILTON PLOGHOFT, director, Center for International Programs and professor of education, Chief of Party (1963-64), AID/Nigerian Project (Kano Teacher Training College)

PAUL ROADEN, assistant professor of education, Chief of Party (1966-68), AID/Nigerian Project (Kano Teacher Training College)

GILBERT STEPHENSON, associate professor of education, campus coordinator, AID/Vietnam Project

Pennsylvania State University

JOSEPH ALLESANCRO, Chief of Party, AID/El Salvador Project

San Diego State College

VINCENT ALOIA, campus coordinator, AID/Brazil Project

PAUL ERICKSON, assistant professor of education, campus coordinator, AID/Jamaica Project

ROBERT R. NARDELLI, professor of education, campus coordinator, AID/Brazil Project and AID/Jamaica Project

San Jose State College

HOBERT BURNS, academic vice president

GERVAIS W. FORD, professor of education, campus coordinator, AID/Dominican Republic Project

Southern Illinois University

JOHN ANDERSON, Chief of Party, AID/Nepal Project
HOWARD L. DEWEESE, campus coordinator, AID/Vietnam Project
A. JUNTZ, campus coordinator, AID/Mali Project and AID/Vietnam Project
WAYNE S. RAMP, campus coordinator, AID/Nepal Project
ROBERT M. REED, foreign student advisor, International Services Division

Teachers College, Columbia University

CAROL CHARLES, education advisor, Peru
RAY GARRISON, former Members of Teachers College, Columbia University in Peru
CARL GRAHAM, director, Office of Overseas Projects; campus coordinator, AID/Peru
   Project, AID/India Project, AID/Afghanistan Project
SYDNEY GRANT, former Chief of Party (now superintendent of schools, Bellevue, Wash-
   ington)
CHRISTINE HOGERT, program officer, India Project
SCOTT KELLY, campus coordinator, AID/East Africa Regional Project
RICHARD KING, Acting Chief of Party, Afghanistan Project
PAUL LEONARD, past campus coordinator, AID/India Project
E. MEDINA, education advisor
ROLLAND PALLSTON, advisor on education research
WILLIAM SAYRES, Chief of Party, USAID, Lima, Peru
DAVID G. SCANLON, director, Center for Education in Africa, Institute of International
   Studies
FRANCIS SHOEMAKER, director, Office of International Programs and Services
CECIL SPEARMAN, Chief of Party, India Project

Tuskegee Institute

JAMES E. FARRELL, administrative consultant, Tuskegee Institute Team
JOHN KROUSE, campus coordinator, AID/Liberia Project
FINLEY McQUEEN, Chief of Party, Tuskegee Institute Team
SAMUEL MONTEE, director, Kakata Training Institute

University of Hawaii

TERURO IHARA, director, Foreign Contracts, associate professor of education, campus
   coordinator, AID/Laos Project

University of Illinois

ROGER BROWN, Chief of Party, Sierra Leone Project
HERBERT DYASI, member of contract team, Njala Project
KARL GARDNER, dean, College of Agriculture, member of original Njala survey team
JOE KASTELIC, professor of animal sciences, member of Njala contract team
O. NEAL LIMING, assistant director, AID Projects
R. ODELL, professor of soils, Chief of Party, Njala Project

University of Southern California

JOHN A. CARPENTER, director, Center for International Education, campus coordinator,
   AID/Malawi Project
IRVING R. MELBO, dean, School of Education

University of Southern California at Los Angeles

JERRY WULK, coordinator, International Programs, Graduate School of Education,
   campus coordinator, AID/Lagos Project

University of Utah

G. S. JACOBSEN, professor of educational administration, Chief of Party, Ethiopian
   Project, 1964-66
W. E. McPHIE, Chief of Party, Ethiopian Project
ASAHEL D. WOODRUFF, professor of educational psychology, campus coordinator, AID/
   Ethiopia Projects

University of Wisconsin

DAN ANDERSEN, assistant dean, School of Education
R. G. HEIDEMAN, campus coordinator, AID/Nigeria Project

F. L. JOHNSON, campus coordinator, AID/Kenya Project
ROBERT KOEHL, professor of educational policy studies
WILLARD LEEDS, director, Laboratory of International Research
DONALD McCARTY, dean, School of Education
PETER MICKELSON, director, International Programs, School of Education
DONALD MILLER, Laboratory of International Research

West Virginia University

NEWTON M. BAUGHMAN, campus coordinator, AID/Keyna Project, director, International Programs

Foreign Educators

JOSEPH W. ABWAO, principal, Chadwick Teacher Training College, Butere, Kenya

H. ALLEN, Minister of Education, Jamaica

MICHAEL ALEFE-ALUKE, vice-principal, Comprehensive High School, Aiyetere, Abeekuta, Nigeria

JOSUE ANGEL, dean, Faculty of Education, University of Valle, Cali, Valle, Colombia

BHUNTHIN ATTAGARA, director of teacher training, Ministry of Education, Bangkok, Thailand

GREGORIA BORLAZA, officer in charge, Office of the Vice-President, Philippine Normal College, Manila, Philippines

MARY BROWN, dean of education, University of Liberia

DEREK BULLOCK, principal, Comprehensive High School, Aiyetere, Nigeria

MAVIS BURKE, lecturer, Faculty of Education, University of the West Indies, Kingston, Jamaica

JOSE CASTILLO, professor, Faculty of Education, University of the Atlantic, Barranquilla, Colombia

AURELIO CESPEDES, director general, Ministry of Education, Bogota, Colombia

A. B. CHANDIRAMANI, joint educational advisor, Bureau of Scholarships & Youth Services, Ministry of Education, India

MELVILLE COTE, administrative consultant, Narvard Team, Comprehensive High School, Aiyetere, Nigeria

SAMUEL F. DENNIS, assistant secretary of education, Liberian Department of Education

IRENE JARA DE SOLORZANO, rector, Pedagogical Universita, Colombia

LEE YOUNG DUG, Graduate School of Education, Seoul National University, Korea

ELEANOR ELEQUIN, secretary, graduate committee, College of Education, University of the Philippines, Quezon City, Philippines

ANIBAL ESPINO, head, Pedagogics Department, Universidad Nacional de Trujillo, Peru

A. B. FAFUNWA, dean, Faculty of Education, University of Ife, Ile-Ife, Nigeria

JOHN FIGUEROA, dean, Faculty of Education, University of the West Indies, Kingston, Jamaica

GEORGE M. FLEMING, tutro, Chadwick Teacher Training College, Butere, Kenya

WERNER GORBITZ, rektor, Universidad Nacional de Trujillo, Peru

HARRY GUPTA, UNESCO expert in education, Liberian Department of Education

PANAS HANNARKIN, acting vice-president, College of Education, Phitsanulok, Thailand

MESTAFA KAMAL HELMY, Under-Secretary of State for University Affairs and Secretary-General of the Higher Council of Universities, Cairo, United Arab Republic

NELLY FESTINI ILLICH, dean, Faculty of Education, Universidad Nacional Mayor de San Marcos, Lima Peru

ALBERTO JIMENEZ S., dean, Faculty of Education, Pedagogical University of Tunja, Tunja, Boyaca, Colombia

J. N. KAUL, development officer (Humanities), University Grants Commission, India

KIM SUNG KEUN, dean, College of Education, Seoul National University, Korea

PAIK HYUN KI, director, Central Education Research Institute, Korea

BENJAMIN KING, principal, Freetown Teachers College, Freetown, Sierra Leone

FOONGFUANG KRUATRACHUE, chairman, division of English and literature, College of Education, Patoomwan Branch, Bangkok, Thailand

CHOI NAK KU, director, textbook bureau, Ministry of Education, Korea

LEE SANG KYU, director, higher education bureau, Ministry of Education, Korea

WON HUNG KYUN, president, Seoul Junior Teachers' College, Korea

J. A. LIJEMBE, director, Kenya Institute of Education, Kenya

YU KYUNG LOH, professor, College of Education, Seoul National University, Korea

AGUSTIN LOMBANA, chief, Personnel Preparation for the INEM Program, Bogota, Colombia

CAMPO ELIAS MARQUEZ, dean, Faculty of Education, National University, Bogota, D.E., Colombia

MR. MASHURI, Director General of Higher Education, Djakarta

JOSHUA S. MEENA, principal, Mpwapwa Teachers College, Mpwapwa, Tanzania

E. K. MEENA, assistant chief education officer, teacher training, Ministry of Education, Republic of Tanzania, Dar Es Salaam, Tanzania

SHIB K. MITRA, joint director, National Council of Educational Research & Training, Ministry of Education, India

JOSEPH MORRIS, director of rural education, Liberian Department of Education

KYALE MWENDWA, chief education officer, acting permanent secretary, Ministry of Education, Kenya

DELIAR NOER, rector, IKIP/Djakarta

AUGUSTO OLARTE, advisor, planning office, Association of Colleges and Universities, Bogota, Colombia

JOHN OSOGO, Ministry of Education, Nairobi, Kenya

GLENVILLE OWEN, principal, Mico Teachers College, Kingston, Jamaica

MARIA PAJUELO, director of teacher education, Ministry of Education, Lima, Peru

AUBREY PHILLIPS, senior lecturer, Faculty of Education, University of the West Indies, Kingston, Jamaica

R. P. QUINTANA, dean, Faculty of Education, Javeriana University, Bogota, Colombia

PAZ G. RAMOS, dean of admissions, University of the Philippines, Quezon City, Philippines

YOON TAE RIM, president, Sookmyung Women's University, Korea

BATUK RJBHANDARI, supervisor of instruction, College of Education, Birgans, Nepal

AHMEN SABRY, chief administrator, Higher Council of Universities, United Arab Republic, Cairo

CHANG IL SE, chief, technical service section, Central National Library, Korea

SELIMAN SHALAAN, Under-Secretary of State, Ministry of Education, United Arab Republic

MR. SHAMSULABUDDIN, Faculty of Education, Kabul University, Kabul, Afghanistan

T. BAI SHERMAN, under-secretary for teacher preparation, Liberian Department of Education

CHUNG WON SHIK, College of Education, Seoul National University, Korea

KIM YOUNG SHIK, Graduate School of Education, Seoul National University, Korea

CHUNG TAE SI, secretary-general, Korean Federation of Education Associations, Korea

MR. SIMANDJUNTAK, IKIP/Djakarta

MR. SOEMARDJO, senior lecturer, Institute for Teacher Training and Education, Djakarta, Indonesia

MR. SOEPANGKAT, chief, Bureau for International Relations, Directorate General of Higher Education, Djakarta

KIM BONG SOO, Seoul Junior Teachers' College, Korea

KIM RAN SOO, professor, graduate school of education, Yonsei University, Korea

LEE CHONG SOO, dean, graduate school of education, Seoul National University, Korea

NARTCHALEO SUMAWONG, head, department of education, College of Education, Prasanmitra Branch, Bangkok, Thailand

GUILLERMO VELEZ, dean, Faculty of Education, University of Valle, Cali, Valle, Colombia

OPAL WATTHA, lecturer, College of Education, Department of Teacher Training of Education, Bangkok, Thailand

ATO ABAIMEH WORKIE, assistant dean, Faculty of Education, Haile Selassie I University, Ethiopia

BIBLIOGRAPHY

ABERNATHY, DAVID, and COOMBE, TREVOR. "Education and Politics in Developing Countries." *Harvard Educational Review* 35 (3) : 287-302; Summer 1965.

ADAMS, DONALD K. "Education and Nation Building." *America's Emerging Role in Overseas Education.* (Edited by Clarence Hunnicutt.) Syracuse, N. Y.: School of Education, Syracuse University, 1962. pp. 51-69.

ADAMS, DONALD K., editor. *Educational Planning.* Syracuse, N. Y.: Center for Development Education, Syracuse University, 1964.

ADAMS, DONALD K. "The Monkey and the Fish: Cultural Pitfalls of an Educational Advisor." *International Development Review* II (2) : 22-24; October 1960.

ADAMS, DONALD K. "The Study of Education and Social Development." *Comparative Education Review* 9: 258-69; October 1965.

ADAMS, DONALD K., and FARRELL, JOSEPH P., editors. *Education and Social Development.* Syracuse, N. Y.: Center for Development Education, Syracuse University, and U.S. Agency for International Development, 1966. (Mimeo.)

AGENCY FOR INTERNATIONAL DEVELOPMENT. *New Initiatives in Economic Assistance— Agriculture, Health, and Education.* Washington, D.C.: the Agency, 1966.

ALEXANDER-FRUTSCHI, MARIAN C., editor. *Human Resources and Economic Growth: An International Annotated Bibliography on the Role of Education and Training in Economic and Social Development.* Menlo Park, Calif.: Stanford Research Institute, 1963.

ALMOND, GABRIEL A., and COLEMAN, JAMES S., editors. *The Politics of the Developing Areas.* Princeton, N.J.: Princeton University Press, 1960.

AMACHREE, GODFREY K. J. "Education in the New Africa." *The American Association of Colleges for Teacher Education 1964 Yearbook.* Washington, D.C.: the Association, 1964. pp. 58-67.

ANDERSON, CHARLES ARNOLD, and BOWMAN, M. J., editors. *Education and Economic Development.* Chicago: Aldine Publishing Co., 1965.

ANDERSON, CHARLES ARNOLD. "Educational Planning in the Context of National Social Policy." *Phi Delta Kappan* 47 (4) : 180-4; December 1965.

ANDREWS, F. EMERSON, editor. "AID Abroad: Some Principles and Their Latin American Practice." *Foundations—20 Viewpoints.* New York: Russell Sage Foundation, 1965.

ANDREWS, STANLEY. "University Contracts: A Review and Comment on Selected University Contracts in Africa, the Middle East and Asia." Technical Assistance Study Group, International Cooperation Administration, Department of State. Washington, D.C.: 1960. pp. 14-17.

ARENSBERG, CONRAD M., and NIEHOFF, ARTHUR H. *Introducing Social Change: A Manual for Americans Overseas.* Chicago: Aldine Publishing Co., 1964. pp. 7-8.

BECKER, GARY S. "Investment in Human Capital: A Theoretical Analysis." *Journal of Political Economy* 70 (5), Part 2: 9-49; October 1962.

BEEBY, CLASENE E. *The Quality of Education in Developing Countries.* Cambridge, Mass.: Harvard University Press, 1966. p. 139.

BEEBY, CLASENE E. "Stages in the Growth of a Primary Education System." *Comparative Education Review,* Vol. 6, No. 1: 2-11. 1962.

BELL, DAVID E. "The Quality of AID." *Foreign Affairs,* July 1966. Reprinted in *International Education: Past, Present, Problems and Prospects.* Prepared by Task Force on International Education, Chairman. Washington, D.C.: U.S. Government Printing Office, 1966. p. 281.

BELL, DAVID E. "The University's Contribution to the Developing Nations." *Higher Education* 15: 7; March 1964.

179

BENJAMIN, HAROLD R. W. *Higher Education in the American Republics.* New York: McGraw-Hill, 1965. 222 pp.

BENSON, CHARLES S. "Economics and Education." *Review of Educational Research* 37: 96-102; February 1967.

BEREDAY, GEORGE Z. F., and LAUWERYS, JOSEPH A., editors. *The World Yearbook of Education* 1965: *The Education Explosion.* New York: Harcourt, Brace and World, 1965. 498 pp.

BIGELOW, KARL S. *Africa, Teacher Education and the United States.* Washington, D.C.: The American Association of Colleges for Teacher Education, 1963. 19 pp.

BIGELOW, KARL S. "Fundamental Education for the Emerging Nations of Africa." *Educational Needs of Sub-Sahara Africa and Latin America.* Washington, D.C.: 1961. pp. 30-40.

BLACK, LLOYD D. *The Strategy of Foreign Aid.* New Jersey: D. Van Nostrand Company, Inc., 1968.

BOWMAN, MARY JEAN, and ANDERSON, CHARLES ARNOLD. "The Role of Education in Development," *Development of the Emerging Countries: An Agenda for Research.* (Robert E. Asher, et al.) Washington, D.C.: The Brookings Institution, 1962.

BOWMAN, MARY JEAN, and ANDERSON, CHARLES ARNOLD. "Concerning the Role of Education in Development." *Old Societies and New States.* (Edited by Clifford Geetz.) New York: Free Press of Glencoe, 1963. pp. 247-79.

BRADEMAS, JOHN, chairman. *Task Force on International Education: Past, Present, Problems and Prospects.* Washington, D.C.: Government Printing Office, 1966.

BREMBECK, COLE S. "Colleges of Education and Overseas Technical Assistance." *Comparative Education Review* 11: 91-94; February 1967.

BREMBECK, COLE S. "Education for National Development." *Comparative Education Review* 5: 223-31; February 1962.

BRENENSTOCK, THEODORE, and SAYES, WILLIAM. *Contribution of Sociology and Anthropology to Education.* Albany: University of the State of New York, State Department of Education, Division of Research, 1962.

BRUNER, JEROME S., editor. "Educational Assistance for Developing Nations: Techniques and Technology." *Education and Training in the Developing Countries.* (Edited by William Elliot.) New York: Praeger, 1966.

BUTTS, R. FREEMAN. *American Education in International Development.* New York: Harper and Row, 1963. 138 pp.

BUTTS, R. FREEMAN. "The African University and Human Resources Development: An Educationist's View." *Documents of the Conference on the African University and National Educational Development, September 8-18, 1964.* New York: Institute for Education in Africa, Teachers College, Columbia University, 1964.

BYRNES, FRANCIS C. *Americans in Technical Assistance: A Study of Attitudes and Responses to Their Role Abroad.* New York: Praeger, 1965.

CALDER, RITCHIE. *Two-Way Passage: A Study of the Give-and-Take of International Aid.* London: William Heinemann Ltd., 1964.

CALDWELL, LYNTON K. "The Universities and International Technical Assistance: The Uses of Government Contracts." *Journal of Higher Education* 36: 266-73; May 1965.

CALDWELL, O. J. "Education for Africanisation." *Phi Delta Kappan* 14 (4): 143-47; January 1960.

CARLEY, VERNA A. *Report of Progress in Teacher Education—Technical Co-operation in Forty Developing Countries.* Washington, D.C.: Office of Educational Services, International Cooperation Administration, 1960.

CASH, WEBSTER C. "A Critique of Manpower Planning and Educational Change in Africa." *Economic Development and Cultural Change* 14 (1): 33-47; October 1965.

CERYCH, LADISLAV. *Problems of Aid to Education in Developing Countries.* New York: Praeger (for the Atlantic Institute), 1965.

CLEVELAND, HARLAN; MANGONE, GERALD J.; and ADAMS, JOHN C. *The Overseas Americans.* New York: McGraw-Hill, 1960. 316 pp.

COLEMAN, JAMES S., editor. *Education and Political Development.* Princeton, N.J.: Princeton University Press, 1965.

COOMBS, PHILIP H. *The World Educational Crisis: A Systems Analysis.* New York: Oxford University Press, 1968.

COOMBS, PHILIP H., and BIGELOW, KARL W. *Education and Foreign Aid.* Cambridge, Mass.: Harvard University Press, 1965.

CORREA, HECTOR. "Quality of Education and Socio-Economic Development." *Comparative Education Review* 8: 11-16; June 1964.

CORREA, HECTOR. *Educational Planning: Its Quantitative Aspects and Its Integration with Economic Planning.* Paris: International Institute for Educational Planning, 1965.

COWAN, LAING GRAY; O'CONNELL, JAMES; and SCANLON, DAVID G., editors. *Education and Nation-Building in Africa.* New York: Praeger, 1965.

CURLE, ADAM. *Educational Strategy for Developing Societies: A Study of Educational and Social Factors in Relation to Economic Growth.* London: Travistock, 1963. 180 pp.

CURLE, ADAM. "Some Aspects of Educational Planning in Underdeveloped Areas." *Harvard Educational Review* 32 (3) ; Summer 1962.

DART, FRANCIS E. "The Rub of Cultures." *Foreign Affairs* 41: 360-68; January 1963.

Education for National Development; Focus: Latin America. Washington, D.C.: 1964.

ELLIOTT, WILLIAM YANDELL, editor. *Education and Training in the Developing Countries: The Role of U.S. Foreign Aid.* New York: Praeger, 1966.

ENARSON, HAROLD L. "The Successes and Failures of Aid." *Phi Delta Kappan* 47 (4) ; February 1965.

ENARSON, HAROLD L. "The United States Commitment to Education in Developing Societies." *National Elementary Principal* 44 (4) ; February 1965.

ENARSON, HAROLD L. "The Universities' Stake in the Developing Nations." *Educational Record* 45: 27-32; 1964.

ESMAN, MILTON J. *Needed: An Education and Research Base to Support America's Expanded Commitments Overseas.* Pittsburgh, Pa.; University of Pittsburgh, 1961.

ESMAN, MILTON J. *The Institution Building Concepts—An Interim Appraisal.* Pittsburgh, Pa.: Inter-University Research Program in Institution Building. Graduate School of Public and International Affairs, University of Pittsburgh, 1967.

FIGUEROA, JOHN J. "Teacher Training for Mass Education in Africa." *The Education and Training of Teachers: The Yearbook of Education,* 1963.

The Foreign Assistance Program Annual Report to the Congress, Fiscal Year 1967. Washington, D.C.: U.S. Government Printing Office, 1967.

The Foreign Assistance Program Annual Report to the Congress, Fiscal Year 1966. Washington, D.C.: U.S. Government Printing Office, 1968.

FRANKEL, CHARLES. *The Neglected Aspect of Foreign Affairs: American Educational and Cultural Policy Abroad.* Washington, D.C.: The Brookings Institution, 1966.

FULBRIGHT, J. W. "Foreign Aid? Yes, but with a New Approach." *New York Times Magazine,* March 21, 1965.

GANT, GEORGE F. "The Institution Building Project." *International Review of Administrative Science* 33 (3), 1966.

GARDNER, JOHN W. *AID and the Universities.* New York: Education and World Affairs, 1964.

GLENNAN, T. KEITH, and SANDERS, IRWIN T. *The Professional School and World Affairs: Report of the Task Force on Education.* New York: Education and World Affairs, 1967. 96 pp.

GOODWIN, LEONARD. *American Professors in Asia: A Study of the Selection and Adaptation of Fifty American Professors Who Went to India, Pakistan and Korea under the Fulbright-Hays Program During 1962-63.* Department of State, Bureau of Education and Cultural Affairs. Washington, D.C.: U.S. Government Printing Office, 1964. 84 pp.

GRIFFITH, ALISON. *The Role of American Higher Education in Relation to Developing Areas.* Washington, D.C.: American Council on Education, 1962.

GROOMES, GWENDOLYN, editor. *Inventory of American Aid to Education in Africa.* Washington, D.C.: American Council on Education, 1962.

HALPERN, JOEL M., and TINSMAN, MARILYN CLARK. "Education and Nation-Building in Laos." *Comparative Education Review* 10: 499-507; October 1966.

HANITCHAK, JOHN J. "A Follow-up of a Technical Assistance Project in Education in West Pakistan" (Unpublished). Indiana University, 1968.

HANNA, PAUL R., and others. *Education: An Instrument of National Policy in Selected Newly Developing Nations Phase I-V.* Stanford, Calif.: School of Education, Stanford University, 1964. 837 pp.

HANNA, PAUL R. "Conventional and Unconventional Education for Newly Developed Countries." *America's Emerging Role in Overseas Education.* (Edited by Clarence Hunnicut.) Syracuse, N.Y.: School of Education, Syracuse University 1962. pp. 21-39.

HANSON, JOHN W. "On General Education for the African Teacher." *Teacher Education* 3 (3) : 181-88; February 1963.

HANSON, JOHN W., and BREMBECK, COLE S., editors. *Education and the Development of Nations.* New York: Holt, Rinehart and Winston, 1966.

HANSON, JOHN W., and GIBSON, GEOFFREY W. *African Education and Development since 1960—A Select and Annotated Bibliography.* East Lansing, Mich.: Institute for International Studies in Education and the African Studies Center, Michigan State University, 1966.

HARBISON, FREDERICK, and MYERS, CHARLES. "Education and Development in the Newly Developing Economics." *Comparative Education Review* 8: 5-10; October 1964.

HARBISON, FREDERICK, and MYERS, CHARLES A. *Education, Manpower and Economic Growth: Strategies of Human Resource Development.* New York: McGraw-Hill, 1964.

HARBISON, FREDERICK. "Education for Development." *Scientific American* 24 (3) : 140-47.

HAVIGHURST, ROBERT J. "Education, Social Mobility, and Social Change in Four Societies: A Comparative Study." *International Review of Education* 4 (2) : 167-83; 1958.

HAVIGHURST, ROBERT J., and ABREU, JAYME. "The Problem of Secondary Education in Latin America." *Comparative Education Review* 5 (3) : 167-74; 1962.

Horizons Unlimited: A Statistical Report on Participant Training. Washington, D.C.: Office of International Training, Agency for International Development, 1968.

HUMPHREY, RICHARD A., editor. *Universities—and Development Assistance Abroad.* Washington, D.C.: American Council on Education, 1962.

HUQ, MUHAMMED SHANSUL. *Education and Development Strategy in South Asia and South East Asia.* Honolulu, Hawaii: East West Center Press, 1965.

HUTASOIT, MARNIXIOS, and PRATOR, CLIFFORD H. "A Study of the 'New Primary Approach' in the Schools of Kenya." Report carried out at the request of the Ministry of Education with the support of the Ford Foundation. (Unpublished). 1965.

International Institute for Educational Planning. *Educational Planning: An Inventory of Major Research Needs.* Paris: UNESCO, 1965.

International Institute for Educational Planning. *New Educational Media in Action: Case Studies for Planners.* Paris: UNESCO, 1967.

JACOBS, ROBERT. "The Interdisciplinary Approach to Educational Planning." *Comparative Education Review* 8: 17-27; June 1964.

JOHNSON, ELDON L. "Consortia in Higher Education." *Education Record* 48 (4) : 341-47; Fall 1967.

KANDEL, I. L. "Comparative Education and Underdeveloped Countries: A New Dimension." *Comparative Education Review* 4 (3) : 130-35; 1961.

LAMBERT, RICHARD D., issue editor. "American Abroad." *The Annals of the American Academy of Political and Social Science.* November 1966.

LEONARD, J. PAUL. "The Development of the National Institute of Education" (Unpublished). Teachers College, Columbia University, 1967.

LEWIS, W. ARTHUR. *Guidelines for the Planning of External AID Projects in Education.* New York: Education and World Affairs, 1967.

LEWIS, W. ARTHUR. "Priorities for Educational Expansion." *Policy Conference on Economic Growth and Investment in Education* 3. Paris: Organization for Economic Cooperation and Development Publications. February 1962. pp. 35-49.

LEWIS, W. ARTHUR. "Education and Economic Development." *Social and Economic Studies* 10 (8) : 113-27; 1961. (Adapted from paper presented to UNESCO Conference on Educational Needs of Africa, Addis Ababa, May 1961.)

LINCOLN, GEROGE A. "Improving AID Program Evaluation." Report to the Administrator of AID. Washington, D.C.: Government Printing Office, 1965.

LOEBER, THOMAS S. *Foreign Aid: Our Tragic Experiment.* New York: W. W. Norton and Company, Inc., 1961.

LYONS, RAYMOND F., editor. *Problems and Strategies of Educational Planning, Lessons from Latin America.* Paris: UNESCO: International Institute for Educational Planning, 1965.

McNOWN, J. S.; HERBERT, TEDDY T.; and LEFRANCOIS, P. C. *The Federal University of Cameroon* (Unpublished). Washington, D.C.: American Council on Education, 1968.

MALIK, CHARLES H. "The World Looks at the American Program." *Education and Training in the Developing Countries: The Role of U.S. Foreign Aid.* (Edited by William Y. Elliott.) New York: Praeger, 1966. pp. 34-42.

MANCONE, GERALD J. "How Can We Better Educate Americans to Work and to Study Abroad?" *Current Issues in Higher Education.* Washington, D.C.: American Association of Higher Education, National Education Association, 1960.

MANCONE, GERALD J. "The Return of the Native—a Hardy Problem of Overseas Education." *America's Emerging Role in Overseas Education.* (Edited by Clarence Hunnicutt.) Syracuse, N.Y.: School of Education, Syracuse University, 1962. pp. 139-48.

MASLAND, JOHN W. *Educational Development in Africa: The Role of United States Assistance.* Education and World Affairs Occasional Report No. 4. New York: Education and World Affairs, 1967.

MEDLIN, WILLIAM K.; CARPENTER, FINLEY; and CAVE, WILLIAM M. *Education and Social Change: A Study of the Role of the School in a Technically Developing Society in Central Asia.* Ann Arbor, Mich.: Office of Research Administration, University of Michigan, 1965. 457 pp.

MEYERS, CHARLES A. *Education, Manpower, and Economic Growth: Strategies of Human Resource Development.* New York: McGraw-Hill, 1964.

MINER, JERRY, and SOLOMON, E. S. *Implications of Population Trends for First-Level Educational Programmes.* Asian Population Conference, New Delhi, India: December 1963.

MOEHLMAN, ARTHUR H. *Comparative Education Systems.* New York: Center for Applied Research in Education, 1964. 113 pp.

MORRILL, J. L., and others. *The University and World Affairs.* New York: Ford Foundation, 1960.

MYERS, CHARLES NASH. *Education and National Development in Mexico.* Princeton Industrial Relations Section, Princeton University, 1965. 147 pp .

NASATIR, DAVID. "Education and Social Change: The Argentine Case." *Sociology of Education* 39: 167-82; Spring 1966.

NASON, JOHN W. *The College and World Affairs.* New York: Education and World Affairs, 1964.

NEFF, KENNETH LEE. *National Development Through Social Progress: The Role of Education.* Washington, D.C.: U.S. Department of Health, Education, and Welfare, 1963.

NEISSER, CHARLOTTE S. "Community Development and Mass Education in British Nigeria." *Economic Development and Cultural Change* 2: 352-65; 1955.

NIEHOFF, ARTHUR H. *A Casebook of Social Change.* Chicago: Aldine Publishing Co., 1966.

Organization for Economic Cooperation and Development. *The Educational Factor for Development.* Paris: The Organization for Economic Cooperation and Development, 1966. Vol. 1, p. 130. Vol. 2, p. 117.

PEASLEE, ALEXANDER L. "Primary School Enrollments and Economic Growth." *Comparative Education Review* 11: 57-67; February 1967.

PESHKIN, ALAN. "Education in Developing Nations: Dimensions of Change." *Comparative Education Review* 10: 53-66; February 1966.

PLATT, WILLIAM J. *Conflict in Education Planning.* Menlo Park, Calif.: Stanford Research Institute, 1962.

PLATT, WILLIAM J. *Toward Strategies of Education.* Menlo Park, Calif.: Stanford Research Institute, International Industrial Development Center, 1962.

PORTER, WILLIS P. "Institution Building: The College of Education in Bangkok, Thailand, and Its Role in National Development" (Unpublished). Bloomington, Ind.: Indiana University, 1965.

PROPP, KATHLEEN M. "The Establishment of Agricultural Universities in India: A Case Study of the Role of USAID—U.S. University Technical Assistance" (Unpublished). Urbana, Ill.: University of Illinois, 1968.

RICHARDSON, JOHN M., JR. *An Analysis of AID-University Relations 1950-65 (With Special Reference to Rural Development Contracts).* Minneapolis, Minn.: Department of Political Science, Center for Comparative Political Analysis, University of Minnesota.

Rogers, Everett M. *Diffusion of Innovations*. New York: Free Press of Glencoe, 1962.

Rosenzweig, Robert M. "Universities and the Foreign Assistance Program." *Journal of Higher Education* 35: 359-66; October 1964.

Rusk, Dean. "Address at the Opening Session of the Department of State." Given at the Policy Conference on Economic Growth and Investment in Education, 1962. *Education and the Development of Nations*. (Edited by John W. Hanson.) New York: Holt, Rinehart and Winston, 1966.

Sanders, Donald P. "Patterns of Educational Change During Economic Growth" (Unpublished). Palo Alto, Calif.: School of Education, Stanford University, 1962.

Sanders, Donald P. *Some Qualitative Aspects of Education in Educational Planning*. Paris: Organization for Economic Cooperation and Development, 1963.

Sanders, Irwin T. *American Professionals Overseas: Academic Specialists, Views of Themselves and Their Roles in Technical Assistance Programs*. New York: The Ford Foundation, 1966.

Sanders, Irwin T., editor. *Interprofessional Training Goals for Technical Assistance Personnel Abroad*. New York: Council on Social Work Education, 1959.

Sarason, Seymour B. "Toward a Psychology of Change and Innovation." *American Psychologist* 22 (3) : 227; March 1967.

Scanlon, David, and Shields, David. *Problems and Prospects—International Education*. New York: Teachers College Press, 1968.

Schultz, Theodore W. "Investment in Human Capital." *The American Economic Review* 51 (1) ; March 1961.

Schultz, Theodore W. *The Economic Value of Education*. New York: Columbia University Press, 1963.

Shiver, Elizabeth N., editor. *Higher Education and Public International Service*. Commission on International Education of the American Council on Education in collaboration with the Department of State Seminar, March 1967. Washington, D. C.: American Council on Education, August 1967.

Taper, Bernard. "National Development through International Education." *Overseas* 3 (9) : 2-14; 1964.

Taylor, Harold, editor. *Conference on World Education*. Washington, D.C.: American Association of Colleges for Teacher Education, 1967.

Taylor, Harold. *The World and the American Teacher*. Washington, D.C.: American Association of Colleges for Teacher Education, 1968.

Teacher Education in Korea. Nashville, Tenn.: George Peabody College for Teachers.

Tewksbury, Donald G. "American Education and the International Scene." *Teachers College Record* 60: 357-68; April 1959.

Thompson, William N., et al. *AID-University Rural Development Contracts and U.S. Universities* (Unpublished). Urbana, Ill.: University of Illinois, 1968.

Tinbergen, Jan, and Box, H. C. "A Planning Model for the Educational Requirements of Economic Development." *The Residual Factor and Economic Growth*. Paris: Organization for Economic Cooperation and Development, Study Group in the Economics of Education, 1964. pp. 147-69.

Training for Leadership and Service. Washington, D.C.: Agency for International Development.

The University Community and Overseas Research: Guidelines for the Future. New York: Education and World Affairs, 1967.

The University Looks Abroad: Approaches to World Affairs at Six American Universities. New York: Walker and Co., 1965.

Ward, Barbara, and Bauer, P. T. *Two Views on Aid to Developing Countries*. London: The Institute of Economic Affairs, 1966.

185

WEEKS, SHELDON. *Divergence in Educational Development: The Case of Kenya and Uganda.* New York: Columbia University Teachers College, 1967.

WEIDNER, EDWARD W. *The World Role of Universities.* New York: McGraw-Hill, 1962.

WELTY, PAUL S. "The World Challenge for Teacher Education." *Teacher Education for the Sixties.* Washington, D.C.: American Association of Colleges for Teacher Education, 1961. pp. 77-82.

WILSON, JOHN. *Education and Changing West African Culture.* New York: Columbia University Teachers College, 1963.

WOOD, RICHARD H. *U.S. Universities: Their Role in AID-Financed Technical Assistance Overseas.* New York: Education and World Affairs, 1968.

PEOPLE CONSULTED

AID/Washington

T. C. CLARK, technical advisory staff, Bureau of Far Eastern Affairs
GLENN COOMBS, Latin American Bureau
ROBERT D. DOLLEY, education advisor, Near East and South Asia Education Bureau
SCOTT HAMMOND, education advisor, Vietnam Bureau
STEWART M. PATTERSON, senior resources officer, Office of International Training
WILLIAM SHUMATE, education advisor, Vietnam Bureau
EDWIN TREATHAWAY, education officer, African Education Bureau
MYRON VENT, acting chief, Education Planning Division

AID/Overseas

MICHAEL ADLER, director, USAID Mission to Nigeria, Lagos
ANSELMA BERNAL, education advisor, AID Mission to Kenya, Nairobi
BEN HILL BROWN, Ambassador to Liberia, U.S. Embassy, Monrovia
JOHN DIETRICH, secondary education advisor, USAID Mission to Nigeria, Ibadan
MARY A. DOYLE, chief, training division, Indonesia, Djakarta
A. H. ELLIS, program officer and assistant director, USAID Mission to Kenya, Nairobi
PHILIP HAINEY, education officer, Dacca, Pakistan
HENRY HERGE, chief education officer, USAID, Jamaica
DAVID G. IMIG, education advisor, USAID, Monrovia
CLIFFORD LIDDLE, education officer, Seoul, Korea
HOWARD LUSK, educational development officer, USAID, Bogota, Colombia
ED MARTIN, education officer, Kabul, Afghanistan
E. K. MEENA, assistant chief education officer, teacher training, Ministry of Education, Republic of Tanzania
NOEL MYERS, chief education advisor, AID Mission to Tanzania
MARY NEVILLE, education advisor, USAID Mission to Nigeria, Ibadan
LAWRENCE NEWBERRY, associate education officer, New Delhi, India
WILLIAM E. REED, director, USAID Mission to Nigeria, Ibadan
WILL SAUNDERS, chief education advisor, AID, Addis Ababa
E. SCHEELEY, deputy education officer, USAID, Bogota, Colombia
EDWARD SCHTEN, higher education advisor, USAID, Bogota, Colombia
MR. SHIN, Kok Bom, program specialist, Seoul, Korea
ROBERT SMAIL, chief of education, USAID Mission to Nigeria, Ibadan
MORROW STOUGH, education officer, Kathmandu, Nepal
JOHN A. ULINSKY, director, USAID Mission to Liberia
WILLIAM WESTLEY, education officer, Manila, Philippines
W. H. WHITTEN, education advisor, AID Mission to Tanzania
MORRIE WILLIAMS, education advisor, Bangkok, Thailand

DATE DUE